THE HISTORY OF LOGIC IN CHINA

Other interview books from Automatic Press ♦ V/I P

Formal Philosophy
edited by Vincent F. Hendricks & John Symons November 2005

Masses of Formal Philosophy
edited by Vincent F. Hendricks & John Symons October 2006

Philosophy of Technology: 5 Questions
edited by Jan-Kyrre Berg Olsen & Evan Selinger February 2007

Game Theory: 5 Questions
edited by Vincent F. Hendricks & Pelle Guldborg Hansen April 2007

Philosophy of Mathematics: 5 Questions
edited by Vincent F. Hendricks & Hannes Leitgeb January 2008

Epistemology: 5 Questions
edited by Vincent F. Hendricks & Duncan Pritchard September 2008

Philosophy of Medicine: 5 Questions
edited by J. K. B. O. Friis, P. Rossel & M. S. Norup September 2011

Narrative Theories and Poetics: 5 Questions
edited by Peer F. Bundbaard, Henrik Skov Nielsen & Frederik Stjernfelt 2012

Intellectual History: 5 Questions
edited by Morten Haugaard Jeppesen, Frederik Stjernfelt & Mikkel Thorup May 2013

Philosophical Practice: 5 Questions
edited by Jeanette Bresson Ladegaard Knox & Jan Kyrre Berg Olsen Friis January 2013

Philosophy of Nursing: 5 Questions
edited by Anette Forss, Christine Ceci & John S. Drummod October 2014

Science and Religion: 5 Questions
edited by Gregg D. Caruso March 2014

Peirce: 5 Questions
edited by Francesco Bellucci, Ahti-Veikko Pietarinen & Frederik Stjernfelt July 2014

Social Epistemology: 5 Questions
edited by Duncan Pritchard and Vincent F. Hendricks, January 2015

See all published and forthcoming books in the 5 Questions series at
www.vince-inc.com

THE HISTORY OF LOGIC IN CHINA
5 QUESTIONS

EDITED BY

FENRONG LIU

JEREMY SELIGMAN

Automatic Press ♦ $\frac{V}{I}$P

Automatic Press ♦ $\frac{V}{\vert}$ P

Information on this title: www. vince-inc. com

© Automatic Press / VIP 2015

This publication is in copyright. Subject to statuary exception and to the provisions of relevant collective licensing agreements, no reproduction of any part may take place without the written permission of the publisher.

First published 2015

Printed in the United States of America
and the United Kingdom

ISBN-10 / 87-92130-54-2
ISBN-13 / 978-87-92130-54-9

The publisher has no responsibilities for the persistence or accuracy of URLs for external or third party Internet Web sites referred to in this publication and does not guarantee that any content on such Web sites is, or will remain, accurate or appropriate.

Cover design by Vincent F. Hendricks

Contents

Preface	iii
Acknowledgements	xv
1 Cuī Qīngtián 崔清田	1
2 Dǒng Zhìtiě 董志铁	7
3 Jù Zōnglín 剧宗林	17
4 Liú Péiyù 刘培育	27
5 Shěn Jiànyīng 沈剑英	35
6 Sūn Zhōngyuán 孙中原	43
7 Wáng Kèxǐ 王克喜	55
8 Yáng Wǔjīn 杨武金	65
9 Zhái Jǐnchéng 翟锦程	71
10 Zhèng Wěihóng 郑伟宏	79
11 Zhōu Shān 周山	95
12 Zhōu Yúnzhī 周云之	103
13 Chris Fraser 方克濤	115
14 Yiu-Ming Fung 馮耀明	121
15 Chad Hansen 陳漢生	129
16 Dan Robins 羅丹	131
17 Hsien-Chung Lee 李賢中	137

18 Jer-Shiarn Lee 李哲賢	145
19 Chung-Ying Cheng 成中英	151
20 Jane Geaney 葛立珍	157
21 Rens Bod 任博德	165
22 Christoph Harbsmeier 何莫邪	171
23 Michiel Leezenberg 李仁伯	175
24 Thierry Lucas 卢卡斯	181
25 Gregor Paul 葛保罗	187
Glossaries	192
About the Editors	218
About the 5 Questions Series	219
Index	220

Preface

The History of Logic in China: 5 Questions

Fenrong: Hi Jeremy, for the preface, let's just record our thoughts as a dialogue. We can think of it as another Skype working session!

Jeremy: I like it. We've spent so much time with other people's answers to our questions. I expect we'll end up not answering most of them, but they'll give some structure to this preface, and we can make some useful remarks on the way.

Fenrong: So these five questions...We didn't have much of an idea about what to ask when we began but I think we got some good answers. My original intention was just to follow the other books in the Five Questions series.

Jeremy: With hindsight, we might have chosen differently, but I now like to think of our project in the way Zhai Jincheng talks about the history of logic: it "grew from nothing, from vague to clear, from fragmentary to complete, and from scattered to systematic."

Fenrong: Very Daoist!

Jeremy: OK, so, the questions. What was the first question and what did you think of it?

1. Why did you begin working on the history of logic in China?

Fenrong: The first question speaks for itself, but there were many different kinds of answer, from the purely academic to the more biographical. Political events shaped the academic careers of many of the more senior Chinese scholars, especially the Cultural Revolution.

Jeremy: I was reassured to learn that logic is "an area that causes less trouble politically" (Shen Jianying) and that when studying logic, "class attributes, political tendencies, political thinking and opinions are washed out as sand; only logical thought remains bright as gold" (Zhou Shan). That's an image worth holding on to.

Fenrong: So how about you, Jeremy? How did you get interested in Chinese logic?

Jeremy: Well, nothing so dramatic. My interest dates back to the mid 90s when I was working at Chung Cheng University in Taiwan. At the time I arrived there I knew nothing about Chinese language or culture, and suddenly I was surrounded by both. I'd heard of the great masters of Chinese philosophy, of course, but knew very little about them; they seemed to me quite exotic and mysterious. It wasn't until Chad Hansen visited and gave a talk to our department that my eyes were opened. He showed that someone with my training in logic and analytic philosophy could have some hope of understanding ancient Chinese philosophy and even that part of it was to do with language and logic. That was a very exciting revelation, and I quickly consumed and digested his books on the subject. And you?

Fenrong: For me, when I was reading the Chinese classics as a philosophy undergraduate, I was fascinated by claims like "*báimǎfēimǎ* 白馬非馬 (white horse not horse)" by Gongsun Long. I wanted to find out why our ancestors could even think that way. That was how I became aware of the Chinese logical tradition, and then later when I studied at the Chinese Academy of Social Sciences, I was surrounded by scholars such as Liu Peiyu, Zhang Jialong, Zhang Qingyu, and Zhou Yunzhi, who have carried on Shen Youding's tradition, applying logical methods to understand the ancient texts. Though my speciality is modern logic, I've tried to read what is going on in the field. It was the relative lack of communication between Chinese scholars and scholars abroad, that got me interested in this project.

Jeremy: You and then me. You were very persuasive when you asked me to be involved! But also, I genuinely wanted to know more about the status of the field and, well, this project seemed like a quick way of finding out. Little did I know how long it would take!

Fenrong: Erm, well, yes, we were thinking it would take about 4 months, not 4 years. But I guess that takes us to the next question.

2. What is the best way to define your area in terms of historical period, textual sources, methodology or other factors?

Fenrong: I'd like to say something about how we defined this project and our methodology. For me, the motivation was to help build a bridge between two scholarly communities: those working primarily in Chinese and those working in other languages, typically publishing in English. Even today, there is only a small minority of those working on the history of logic in China who can function well in both languages.

Jeremy: And so, primarily, our task was that of translation. Before we began I had no idea how hard it would be to translate the Chinese answers we received into English.

Fenrong: Neither did I. So, we should explain to the reader that we first thought that we could get a lot of help with this. We divided up the responses we got to our questions and asked various people to give us an initial translation. But it didn't really work.

Jeremy: No. Some of the translations we got were good but even really good ones didn't save us much work. We still had to go through everything word by word to check that the translation was ok, and that involved us rewriting most if not all sentences, many whole paragraphs, and paraphrasing larger units to fit the space we had available.

Fenrong: The technical parts were especially difficult, and anything referring to ancient texts.

Jeremy: Yes, those were...challenging. The way Chinese scholars usually refer to ancient texts is just by including them with what they're saying in modern Chinese, perhaps with some additional comments to follow, explaining particular words. But for an English version, we had to give both the ancient text and an English translation, in a way that reflected the authors understanding of the passage. I think we must have spent as much time on those parts as on all the rest.

Fenrong: Of course, we relied heavily on A. C. Graham's book[1] and, let's say it now, the Chinese Text Project website (www.ctext.org) was also invaluable.

Jeremy: Totally agree. Thanks Donald! It is such a great resource for anyone working on ancient Chinese texts.

Fenrong: The question also asks about defining the field. We got a lot on that...

Jeremy: Right! There are so many different views. That was a bit of a novelty for me, perhaps because I'm used to working in modern logic, where there is a lot more common ground. Remember the problems we had in translating "中国逻辑史"? Should it be "history of Chinese logic" or "history of logic in China"; the difference seems small but it is anything but. Even the phrase "logic in China" is problematic; does it just refer to the introduction of western (including Indian) ideas into China or to the Chinese tradition dating back to the pre-Qin period? Is it right to call that "logic"?

Fenrong: Well, there is a long list of different proposals for translating "logic" into Chinese.[2] Some of them, like the modern *luóji* 逻辑, are purely phonetic, others like *míngbiànxué* 名辯學 refer back to Chinese tradition. But the problem is much deeper than just a matter of translation.

Jeremy: "Logic" is deeply embedded in the European intellectual cultural, all the way back to the ancient Greeks, with its emphasis on the exercise of rigorous, rule-based ways of thinking, close association to grammatical patterns, and even the legalistic structure of academic debate with its objections and counterexamples. As Rens Bod reminded us, for centuries, logic was part of the *trivium*, the central curriculum throughout mediaeval Europe.

Fenrong: I think everyone agrees that the style of thinking in the Chinese tradition is quite different. Foundational texts like the *Analects* of Confucius and the *Daodejing* don't give argumentation a central place. They get you to think deeply about the human condition, our place in the world, but prefer to use carefully chosen metaphors and illustrations rather than explicit argument.

---

[1] *Later Mohist Logic, Ethics and Science*, Hong Kong: The Chinese University Press, 1978; reprinted 2003. We use Graham's numbering system (A11, B27, etc) for easy reference to the translations in this book.
[2] A few of them are listed on the back cover of this book.

Jeremy: And that's a challenge for any student of Chinese philosophy, let alone Chinese logic. On the face of it, the very idea of looking for such a western idea as "logic" in Chinese culture seems very strange.

Fenrong: But, as we know, there *was* a tradition of debate in ancient China, and a lot of interest in the relationship between language and reality. And that's why scholars in this field should look for "logical thought", rather than in an exact parallel with the logical thought of the Greeks or ancient Indians.

Jeremy: Well, Gregor Paul takes it to be essential that we regard all cultures as sharing at least some common understanding of logic. Denying that, he says, is "denying the unity of mankind and the basic identity of all members of the species homo sapiens sapiens". And Sun Zhongyuan would agree, I think. With a virtuoso display of the Chinese argumentative method of parallelism, he explains: "The stones on other hills can be used to work jade. Human anatomy contains a key to the anatomy of the ape. Likewise, western logic, systematic, developed, and refined as it is, can be taken to provide the correct perspective and methods for the study of ancient Chinese logic."

Fenrong: Yet some scholars focus on the comparative *absence* of logical development in Chinese history. Yang Wujin recalls the Needham question of "why the modern scientific revolution didn't happen in China" and remarks that although there are economic and political reasons, he has "always believed that the more fundamental cause was cultural". Ju Zonglin even takes the minor role of logic in Chinese culture as a serious social problem: "why don't we care about its lack in our speech, writing and actions? Why can't we use logic to constrain our thinking and language to avoid irrational behaviour?"

Jeremy: Others suggest rather that scholars focussing on western formal logic are just looking for the wrong thing and so failing to see what's there. Wang Kexi, for example, asks "whether there is anything like western logic in Chinese culture" not to conclude that Chinese culture is impoverished, but to suggest that western formal logic is the wrong interpretative framework. He says that "the feeling of this research is something quite independent of Chinese culture". Offering a comparative alternative, Liu Peiyu says that Chinese logic is "closer to 'informal logic' or 'critical thinking', having inference by analogy as the main reasoning method."

Fenrong: The view that the *Mobian* is not concerned with logic at all, at least not in the western sense of "logic", is shared by a number of the non-Chinese scholars, including Chris Fraser, Jane Geaney and Dan

Robins. Yet others, such as Yiu-Ming Fung criticise the view that "main function of Chinese language is figurative or poetic" and emphasises the commonalities with logical thought in non-Chinese traditions.

Jeremy: Cui Qingtian also emphasises both the commonalities and the specialness of Chinese ideas about logic. He says that "logic has both general and particular features" where "the particular features are those that vary according to different cultural histories and backgrounds."

Fenrong: And that cross-cultural perspective on logic also lies behind the common phrase "three world systems of logic", referring to the logic of ancient Greece, *hetuvidyā* from ancient India, and Chinese *míngbiànxué*. Liu Peiyu reminds us that the interaction of ideas from these three sources in China is "something that has not happened elsewhere."

Jeremy: Chung-Ying Cheng focusses more on the interplay between logic and other parts of philosophy, notably ontology and metaphysics: "no philosophy is separable from logic; logic itself is not separable from philosophy". He thinks this connection can be traced right back to the *Zhouyi*,[3] and prefers to see Chinese logic as emerging from the same process-oriented metaphysics of change that informs every other branch of Chinese philosophy.

Fenrong: Well, I know we have only scratched the surface of this debate, but we should move on. Our reader will find a lot more inside.

Jeremy: Time perhaps to consider some examples?

3. What is your favourite example of logical acumen by an early Chinese thinker?

Jeremy: We had lot of good suggestions from those we interviewed. I'm really not sure which I like best. How about you?

Fenrong: No, I'm not going to chose one here. We can just invite our readers to go look. But maybe we can talk about what we mean by "logical acumen".

Jeremy: Well, that gets us straight back to the question of what is meant by "logic" when applied to the Chinese tradition. But I think that whatever

---

[3] *Zhōuyì*《周易》Chou-i (Zhou Book of Changes), early Zhou divinatory text in which lines of — and -- are combined in combinations of 6 to produce 64 symbols, and brief lines of interpretation; later combined with a series of commentaries in the *Yijing*.

one's theoretical stance on that issue, it is relatively easy to recognise the signs of a logician at work, taking delight in the trickery of language and the force of good argument.

Fenrong: Ha! Yes. It is interesting that almost everyone had much less difficulty in picking good examples.

Jeremy: O.K. So instead of picking an example here, we could mention the three-way distinction that we often talked about—the one that Johan put so clearly—and which helped us to retain a fairly liberal view of what passes as "logical". At least in a footnote.[4]

Fenrong: Well, I want to talk about one line from an ancient text: the one on our cover! 以故生以理長以類行 from the *Xiaoqu*. Sun Yirang suggested to insert 夫辭 in front of this line, to provide a subject for the sentence. This was followed by A. C. Graham and later researchers. Whatever the original text is, most researchers agreed that *gù* 故 (reason/cause), *lǐ* 理 (principle) and *lèi* 類 (kind) in this line compose the core notions of Chinese logic. Our readers will meet these notions many times through this book.

Jeremy: But basically, it means something like "born from reason, raised by principle, and proceeding from kinds". I like that. It could be a Bruce Springsteen song. And Sun Yirang is suggesting that this describes "propositions". Now I know that the meaning of 辭 is disputed: "proposition" (i.e., something logical) or "phrase" (purely linguistic)? But let's not go there. (Reader: have a look on what, for example, Jane Geaney has to say about this and compare with others.) An interesting point is that the *subject* of the phrase is missing, or in any case, someone as learned as Sun Yirang thought it necessary to add one. This addition of characters and other emendations is something a number of our interviewees have commented on, and it bring us neatly to the next question.

---

[4] Johan van Benthem (private communication, 29 April 2014): "(a) implicit logic in use, whenever there is planning and intelligent behaviour (this was already true for the mammoth hunt in prehistoric times, but also for shopping today), (b) explicit logic in use, like when people explicitly give reasons, draw conclusions, argue about whether something follows, point at consistency as a virtue in thinking, show that something is self-refuting, etc. (c) logical theory as such, evidenced in introducing technical terms, making distinctions, defining validity, system building."

4. In your opinion what is the most difficult or problematic aspect of studying logical thought in China?

Fenrong: Well, as you hinted, it must be the poor state of the ancient texts, especially the *Mobian*. As Chris Fraser puts it, they are a "philological minefield, full of lacunae, miscopied words, transpositions, and unknown, archaic graphs".

Jeremy: Yes, and I liked Jane Geaney's version. She called the corruption of the texts "the interpretive equivalent of quicksand". It's a severe limitation on what can be done, and yet, ironically, it's probably the reason for their survival.

Fenrong: Oh, yes, if they were properly understood, they may not have been included in the *Daozang*.[5] It wasn't until the nineteenth century that Chinese scholars made any progress in decoding them, with Sun Yirang's breakthrough as late as 1895.

Jeremy: And again ironically, it was the sudden awareness of logic as a subject of importance in the West that first drew the attention of such luminaries as Liang Qichao[6] and Hu Shi.[7] And only after that was there significant interest in China concerning logic in ancient texts such as the *Mobian*.

Fenrong: So it is very exciting that China *has* a history of "logical thought" but disappointing that there is so little of it, and what there is so difficult to interpret.

Jeremy: And that brings us back to methodology, which I know is important to you.

Fenrong: My own view is that we shouldn't place too many restrictions. Basically, when we face the old texts, corrupted as they are, we want to understand them—how the Mohists really thought. And the best way to do this is to be open, using as many tools as are available. Traditional western

---

[5] *Dàozàng* 《道藏》 Tao-tsang (Daoist Canon), Collection of 1476 texts, assembled by daoist monks c. 400, and containing the oldest known version of the *Mobian*.
[6] Liáng Qǐchāo 梁啟超, 1873-1929, prominent scholar and reformist who had significant philological insights into the structure of the *Mojing*, whose connection to western logic he was one of the first to recognise; one of the four principal scholars of the Tsinghua academy of *guóxué*.
[7] Hú Shì 胡適, 1891-1962, influential scholar, writer, philosopher, and literary reformist, who studied at Columbia University under John Dewey; his dissertation *Xianqin Mingxueshi* was the first book on the history of Chinese logic in English.

logic and the great variety of logical systems and techniques available today have the potential to be used as tools to help us understand the text. To restrict oneself to one particular tool form logical research, such as the notion of a deductively valid formula from classical predicate logic, is unnecessarily limiting.

Jeremy: Absolutely. Thierry Lucas tells a nice story about how he was challenged to explain the logic of a sign that says "keep off the grass", which means more than it literally says. He responded, quite rightly in my view, that this is exactly the sort of challenge that logicians enjoy and rise to. It is also a common complaint that ideas from temporally or spatially remote cultures are inappropriately used by scholars to interpret ancient Chinese texts. And one must be very alert to that possibility, and open to reexamining assumptions. But one cannot avoid using them altogether. After all, our subject is the history of logic in China, which is essentially comparative. But in choosing tools with which to make comparison, I'd say that there are no absolute prohibitions; anything that promotes understanding is worth at least an initial trial, even if it is rejected on closer examination. I think Dong Zhitie has it right when he says we should "let the text speak".

Fenrong: And it is not only tools from logic that are useful. As Cui Qingtian, Zhai Jincheng, Wang Kexi, Zhou Shan and others have said, it is important to see the history of logic in China as part of the development of Chinese culture more generally, and so other interpretative frameworks within Chinese intellectual history are just as, if not more, relevant.

Jeremy: I found it interesting that this point was taken up also by Rens Bod, who draws comparisons between the history of logic in China and the history of other more theoretical parts of the humanities such as art theory, music theory, and the "rules" of written composition and style, all within the Chinese tradition. If we approach the ancient texts with a fixed idea about what counts as "logic", we may miss a lot. But if we don't attempt to try to understand them using our own tools, our interpretation risks being too shallow. It's a difficult balancing act.

Fenrong: Yes, and that reminds me of the problem of textual emendations. There are sound philological principles, which involve looking for evidence for conjectured emendations based on usage in other texts from a similar period, but very often the evidence is too weak to make a convincing case. And in the case of the *Mobian* this often happens.

Jeremy: Many of those interviewed in this book make that point. Still, one can either take that as a reason to stop our efforts to understand the text or seek other methods. Chad Hansen quotes the interpretative principles of charity and humanity as useful in this respect, and A. C. Graham is known for using his global theory of the structure of the text to make decisions on particular textual issues.

Fenrong: I know there is a lot of disagreement about this, and it is not our place to resolve it here. All we can do is to highlight it for the reader.

Jeremy: Perhaps we should summarise our policy about handling quotations from the ancient texts.

Fenrong: Our aim was to provide explicit quotations, in traditional characters, with all emendations marked. And for that, we mostly used the digitised sources on Chinese Text Project.

Jeremy: We checked quotations from the *Mobian* against the facsimile copy of the *Daozang* edition, so we would be sure to show which if any emendations were being used. In some cases, the way in which the quotation was being used clearly indicated that a different edition was being used, and so we showed the required emendations and translated into English in a way that made most sense.

Fenrong: The result is that readers will see different translations of the same passage in different places in the book. That could be a little confusing.

Jeremy: Well, we tried to stick to "standard" translations, such as A. C. Graham's, if possible, and only modified when necessary. So long as we make the reader aware of this issues, as we are doing now, I think that's ok. Since we included the Chinese text, someone who wants to go into further depth can do so. We also included some cross-references to discussions of the same passage by different people.

Fenrong: And the glossaries!

Jeremy: The glossaries! I think we might be able to put our remarks on them under the heading of the final question.

5. Which other areas of study could benefit from a better understanding of Chinese logic, or vice versa?

Jeremy: In asking this question, we were looking for comments on the wider role of a study of the history of Chinese logic, or "logical thought in

China", and had many comments on that. But how about saying something about what we think of the "wider role" of this book?

Fenrong: I see where you are going. Yes, this book is in a way a trial run for our larger project: the *Handbook of the History of Logical Thought in China*. Our co-editor on that project, Zhai Jincheng is represented here, as are many of the authors of the handbook chapters. We hope that the experience of putting this small book together will help us coordinate the final stages of producing the handbook.

Jeremy: And that's where the glossaries may have a wider role. We should point out to the reader that almost all personal names, the names of texts, and technical terms related to logic are stored in a database and automatically inserted into the text with various commands allowing more or less information to appear.

Fenrong: Gradually, we hope to expand those databases. At this point they're certainly not comprehensive. Entries were chosen just to help in the reading of this book and there are many important scholars, books and technical terms that we didn't cover.

Jeremy: Indeed. Please don't be offended if your name is omitted or if the topic of your last book doesn't appear!

Fenrong: Now I've a test for you, Jeremy. Do you still remember our rules for using simplified or traditional characters?

Jeremy: Let's see. For ancient texts, we used old characters, for texts published post-1950, simplified characters. For people's names, scholars from Hong Kong, Taiwan and mainland China but born before 1900, we also used traditional characters. For rest we used simplified characters. Technical terms found in ancient texts: traditional. Expressions and technical terms from modern times: simplified. It's a little complicated but we hope it seems natural in context. I'd test you on the bibliographical format we used for Chinese journals, but it's getting late and we may be trying the patience of our readers.

Fenrong: You may well be right! So…any last comments?

Jeremy: I'd like to give Christoph Harbsmeier the last word. Seeing an abundance of interesting topics to pursue, he reminds us that it "is far from having made the kinds of contributions to comparative philosophy of language and indeed comparative philosophy more generally that one would think it should be capable of." I share his hope, and invite the reader to enter the world of history of Chinese logic.

Acknowledgements

We thank all the scholars we interviewed for their willingness to participate in this book project, for presenting their views openly, and, in many cases, for trusting us to translate and present their ideas in English. The project has taken us about four years and we appreciate their collaboration in such a long process and especially for their patience and understanding of the inevitable editorial economies we had to impose.

We are grateful to Song Saihua, Tang Mingjun, Zhang Li, and Ma Minghui for their help with the initial translations. In particular, Tang Mingjun and Ji Ying provided a very thorough initial translation of Zheng Weihong's contribution, as did Song Saihua with Sun Zhongyuan's.

Tang Mingjun, Zhai Jincheng, Yang Wujin, Thierry Lucas, provided detailed comments and corrections to our glossaries, for which were are also very thankful.

Liang Zhen helped with type-setting when we moved from word processor to LaTeX, and Dan Robins helped fine-tune some of our code. Thanks also to them.

A special acknowledgement is reserved for Chinese Text Project (www.ctext.org) and its creator Donald Sturgeon, also for permission to use some of the images of the text of the *Mobian* on our front cover.

The cover was designed by our editor-in-chief Vincent Hendricks, without whom this series of 5 question books would not have existed. So a great thanks goes to him for his support and inspiration.

Fenrong Liu & Jeremy Seligman
Beijing and Auckland
August 2015
www.holicnet.net

Chapter 1
Cuī Qīngtián 崔清田

Nankai University, Tianjin

---

1. Why did you begin working on the history of logic in China?

I have been drawn to study the history of Chinese logic by several considerations. But my main motivation is an ongoing confusion over the issue raised by an author who wrote under the pseudonym "Old Overseas Chinese". He said that "a cultural tradition excluding logic and rational reflection has been dominant in China for more than two thousand years."[1] This issue remains alive today. What is called "rational reflection" involves logical thinking - a mode of analytical thought that is different from mere feeling; in fact, we can just take it to be "logical thinking". So the suggestion is that there is no logic or even logical thinking in traditional Chinese culture.

Yet others believe that there really was logic in ancient China, and that even the study of logic, that is *formal* logic, occurred in China before the time of Aristotle, with the study and discussion of logical form, including constants and variables.

Now the following questions arise:

First, was there logic in ancient China or in Chinese traditional culture?

Second, what does it mean to say that there was no logic in Chinese traditional culture? Why is that in any way plausible? Culture is the totality of human practical activities and their products. Practice consists of action and thinking. Action without thinking is hard to imagine. If there was no logical thinking in Chinese traditional culture, how could

---

[1] *Yīgè xiǎogùshì yǐngxiǎng Zhōngguó liǎngqiān duōnián* 一个小故事影响中国两千多年 (A short story influencing China for more than two thousand years), in *Ottawa Chinese*, July 31, 2009.

Chinese culture have arisen, been developed, and produced such fruitful and glorious products?

Third, if we say that there *was* logic in Chinese traditional culture, what was its specific content? How was it represented? And how did it compare to ancient European logic?

These questions are not only important for understanding Chinese logic and its place in traditional culture, but are also relevant to comparative studies of logic and culture in China and the West. Research on these topics can also make a valuable contribution to the cultural development of society today.

It is my confusion over these issues that has led me to continue studying the history of Chinese logic.

2. What is the best way to define your area in terms of historical period, textual sources, methodology or other factors?

Any basis for understanding the phrase "the History of Chinese Logic" must involve understanding the terms "logic" and "Chinese".

First, let's look at the term "logic", which refers to the science of logic, a science which takes logical thinking as its object.

Logical thinking is thinking on the basis of reason rather than mere feeling. It is displayed in the process of moving from "because" to "therefore". So we may also say that logic is the science of inference or reasoning. An inference is made up of names and propositions and so studying inference inevitably involves a consideration of these things. Nonetheless, the essence of inference is a process.

Logic studies inference. It is not concerned with the specific content of thought but with general forms and laws. An inference form is the common structure shared by inferences with different specific contents, or any way of showing what the contents of different inferences have in common.

Inference forms can be represented by formalisation but the form itself should not be confused with this process. The formalisation of inference is a specific method of representing inference forms using a system of special symbols whose meaning can be clearly explained. What we get from formalisation is an inference structure expressed in an artificial symbolic language.

An alternative way of studying inference is to use ordinary language to express these general patterns. It is easy to see that the former is better because it is more precise, although there is no difference in *what* they study. They both belong to logic, and neither is concerned with particular inferences, but rather with an inquiry into the general forms of inference.

Second, let's look at the term "Chinese". The word "Chinese" in the phrase "history of Chinese logic" can be interpreted along the dimensions of both time and space.

As far as space concerned, there two aspects. First, "Chinese logic" denotes the study by Chinese scholars of logical thought whose origin lies outside China. Indian logic and western logic are the main examples. Second, it denotes logical thought that was produced and evolved in China. The main example of this is Mohist logic, which was developed in the pre-Qin period.

As far as time is concerned, "Chinese logic" denotes the history of the development of logic in China from ancient to modern and on to the contemporary era.

In summary, we can say that the history of Chinese logic is the history of the production and development of logic in China, as well as the transmission of non-Chinese logic within China. Its core is the history of ancient Chinese logic before the modern import of western logic into China, which was born from and constrained by the background of traditional Chinese culture.

3. What is your favourite example of logical acumen by an early Chinese thinker?

The dominant type of inference in ancient China was *tuīlèi* 推類. In the *Mojing*,[2] the Mohists summarised this form of inference as follows: when things are of the same kind, one makes an inference according to kind. That is, from some premise, using a principle of similarity, draw a conclusion of the same kind. This is exactly what is stated in the *Daqu* as "the proposition is something which 'proceeds' according to the kind"[3] and in the *Xiaoqu* as "accepts according to the kind; proposes according to the kind."[4]

The Confucians and Mohists, the two most prominent schools of the pre-Qin period, made good use of *tuīlèi* in formulating and justifying their political claims and ethical thoughts. To support their doctrine of "rejecting fate"[5] against the Confucian doctrine of "there is fate", for example, in the *Xiaoqu* the Mohists use the argument:

> 且出門非出門也，止且出門止出門也。。...若若是，...有命非命也，非執有命非命也，無難矣。。...此與彼同，世有彼而不自非也，墨者有此而罪非之，無也故焉。所謂內膠外閉，與心毋空乎內，膠而不解也。此乃{不}是而然者也。(NO 16)

---

[2] *Mòjīng*《墨經》(Mohist Canons), the four chapters of the *Mozi* containing a definition-like systematisation of Mohist thought: *Jingshang, Jingxia, Jingshuoshang,* and *Jingshuoxia*; Chinese scholars also include in this list the remaining two chapters of the *Mobian*.
[3]《墨子·大取》：夫辭以類行者也 。(NO 10)
[4]《墨子·小取》：以類取，以類予 。(NO 11)
[5] *fēimìng* 非命 (anti-fatalism), doctrine of Mo Zi opposing the Confucian idea that human effort is essentially overwhelmed by that of *tiān* 天 Heaven/sky, so that in unfavourable times the gentleman can only retire from society.

Being about to go out is not going out. Stopping (someone) about to go out is stopping (someone) going out....If it is like this..."there is fate" is not fate. Rejecting "there is fate" *is* rejecting fate. This is without difficulty. ...This and that are the same. All the world (assert) that and do not themselves deny (it), (whereas) the Mohists assert this and the multitude deny (it), lacking any reason. This is called being stuck inside and closed off from the outside, a mind with no space, stuck inside and incapable of being freed. These are cases of *búshì érrán* 不是而然 (not this and it is so).

First, the Mohists note that although being about to go out is not going out, nonetheless, stopping someone about to go out is stopping someone going out. And what's more, everyone agrees to this. This pattern is called "not this and it is so". Then by the principle of *lèitóng* 類同 (sameness of kind), they claim similarly, that although (the Confucians) have a doctrine of fatalism but no fate, their rejection of that doctrine is a rejection of (the existence of) fate, again following the pattern of "not this and it is so".

This is an application of the principle of *lèitóng*, which tells us that things of the same kind have identical or similar attributes.

4. In your opinion what is the most difficult or problematic aspect of studying logical thought in China?

There are two difficulties in the study of the history of Chinese logic. One is to identify the theoretical scope of one's research, and the other is to explain Chinese logic as a kind of logic. The first question is a why-question (why study this, not that?), while the latter is a what-question (what is it?).

First, let us talk about scope. As I said before, the term *zhōngguó luóji* 中国逻辑 (Chinese logic) has a wide range. It includes both ancient Chinese logic and the science of logic imported into China from abroad, such as *yīnmíng* and western logic. The history of Chinese logic is the history of the origins and development of the former and the dissemination and study of the latter; but its core is ancient Chinese logic, which was born, cultivated within and constrained by Chinese tradition. One difficulty in our subject is that the term "*zhōngguó luójí*" is also often used in a more specific sense, as a name only for ancient Chinese logic, so as to distinguish it from logic originating abroad. The difficulties in studying the history of Chinese logic come from this ancient Chinese logic sense of "*zhōngguó luójí*", because we must decide which conception of "logic" is appropriate for such a study.

One conception of logic is the science of structures and forms of logical thinking, which are not influenced by culture. On this conception, there is a unique and general logic for all human beings, which is the object of study of western traditional logic and modern symbolic logic. Accordingly, there can be no specifically *Chinese* logic, and the only scope for a history of Chinese logic is the study of ideas from western logic that can be found in the Chinese tradition.

Another conception of logic is as the science of structures and forms of logical thought that are influenced by culture. On this conception, logic has both general and particular features.⁶ The general features are those that are essential for the science of logic, among which having a common object of study is fundamental. The particular features are those that vary according to different cultural histories and backgrounds, such as the dominant types of inference and methods of explaining inferential forms. According to this conception of logic, western traditional and modern symbolic logic are not the only kinds of logic, and we can recognise different logics arising from different cultural backgrounds. Thus we can say that Chinese logic is a part of the study of traditional "Chinese classical studies", and not merely the study of western ideas found in the Chinese tradition.⁷ Chinese logic has some general features shared with western logic while it also has particular features different from western logic.

The scope of the history of Chinese logic is therefore determined by one's conception of logic. Different conceptions of logic will result in different ways of understanding "Chinese logic", and so different ways of thinking, different methodologies and ultimately a different content to the history of Chinese logic.

Next, let's consider the question of what ancient Chinese logic is. If one thinks there is no logic in the Chinese tradition, the question does not arise. If one thinks that there is a logic in the Chinese tradition that shares common features with western logic and also has its own special features, then one must specify the content and status of this logic. The content includes an account of structures and forms of inference. The status includes an account of the use of inferential forms in ancient Chinese politics, science, technology and other related areas.

Finally, if one thinks that the only logic in China consists of those ideas from western logic that can be found in the Chinese tradition, one must also specify the content and status of this logic.

5. Which other areas of study could benefit from a better understanding of Chinese logic, or vice versa?

Before answering these two questions, let me give two examples.

The first example concerns the discussion of Chinese traditional mathematics by Wu Wenjun.⁸ In the 1970s, Wu Wenjun, proposed the Wu Method, which is rooted in ancient Chinese mathematics, but which opened a new direction of research within the international mathematical community, namely the "mechanisation of mathematics"⁹. He pointed out that

---

⁶For a contrasting view, see Sun Zhongyuan on page 45.

⁷*guóxué* 國學 (Chinese classical studies), used in the late Qing dynasty to refer to the sum of Chinese traditional knowledge and culture in contrast to that being introduced from outside, becoming popular again in recent times with the establishment of a *guóxuéyuàn* 国学院 (academy of guoxue) in most major Chinese universities.

⁸Wú Wénjùn 吴文俊, 1919-, prominent mathematician and fellow of the Chinese Academy of Sciences who studied in Strasbourg in the 1940s; also active in the history of Chinese mathematics.

⁹*shùxué jīxièhuà* 数学机械化

there is no axiomatic deductive system in Chinese traditional mathematics:

> The approach of Chinese mathematics is different from the Euclidean axiomatic approach of western mathematics. China has no axioms, no axiomatic system, no consideration of theorems at all.[10]

In another article concerning Wu Wenjun's research, Ji Zhigang wrote:

> Chinese traditional mathematics is an algorithmic system which takes solving problems as its main aim. In the process of going from problems to solutions, algorithmically, this system developed special constructive and mechanical features. This is a big contrast with the so-called axiomatic deductive systems of western mathematics such as Euclid's *Elements*.[11]

The second example is from a study of western political thought by Tang Shiqi:

> Compared with Eastern, especially Chinese, political thinking, which reaches all kinds of political conclusions by comparing humanity with nature and reasoning about human affairs, western political thinking starts with assumed premises, and by logical reasoning, derives a series of political concepts, such as order, rights, obligations, equality and freedom, and then using these concepts, establishes rigorous theoretical systems.[12]

Some people thinks that cultural differences are rooted in different modes of thinking, and that these differences have something to do with logical thinking specifically. And so cultural studies, especially comparative ones, cannot avoid a connection with logic. The above examples have proved this point, and so we have reason to think that research in the history of Chinese logic can both benefit and benefit from research on Chinese traditional culture and comparisons with western culture. Among the humanities and social sciences, the history of philosophy, politics and ethics, and among the sciences, the history of mathematics and medicine: all these have a close relationship to the history of Chinese logic.

Related publications

Míngxué yǔ Biànxué 《名学与辩学》(Studies of Names and Argumentation), Taiyuan: Shanxi Jiaoyu Chubanshe, 1997.

Mòjiā Luójí yǔ Yàlǐshìduōdé Luójí Bǐjiàoyánjiū 《墨家逻辑与亚里士多德逻辑比较研究》(Comparative Research on Mohist Logic and Aristotelian Logic), Beijing: Renmin Chubanshe, 2004.

---

[10] CCTV, the program of *The Masters*, Wu Wenjun: My inequalities, 中央电视台 "大家" 栏目: 吴文俊·我的不等式.

[11] Jì Zhìgāng 纪志刚, *Wúwénjùn yǔ Shùxué Jīxièhuà* 吴文俊与数学机械化 (Wu Wenjun and the Mechanization of Mathematics), Shanghai Jiaotong Daxue Xuebao 上海交通大学学报, 3:13-18, 2001.

[12] Táng Shìqí 唐士其, *Xīfāng Zhèngzhì Sīxiǎngshǐ* 《西方政治思想史》(The History of Western Political Thought), Beijing: Beijing Daxue Chubanshe, 2003, p. 6.

Chapter 2

Dǒng Zhìtiě 董志铁

Beijing Normal University, Beijing

---

1. Why did you begin working on the history of logic in China?

About this question, I have a little story to tell.

After my graduation in 1969, I became a teacher in Beijing Normal University. The Head of Department asked us newcomers to propose a field for our future research and teaching. I put down "Chinese philosophy" but as it turned out, I was assigned to the logic group. The real reason for this was that the logic group leader, Wu Jiaguo,[1] had said to the Head, "If you give us two people, the Department can decide which ones, but if you only give us only one, I want to decide for myself." The Head answered, "We'll only give you one; who do you want?" So this is how I came to the logic group and started my study and research in logic.

In 1977, after the resumption of the University Entrance Exam, the logic group held an important meeting, requiring us to do a good job teaching general logic but also, in research, to have a focussed direction. There were already people who were working in mathematical logic, the history of western logic, dialectical logic, and inductive logic, so Wu Jiaguo said to me: "How about the history of Chinese logic? Didn't you originally want to study Chinese philosophy? These two fields are closely related and, anyway, you have a good grasp of classical Chinese."

At that time, I had no idea about Chinese logic, but I promised to do it all the same. Except for some things I had read in books on Chinese philosophy, I had no understanding of my new subject. But since I had

---

[1] Wú Jiāguó 吴家国, 1936-, philosopher and professor at Beijing Normal University; one of the authors of *Putong Luoji*.

promised, I wanted to do a good job. At that point, I took my first step along the road of research and teaching in the history of Chinese logic.

My first task was to get to know what had already been done in the field and its current state. I plunged head-first into the library catalogue and directory of journal articles, concentrating on those articles and books written since 1949. It so happened that Liu Peiyu and Zhou Yunzhi[2], from the Institute of Philosophy at the Academy of Social Science were doing the same thing. This led to two books, coedited by the three of us, chronicling the previous thirty years of research on the history of Chinese logic.[3] But for thirty years of work, I was shocked to find that those books were rather thin. From the list of authors alone, it is clear that the research community was very small. There were about 20 people, mostly from the older generation, some of whom had already passed away. Considering the 5000 years of history of civilisation and the 2000 years of recorded history in China, the width and depth of existing research in my field was much too small. Why was that?

As a research area, is the history of Chinese logical thought fertile or barren? This cannot be answered in one or two sentences. One has to sit down, concentrate, and study seriously to discover the answer.

There came an opportunity for me in 1986, when the Ministry of Education asked our logic group at Beijing Normal University to hold national further education classes on logic for several years. I taught a course called *History of Chinese Logical Thought*, a topic that was still new to me. Well, I did the best I could, and when preparing for the course, I found a lot of material which also stimulated my interest in the subject and inspired my own research. I was determined to study them thoroughly.

The German philosopher Theodor Ziehen (1862-1950) said, "As far as we know, China's philosophy books seem to completely ignore logic and epistemology. Only Lao Zi, who lived about 50 years before Confucius and who founded Daoist philosophy (*dào* ≈ logos) said something about logic and epistemology."[4]

Also, the Japanese scholar Ōnishi Hajime said, "In the West, logic originated in Greece, with Aristotle as its founder. In Asia in the ancient period, this can only be matched by *hetuvidyā* from India. Throughout the whole world, probably the only people who thought about it are these. At other times, all thoughts about logic were derived from people in these two places."[5]

---

[2] Liú Péiyù 刘培育 1940- and Zhōu Yúnzhī 周云之 1934- are both scholars in the history of Chinese logic and now fellows of the Chinese Academy of Social Sciences. They are interviewed later in the book.

[3] *Zhōngguó Luójí Sīxiǎng Lùnwénxuǎn*《中国逻辑思想论文选》(A Collection of Papers on Chinese Logical Thought, 1949-1979) Sanlian Chubanshe, 1981, and *Yīnmíng Lùnwénjí*《因明论文集》(A Collection of Papers on Yinming), Gansu Renmin Chubanshe, 1982.

[4] Wáng Xiànjūn 王宪钧 et al. translators, *Luójíshǐ Xuǎnyì*《逻辑史选译》(Selections from the History of Logic), Sanlian Shudian, 1961, p. 15.

[5] pnodaxizhu, *Lùnlǐxué*《論理學》(Study of Rational Discourse), translated into Chinese by Hú Màorú 胡茂如, and published in Shanghai by Taidong Tushuju, 1906.

Foreigners said these things, but the Chinese also have similar views. Jiang Weiqiao said, "In East Asia, there has never been *lùnlǐxué*.[6] In Buddhism, *yīnmíng* looks like logic, as does the work of the School of Names in ancient China; but it is not."[7] Xu Zongze said "As far as *mínglǐ*[8] is concerned, there has been little research by Chinese scholars. In ancient times, although there were Deng Xi, Hui Shi and Gongsun Long at the centre, they just pick things up or discuss them here and there, serving only the purpose of sophistry, holding statements without evidence, speaking without reason."[9]

Is what these scholars say really true? This demands a serious answer.

Well, among the audience for my class, there were further education students, undergraduate philosophy students, and postgraduate logic students. The class was popular and well-received. For me, this somehow answered the above question.

2. What is the best way to define your area in terms of historical period, textual sources, methodology or other factors?

To define the history of Chinese logic, ultimately, we should let the literature speak for itself. Of course, any subject has its own origins and development, which constitute its history. As I understand it, logic studies both modes of thinking, abstracted from concrete content, and laws of thought, which are the basic requirements one must follow when one uses these modes. By "modes of thinking" we usually mean concepts, statements (which below, we also call judgements), inferences and argumentation. Laws of thought include the Law of Identity, the Law of Non-contradiction, and the Law of Excluded Middle. Were there any scholars in ancient China who studied these issues? The answer is positive. Thinking is carried out by brains; the content of thinking is expressed by language. Liu Xie wrote a famous book on art and literature called *Wenxin Diaolong* which contains some lines about words, sentences, paragraphs and complete texts:

> 《文心雕龍》卷七章句第三十四: 夫人之立言，因字而生句，積句而成章，積章而成篇。篇之彪炳，章無疵也；章之明靡，句無玷也；句之清英，字不妄也。

> People use sentences to express thoughts. Once you have words[10] you can form sentences. Putting sentences together forms paragraphs. Putting paragraphs together, one gets a complete essay. The whole essay is splendid

---

[6] *lùnlǐxué* 論理學 (study of rational discourse), Japanese term for 'logic' from 1869, used in translation to Chinese from 1898.
[7] Jiang Weiqiao, *Lùnlǐxué Jiǎngyì* 《論理學講義》(Lecture Notes on Logic), Shangwu Yinshuguan, 1924, p. 1.
[8] *mínglǐ* 名理 (names and reasons), term for 'logic' dating from 1631 and used in the *Mínglǐtàn*.
[9] Xú Zōngzé 徐宗澤, Preface to the Second Edition of the *Mínglǐtàn*《名理探》(Exploration of Names and Principles), Sanlian Shudian, 1959.
[10] Classical Chinese is mostly monosyllabic, having one character to express each word.

because every paragraph lacks imperfection. Every paragraph is bright and rich, expressing ideas precisely, because every sentence contains no mistakes. Every sentence is precise and vivid because the usage of each word is correct.

The logical requirements for these relationships are that concepts should be defined clearly, so that one can make appropriate statements, and that statements must be appropriate so that the inferences we make conform to logic, and are thereby convincing.

Liu Xie observes that when people express their thoughts they use words, sentences and larger linguistic units of interconnected sentences. Logic is about concepts, propositions, inference and argumentation - the modes of thinking - and the basic laws one has to follow when using them. There is an intimate relationship between these linguistic forms and modes of thinking but there are also clear differences. Generally speaking, the linguistic form of a concept is a word, that of a proposition is a sentence, and that of an inference or argument is a paragraph. The question is whether in ancient China there were definitions and studies of these modes of thinking. Of course there were! But they did not use the terms "concept", "proposition" and "inference". Instead they used *míngcíshuōbiàn* 名辭說辯 (logico-linguistic categories).

《墨子·小取》：以名舉實，以辭抒意，以說出故。(NO 11)

> One uses *míng* 名 (name) to represent objects, *cí* 辭 (phrase) to express thoughts, and *shuō* 說 (reasoning) to provide evidence or reasons for statements.[11]

This translation is based on the explanation of this definition given in *Mozi*, so I will not discuss it in detail here. If it seems too unspecific, Xun Zi's account is more precise:

《荀子·正名》：名也者，所以期纍實也。辭也者，兼異實之名以論一意也。辯說也者，不異實名以喻動靜之道也。

> A *míng* is that with which *shí* 實 (reality/stuff) is conventionally grouped together. A *cí* is what combines the *míng* of different *shí* into a single thought. *Biànshuō* is to regulate the relationship between *míng* and *shí* so as to reveal the way things change.

The first sentence is a definition of "*míng*" as something referring to many objects of the same kind, by a process of abstraction and generalisation. The second sentence is a definition of "*cí*" as the mode of thinking that connects two different *míng* to express one thought. This definition tells us that *cí* consists of *míng*, and that the structure of *cí* is formed by connecting *míng*. It is hard to know the meaning of an isolated *míng*; we have to connect it (either positively or negatively) with another *míng* to form a sentence. Only by expressing a complete thought can we make the meaning (intension) of a *míng* explicit. In ancient China, this form of expressing thought is called "*cí*". The third sentence is a definition of "*biànshuō*" as inference or argumentation aimed at determining whether

---
[11] For more on the idea of *míngcíshuōbiàn*, see Liu Peiyu, p. 32.

or not something can be attributed to a given object. The process of *biàn* 辯 (disputation) requires *shuō* 說 (reasoning).

In classical Chinese there are words, sentences, paragraphs and the whole discourse. These linguistic forms correspond to the modes of thinking: *míng*, *cí*, *shuō* and *biàn*. Those who thought about logic in ancient China came up with definitions of these categories by reflecting on thinking itself, with the various schools or their representatives reaching their own conclusions either systematically or bit-by-bit. Examples include Confucius' proposal for the theory of *zhèngmíng* 正名 (correcting names), the essay *Mingshilun* by Gongsun Long, the course on "argumentation" that Mo Zi used to teach his students, and Xun Zi's chapter *Zhengming*.[12] After Mo Zi died, his school divided into three factions but they all read the *Mojing*. Lu Sheng tells us that "Mo Zi wrote the *Bianjing*[13] in order to secure the foundations of *mìng*."[14] All these examples are concerned with *míng* and *biàn*.

The ancient Chinese logicians also came to their own conclusions about laws of thought. Gongsun Long, of the School of Names, and Mo Zi all required that the process of thinking must follow the Law of Identity. The Mohists stipulated that "*biàn* is contending (about) contradictories"[15] and then elaborated: "Contradictories are neither both admissible nor both inadmissible."[16] These we can take to express the Law of Non-contradiction and the Law of the Excluded Middle respectively.[17]

Research on the history of Chinese logic has focussed on these central topics of logical thought in ancient China, and so it is no surprise that our forebears used "*míngxué* 名學 (study of names)" or "*biànxué* 辯學 (study of disputation)" in the titles of their translations of works of western logic. For example, Yan Fu translated Mill's book *A System of Logic* as "Mule Mingxue" and Jevons' book *Studies in Deductive Logic* as "Mingxue Qianshuo". Wang Guowei translated his *Elementary Lessons on Logic* as "Bianxue". Hu Shi's American doctoral thesis was called *The Development*

---

[12] *tánbiàn* 談辯 (argumentation), used, but only once, by Mo Zi: "one who can argue argues, one who tells stories tells stories" 《墨子・耕柱》: 能談辯者談辯, 能說書者說書.

[13] *Biànjīng* 《辯經》 (Classic of Disputation), alternative name for *Mojing* or *Mobian*, used by Lu Sheng.

[14] Lǚ Shèng 魯勝 *Preface to the Mohist Dialectical Chapters* 《墨辯注序》: 墨子著書作辯經以立名本

[15] 《墨子・經上》: 辯, 爭 (攸)*{彼} 也。(A74)

[16] 《墨子・經上》: (攸)*{彼} 不可兩不可也。(A73)
There are two issues we would like to mention here. First, the character 攸 in the text is widely interpreted as an error, but there is some disagreement about what to replace it with. Modern Chinese scholars tend to prefer *bǐ* 彼 (that) whereas A. C. Graham prefers *fǎn* 反 (opposite). We translate it here as "contradictory" to align with the current discussion. Second, there is also a disagreement about whether a character 兩 (between the first 不可) is missing from the original text, here again our translation is in line with the author's opinion of taking the text to be 不兩可不可也.

[17] See also the discussion of this passage by Wang Kexi on page 1. *wéihūqíbǐcǐ* 唯乎其彼此 (Law of Identity), *bùmáodùnlǜ* 不矛盾律 (Law of Non-contradiction) and *páizhōnglǜ* 排中律 (Law of the Excluded Middle) are all modern Chinese translations of the terms from western logic, as represented in, for example, *Putong Luoji*.

of the Logical Method in Ancient China, which he translated into Chinese as "Xianqin Mingxueshi". Later Guo Zhanbo wrote a book called "Xianqin Bianxueshi".

Thus ancient Chinese logic just is *míngxué* and *biànxué*, or as it may also be called, "*míngbiànxué*", and so one cannot deny that there was logical thought in ancient China. This was also emphasised, by Joseph Needham[18] who said that "In any case, what is left, together with the many other evidences of geometrical thought in ancient and medieval China, precludes any suggestion that this was wholly lacking–though it was a knowledge of facts rather than of the logical reasons for them, and the algebraic trend, with its own form of logical reasoning, always dominated"[19] Needham clearly accepts that China has its own forms of logical reasoning. My own opinions on Chinese logical thought are contained in my book *The Art of Mingbian and the Logic of Thinking*.

3. What is your favourite example of logical acumen by an early Chinese thinker?

One of the brightest stars of Chinese thought, whose wisdom greatly impresses me, is the one who gave a brilliant explanation of *pì* 譬 (analogy), namely Hui Shi. He was born in the state of Song and then served as a minister for King Hui of the state of Wei for more than ten years. In contrast to the more usual emphasis on ethics and morality, he was interested in the natural world, and never tired of talking about the ten thousand things,[20] remaining constantly fascinated by the mysteries of nature.[21]

We are told of an occasion when he met King Hui of Liang and gave a brilliant defence of his own methods:

> 《新序說苑・善說》明日見，謂惠子曰："願先生言事則直言耳，無譬也。"惠子曰："今有人於此而不知彈者，曰：'彈之狀何若？'應曰：'彈之狀如彈。'諭乎？"王曰："未諭也。""於是更應曰：'彈之狀如弓而以竹為弦。'則知乎？"王曰："可知矣。"惠子曰："夫說者固以其所知，諭其所不知，而使人知之。今王曰無譬則不可矣。"王曰："善。"

The king asked Hui Shi, "When you speak of affairs, sir, I wish you would simply speak directly, with no *pì* 譬 (analogy)"

"Let's suppose we have a man who does not know about *dàn*," he replied. "If he says 'What are the characteristics of a *dàn* like?', and you answer 'Like a *dàn*', will it be communicated?"

"It will not."

---

[18] Joseph Needham (Lǐ Yuēsè 李约瑟), 1900-1995, British biochemist and sinologist noted for his work on the history of science in China in particular as the main editor of *Science and Civilisation in China*, 27 volumes, Cambridge University Press, 1954-2008.

[19] *Science and Civilisation in China*: Volume 3, *Mathematics and the Sciences of the Heavens and the Earth*, 1959, p. 94.

[20] *wànwù* 萬物 (ten thousand things), referring to all that is part of the natural world.

[21] 《莊子・天下》："弱於德，強於物"，"散於萬物而不厭"，"逐萬物而不返"。

"If then you answer instead 'A *dàn* in its characteristics is like a bow, but with a string made of bamboo', will he know?"

"It could be known."

"It is inherent in *shuō* (explanation)," continued Hui Shi, "that by using what he does know to communicate what he does not, you cause the other man to know it. For Your Majesty now to say 'No *pì*' is inadmissible."

"Good," said the King.[22]

In ancient China, a *dàn* and a bow are two devices, differing in that a bow shoots arrows and a *dàn* shoots something round, like stones. The process of thinking by analogy involves using what one knows to reason about what one does not know. Hui Shi's particular method of *pì* enables those who know something to explain it to those who don't. It presupposes that someone knows that A and B have common features, and someone else knows only A but not B. The first uses his knowledge about A to draw an analogy, which allows the second to learn about B. We can summarise the whole process as follows:

Jia knows that A (bow) and B (*dàn*) have common features (similar shape).
Yi knows A but not B.
Jia tells Yi that B has a similar shape to A but with a string made from bamboo.
Yi infers that B is an A-shaped device with a bamboo string.

Following this example, Hui Shi gave a general explanation of his conception of inference: that by using what someone does know to communicate what he doesn't, you thereby get him to know it. Such a general definition is valuable in itself but also explains the importance of the method of *pì*. By listening to the complaints against him, we learned that Hui Shi is so good at using this method that he cannot speak without it!

There are many examples of Hui Shi's using analogies for political purposes and so his knowledge of their essential features is not so surprising. There are too many to list here, but they can be found in the *Zhanguoce*, *Hanfeizi* and *Lüshichunqiu*.

4. In your opinion what is the most difficult or problematic aspect of studying logical thought in China?

In the last 30 years, we have made progress in studying the history of Chinese logic but we have also encountered some problems, not only in the field itself but in the very definition of "logic". At one extreme, there are those who think that logic is the science of necessary relationships between strings of symbols; in other words, that the only logic is deductive

---

[22] Translation: A. C. Graham, *Disputers of the Tao*, Open Court, 1989, p.81.

logic. Whatever fits this criterion is logic; what doesn't fit is not logic. But there are no deductive systems in ancient Chinese literature, with the possible exception of the *Yijing*, according to some scholars whose view is not widely accepted. And so, in this way, the very existence of our field can be denied.

In my opinion, the relationship between thinking and the content of thinking is very complicated. The relationships (correlations or conditional relations) between things (events and objects) can be necessary or merely probable, and when considering the process of thinking there are fours cases of inference: from general to specific, from specific to general, from specific to specific, and from general to general. So we should not expect there to be only one kind of inference form, and logic, as the study of inference, cannot be just one system. This opinion has been accepted by most scholars.

A further question concerns the comparison of Chinese *míngbiànxué* to Indian *hetuvidyā* and western logic. If one of the origins of logic lies in China, then what are its distinguishing features? Several decades of research by scholars such as Wang Dianji, Wen Gongyi, Shen Youding, Zhou Wenying, Liu Peiyu, Zhou Yunzhi, Cui Qingtian, and Sun Zhongyuan[23] have shown that *tuīlèi* 推類 (kind-based inference) is the main form of inference and argumentation in ancient China. This view has been widely adopted within the field. Yet one can ask further questions: What is *tuīlèi*? What is the structure of *tuīlèi*? Can it be formalised? What are the categories or kinds of *tuīlèi*? What are the logical properties of *tuīlèi*? Is it deductive, inductive, analogical, or some combination of these? What is the essence and function of *tuīlèi*?

Until now, research in the field has either not mentioned or said too little about this series of questions, and among those who have said something there are very different opinions. Over the years, I have given my own answers, and more recently, a younger generation of scholars is also addressing them. Yet, unfortunately, we still lack an account that is generally accepted.

A special feature of the history of Chinese logic concerns its relationship to the outside world. Although ancient Chinese civilisation had its own ideas about logic in the Spring and Autumn and Warring States period (770-221 B.C.E.), there is also a long-standing and well-established history of communication with other civilisations. Indian *hetuvidyā* was first encountered in the Han dynasty but it had little influence. During the Tang dynasty, in the 7th Century, Xuan Zang[24] introduced a system of *yīnmíng* that proved to be popular but later declined, and interest in this kind of logic only resumed after being re-introduced from Japan at the end of the Qing dynasty. Western Aristotelian logic was first translated at

---

[23] These are all scholars from China from the 20th century, many of whom are interviewed in this book. Consult the glossary for further details.

[24] Xuán Zàng 玄奘, 602-664, monk, scholar, traveller and teacher, who studied in India and translated many Buddhist texts, including the logical texts *Zhenglimenlun* and *Ruzhenglilun*.

the end of the Ming dynasty but without significant impact and was only introduced systematically at the end of the Qing dynasty. This inspired Chinese intellectuals to engage in many comparative studies of the three world traditions of logic: Indian *hetuvidyā*, western logic and Chinese *míngbiànxué*. So this feature of the history of Chinese logic is also both important and a source of further difficulty.

5. Which other areas of study could benefit from a better understanding of Chinese logic, or vice versa?

This is a big question, which cannot be answered clearly in a few lines. Generally speaking, in ancient China there was no division of subjects of the kind we have today, so one rarely finds classical texts that are purely about logic. Ancient western logic and Indian *hetuvidyā* are similar in this respect. Consequently, the history of Chinese logic is sure to encounter material which, from a modern perspective, we see as different subjects, such as philosophy, politics, military affairs, and natural science (mathematics, astronomy, geography, physics, medicine, biology, engineering, etc.) The detailed division of subjects appeared only in the modern period, and it is very natural to find many subjects in one book.

By drawing from these other subjects, logic can better advance its own research agenda. All those who research Chinese philosophy know the *lìwùshíshì* and *biànzhě èrshíyīshì*,[25] and everyone in the history of Chinese Science reads the *Mojing*. These are also important for Chinese logic and Chinese *míngbiànxué*. The differences lie in the perspective one adopts, and this leads scholars from different areas to different conclusions.

Every science includes applications of logic, which is foundational. So understanding and then using research in logic can definitely benefit the development of other sciences. Of course, these are very general comments. Also, research in the history of Chinese logical thought can benefit form neighbouring and interdisciplinary subjects, such as the history of thinking, the history of thought, the history of epistemology, and the history of scientific method. For example, an important issue in epistemology concerns the relationship between *míng* and *shí*, which is also discussed extensively in the history of Chinese logic. But to continue discussing this issue would take much more time and many more words.

---

[25] *lìwùshíshì* 曆物十事 (Huishi's 10 theses), sequence of ten propositions attributed to Hui Shi in the *Tianxia* chapter of *Zhuangzi*. *biànzhě èrshíyīshì* 辯者二十一事 (dialecticians' 21 theses), the 21 propositions held by various *biànzhě*, mentioned in the *Tianxia* chapter of *Zhuangzi*.

Related publications

Míngbiàn Yìshù yǔ Sīwéi Luójí 《名辩艺术与思维逻辑》(The Art of Mingbian and the Logic of Thinking), Beijing: Zhongguo Guangbo Dianshi Chubanshe, 1998.

Yándào、*Yánshì yǔ Yǐnpì*、*Yuánlèi* 言道、言事与引譬、援类 (Speaking of the "way" and "object" with "analogy" and "adducing"), *Xinyang Shiyuan Xuebao* 信阳师院学报, No. 2, 2003.

"Fúyìérdòng, Tuīlǐérxíng"—Yǐnpì、*Yuánlèi Zàitàntǎo* "扶义而动，推理而行"—引譬、援类再探讨 (Revisiting "analogy" and "adducing" through "fuyierdong tuilierxing"), in Zhou Shan, ed., *Zhōngguó Chuántǒng Sīwéi Fāngfǎ Yánjiū* 《中国传统思维方法研究》, Shanghai: Xuelin Chubanshe, 2010, pp.43-50.

Tuīlèide Gòuchéng、*Běnzhì yǔ Zuòyòng* "推类"的构成、本质与作用 (The Composition, Essence and Function of "kind-based inference"), *Guizhou Bijie Xueyuan Xuebao* 贵州毕节学院学报, No. 7, 2010.

Chapter 3

Jù Zōnglín 剧宗林

Minzu University of China, Beijing

---

1. Why did you begin working on the history of logic in China?

There are two things that influenced me to study the history of Chinese logic:

Firstly, my training in logic, which has made me sensitive to logical issues in whatever I read or hear. When, in the 1960s I worked as a translator for the Tibetan Daily, I much preferred those articles sent from Xinhua, the national news agency, to those written locally. I even preferred to translate political and classical literary essays to those local stories. The reason was simple: I could translate them much faster, at a rate of 1000 words an hour compared to only 300-500. The locally written material couldn't be translated without preliminary and lengthy discussions with an editor, mostly concerning logical issues: vague concepts, internal contradictions, and a lack of clarity in transitions and logical structure. Most of the authors were from major news agencies, with a university education and presumably a training in logic—what a tragic situation! You can imagine the quality of the articles written by those without such a background.

Secondly, the attitude of the Chinese to Confucianism. In his lifetime, Confucius was rejected by all the rulers he spoke to and during the reign of the first emperor, his books were burned and his followers buried. Shortly after, in the Han dynasty, Confucian teaching was established as orthodoxy for two thousand years until the May 4th movement in 1919 proclaimed "Fight Confucianism!" and rejected the old morality and literature for new ways. When the new China was established in 1949, Confucius was rehabilitated and most universities taught the *Analects*, saying "he who reads even half of the *Analects* can rule the whole world." But then during the Cultural Revolution, of course, every word from this old text was criticised, and after Opening and Reform, once again, Confucius has became a national hero. How many twists and turns! And each one far from gentle! What is Confucianism that it should be burnt, revered, beaten, exaggerated, criticised and praised? There must be a convincing reason. It reminds me of the old military slogan: "If I say you are then you are, even if you're not and if I say you're not then you're not, even if you are."[1]

One cannot say that Chinese people lack the capacity for logical thought. We have brains like people from the rest of the world. And one cannot say that we lack a logical tradition. In addition to Mohist logic from ancient times, Buddhist logic was introduced in the Tang dynasty by Xuan Zang[2] and western logic in the Ming dynasty by Li Zhizao.[3] So, with a capacity, our own tradition, and even exposure to logic from other parts of the world, why don't we care about its lack in our speech, writing and actions? Why can't we use logic to constrain our thinking and language to avoid irrational behaviour? In order to answer such weighty questions, one has to study the history of logic in China. And this is the reason for my own decision to work in the field.

2. What is the best way to define your area in terms of historical period, textual sources, methodology or other factors?

Within the history of Chinese logic, my focus is on *yīnmíng*,[4] not as a subject of pure research but as a methodology for life. Logic can guide our thinking, help us establish a position, criticise opponents and act correctly. In my view, researchers in logic should have a strong sense of historical and social responsibility. *Yinming* is not only a reliable tool for understanding the world and making history, but the spirit of our time. We have two tasks: to study its content and grasp its principles, and then to take these out of the ivory tower, making them understood by the community at large. Applying its principles to society will benefit our spiritual civilisation, bring happiness to human kind, and promote harmony and peace throughout the world.[5]

---

[1] 说你是，你就是，是也不是，说不是，就不是，是也不是。

[2] Xuán Zàng 玄奘, 602-664, monk, scholar, traveller and teacher, who studied in India and translated many Buddhist texts, including the logical texts *Zhenglimenlun* and *Ruzhenglilun*.

[3] Lǐ Zhīzǎo 李之藻, 1564-1630, translator of the *Minglitan* with Francisco Furtado.

[4] *yīnmíng* 因明 (*hetuvidyā*, theory of reason), style of reasoning originating in India and introduced to China in the 7th century, also known as "Buddhist logic", divided into an ancient phase including the *Nyāyasūtra* and a new phase from Dignāga and onwards; the sanskrit term "hetuvidyā" is reserved for the later phase.

[5] This last remark is a translation of a passage in "The Spirit of Yinming and the Development of Modern Society".

Of course, I am not suggesting some kind of ideology that would compete with the scientific methodology of Marxism. But I believe that in the current period of history, given that people have more or less the same understanding of the world, society and life in general, there is a need for a uniform methodology. In China, only with such a methodology, and only when people willingly follow it, can we have some order in our ways of thinking and rules to guide us. (Some scholars reject this call for uniformity, thinking that each should blow his own trumpet. This they take to be freedom.) Only when these methodological prerequisites are met can the logical education of the Chinese people be advanced. Without them, acting irrationally and in a way that is not guided by rules or ordered thought, we will never reach our ideals.

I love the Chinese nation and hope that we will lead the world as soon as possible, but whether a nation is advanced cannot be made true merely by boastful and flattering statements. What is important is the general level of logical thinking, creativity, the capacity to avoid logical confusion in speech and writing, and the degree of rationality in action. These are all part of the methodology that I have sought to promote on the basis of my research in *yīnmíng*.

3. What is your favourite example of logical acumen by an early Chinese thinker?

Aristotle praised Democritus for saying that everything happens according to necessity. A similar thought is expressed by Gautama Buddha, who defined karma as what results from what you do and what you fail to do. This was then developed in Buddhism as the idea that good follows good action and bad follows bad action. But we can also find a similar idea in Mo Zi's *Daqu*:

《墨子・大取》：{夫辭} 以故生，...立辭而不明於其所生，妄也 。

> Propositions originate from reasons. ...To put forward propositions without a clear understanding of the reasons is foolish.

In this way, Mo Zi provides a very concise and exact description of *yīn* 因 (*hetu*, reason), which is the central topic of logic. It is also the key to applying logic to society and to developing a methodology to guide us in our thinking and action.

While the logical tradition of the Greeks became a powerful tool when applied to politics and economics, in China it remained locked away in the ivory tower and largely ignored. Initially transmitted only between monks, *yīnmíng* still has a history of development within China. But what about *mòbiàn*?[6] Although, in the pre-Qin period Xun Zi, Gongsun Long and others all studied Mo Zi, they did not reach his level of understanding. Even recent scholars, such as Liang Qichao and Hu Shi, have only

---

[6] *mòbiàn* 墨辯 (Mohist disputation), later Mohist theory of *biàn* 辯 (disputation) .

interpreted and evaluated Mo Zi's ideas; they have not made it a tool comparable with western logic. Today there are few who have heard of Mo Zi's dictim, fewer who understand it, and even fewer who can apply it in practice. And yet it is absolutely necessary to establish a methodology for living. Logical errors abound in ordinary sayings and inference. It is quite common to infer, for example, that all animals with wings fly from the example of an eagle, forgetting completely about chickens and ducks! And many people believe that "false words repeated three times can become the truth."[7] Such mistakes demonstrate the value of Mo Zi's insight even today.

Ten centuries after Mo Zi, in India, Dignāga and Dharmakīrti, finally provided a systematic theory of *yīn*. From this we can see how far ahead of his time Mo Zi was.

4. In your opinion what is the most difficult or problematic aspect of studying logical thought in China?

The most difficult problem we face is knowing how to apply logical theory to circumstances in China. Logical theory demands well-defined concepts, truthful judgements, and arguments that are supported by evidence and correct inference. In order for Chinese society to begin to satisfy these strict demands, those who understand logic and its history must be more active in society. It is the responsibility of historians of logic in China to popularise their subject so as to improve the logical literacy of the Chinese people by teaching them to think, speak and behave logically.

The difficulty arises for a two main reasons.

A. The lack of development of logic in China

In China, the emperor dominates the political system and the political system dominates logic. The traditional Chinese logic known as *mòbiàn* lacked the right social environment to be further developed and both western logic and *yīnmíng* were never well known to the Chinese public. So, unlike in the west, logic remained a stranger to the people. During the age of slavery there was much conflict between slaves and owners, between the owners, and between different states, and this conflict created a purpose for the tools of argumentation. When Aristotle collected these tools, he intended for them to be used, and they were. Throughout the history of western thought their development was further encouraged by the growth of technology. By contrast, Chinese *mòbiàn* was suffocated by feudalism and lacked any proper interpretation for two thousand years. Although some say that even without the development of a Chinese logic, the Chinese people had access to western logic and *yīnmíng*, in fact, the low general level of education

---

[7] 假话重复三遍就可以变成真理, a common idiom.

prevented their dissemination. This was not helped by the choice of *luójí* 逻辑 (logic) as the name for this subject, which in my opinion is a much worse term than its many predecessors, such as *mínglǐxué* 名理學 (study of names and reasons), *míngxué* 名學 (study of names), *biànxué* 辯學 (study of disputation), *lùnlǐxué* 論理學 (study of rational discourse), *lǐzéxué* 理則學 (study of rational principles), etc. And *yīnmíng* is even less clear; not even highly educated Chinese people know about it and the subject is doomed to extinction. Under such social and historical conditions, the lack of logic among the Chinese people is no surprise.

B. Logic faces serious challenges

(i) The habit of revering the emperor is unnerving to logicians. Logic aims to eliminate falsity, to follow truth, to reject what is wrong and to establish what is right. Yet for over two thousand years, the emperor's speech and actions were not evaluated by logic. Every imperial edict was taken to be correct and death was the only option for those with a different opinion. Because of this situation, the wisdom of ignorance and the spirit of Ah Q[8] was transmitted across the generations.

(ii) The lack of stability in the dominant attitudes of Chinese culture makes it hard to apply logical methods. The history of views about Confucius, mentioned above, is one of many examples. In China, although the foundations of culture are very deep and the scope of thinking very broad, they do not follow the way of logic. There is too little tolerance or too much; both leave logic behind.

(iii) The trend of increasing conceptual confusion. Names in Chinese are not merely signs for objects but are associated with feelings and emotions, and this is obvious to any speaker. When we substitute different words within a sentence we can change the feeling of it completely, often because of semantic or phonetic associations. And yet many words used today have been introduced carelessly. The word *kù* 酷 (cool) just looks ugly when pronounced because of its effect on one's facial expression, but it is used as praise! This is particularly problematic with translation. The terms *fó* 佛 (Buddha) and *púsà* 菩萨 (Bodhisattva) are unnecessarily confusing, not revealing the difference between these concepts. They just sound mysterious when clearer terms could have been used (as in, for example, Tibetan). Also, perfectly good words, such as *lǐxiǎng* 理想 (ideal) have been dropped from our dictionaries, and other important words, such as *gémìng* 革命 (revolution) are either literally or mentally deleted from sentences because they make people feel uncomfortable. Such an irrational basis for selecting our basic words

---

[8] 阿 Q (Ah Q) is a character in stories by Chinese novelist Lǔ Xùn 鲁迅. Poorly education and of rural origin, Ah Q is famous for his self-deceptive "spiritual victories" in the face of a humiliating defeat.

and concepts is unacceptable. Concepts are the foundation stones of judgement, inference and argument. If there are problems with the foundations, how can we trust the theoretical constructions we build on them?

(iv) People dare not tell the truth. Why? When Wen Jiabao[9] discussed the difficulties of reform with Wu Kanmin, a representative of the National People's Congress in Hong Kong, he said that there are two factors that cause people not to tell the truth and which must be corrected: feudalism and the cultural revolution. Since our leader realises this, the common people should realise it too. This is a great challenge for logic because if the premises of an argument are not true, the conclusion is also not reliable. So many falsehoods and lies bring a loss of trust, confusion and blindness and eventually the destruction of society.

(v) When one tries to suppress contradictory propositions they just pop up again. With contemporary issues in social security, the judicial system, anti-corruption, unjust distribution, house price control, medical reform, price control, environmental pollution, food safety, education reform and so on, there are many contradictions. For example, to improve social security the government needs to spend a lot of money, but the country doesn't have enough; to achieve justice in the judicial system it must be complete, and yet injustice in the system is typically blamed on the incompleteness of the system; to guard against corruption, we need a strong supervisory mechanism, but when faults are exposed, the lack of supervision can always be blamed. At popular request, the government decided to control prices, but economists question this, saying that it is a repression of the market economy. Among the alumni of Beijing University there were reported to be 79 billionaires. The purpose of a great university is to produce great scholarship, and yet it celebrates great wealth. These contradictions are a big challenge to the organisation of society but they also presents a challenge to logic.

To address these problems, we should improve people's reasoning via logic education, enabling them both to argue rationally and to have the courage to do so. With reason one can cross the world; without it one cannot take a single step. The continual development of logical theory is also necessary, so as to engage with society in the production of a logic for the general public that is simple, concise, and understandable.

---

[9] Wēn Jiābǎo 温家宝, 1926-, premier of the People's Republic of China from 2003 to 2013.

5. Which other areas of study could benefit from a better understanding of Chinese logic, or vice versa?

Scientific theories consist of concepts, judgements, inferences and arguments, and the correct use of these is what logic studies. So, not only natural science but also social science can learn from the history of logic. And in particular, the design of systems of general education can benefit from a study of logic.

A. Using the law of cause and effect and the Principle of Sufficient Reason.

Someone who lacks reciprocity is a dreadful person; a society that lacks reciprocity is a dreadful society. So as to improve the lack of reciprocity in society, as a matter of general education, we can reasons according to different types of people, as follows:

For children:
Major premise: one should repay kindness
Minor premise: my parents were kind in raising me
Conclusion: I should repay my parents

For current employees:
Major premise: one should repay kindness
Minor premise: retired cadres worked their whole life to create a good conditions for us
Conclusion: we should repay them by encouraging them to continue to play a role and by trying to address their problems

For soldiers:
Major premise: one should repay kindness
Minor premise: the people raised us soldiers
Conclusion: we soldiers should defend people's property

For the rich:
Major premise: one should repay kindness
Minor premise: society made me rich
Conclusion: I should repay society

(Those who do not repay kindness, although rich, are still poor.)

For the powerful:
Major premise: one should repay kindness
Minor premise: my power is given by the people
Conclusion: I should serve the people

(Using power for personal benefit is corrupt, a betrayal of principle, and is not permitted either by law or by the Party.)

For those who lack traffic morality:

Major premise: harming others results in harm to oneself
Minor premise: drink driving, obstructing traffic while talking and such things are all harmful to others
Conclusion: this will necessarily harm yourself, such as by getting in a car accident

(We start by harming other but end up harming ourselves.)

For the achievement of impartial justice:

Major premise: those who do good are rewarded; those who do bad are punished
Minor premise: individuals or organisations do good/bad
Conclusion: we should reward those who do good and punish those who do bad

(In the past, the highest members of society never received punishment and the lowest never received benefits, but this principle is ridiculed by developed societies and despised by Communist Party members.)

Many significant social issues can be addressed by constructive argument, aiming at the unification of the people's ideas. Only with such unification can law be an effective instrument for solving problems. Without such unification, the law alone is not enough. There are bound to be gaps in the law, and in trying to fill them, it is hard to avoid contradiction. These make the problem even more difficult to solve: we push it down and it springs back up.

B. Using the Principle of Sufficient Reason and the Law of Non-contradiction.

By following logical principles you will not necessarily get to the truth, but if you do not follow them, you will be sure to make mistakes. In China today, there are many dictums that conflict with logic: "if you have power you have everything", "money can do anything", "great things cannot be achieved without lying", "eat and drink until you die."[10] All these should be rejected using the principles of logic.

If someone says "if you have power you have everything" you can reply: No! One who has power can do good but also bad, and certainly cannot do everything. Qinshihuang, the first emperor of China, had more power than anyone but could neither find an elixir of immortality nor prevent the downfall of Qin. And, in modern times, even powerful leaders and officials are unable to save themselves from their enemies.

If someone says "money can do anything" you can reply: No! Money can be used to buy cars, houses, luxurious food and commodities, and sometimes even political position. But there are some things one cannot buy. He Shen had lots of money, enough to conquer a whole

---

[10] 有权就有一切; 金钱万能; 不说假话办不成大事; 吃喝等死 。

country, but he was unable to buy his life from Jia Qing.[11] And most of those executed for financial crimes and drug trafficking had plenty of money but were also unable to save themselves.

If someone says "great things cannot be achieved without lying" you can reply: No! Some people gain their leader's trust by lying so as to get promotion or a higher salary. Some lie to cheat others. Some businessmen lie and harm others to increase their wealth. Nonetheless, many great things are achieved without lying. Led by the Communist Party, the Chinese people banished the "three mountains"[12] and established a new China. These things could not have been achieved by telling lies. The plan of "two bombs, one satellite"[13], likewise, could not have been achieved by telling lies.

If someone says "doing great things is hard, doing small things is senseless, eat and drink until you die" you can reply: No! Time is not easy to get; life is not easy. Since other engage in productive work for my benefit, why should I do nothing for them, eating, drinking and waiting to die like an animal.

All the above examples show that conclusions which are not based on the Principle of Sufficient Reason are mistaken and should be rejected. The existence of theories full of mistakes is the fundamental reason for conceptual chaos and aimless practice.

C. Logical analysis helps identify the *zhǔyào máodùn* 主要矛盾 (main contradictions), their principal features and how to resolve them.

There are contradictions in social security, the judicial system, the anti-corruption movement, unjust distribution, house price control, medical reform, price control, environmental pollution, food safety, and education reform. By logical analysis we can see that unfair distribution is the main contradiction. The main aspect of this contradiction is that the income of the poor is too low. If we resolve the main aspect of the main contradiction, the other contradictions can easily be resolved.

D. The cultivation of habits in logical thinking, a calm state-of-mind and an ability to act rationally are all improved by training in logic. As a consequence of logical training:

(i) A person gradually comes to think more deeply and less superficially. Only by doing this can we learn to distinguish truth from falsity in our complex society. Hence logic education is needed to establish a rational society.

---

[11] Hé Shēn 何珅, 1750–1799, served as a high official of the Qianlong 乾隆 emperor in the Qing dynasty was exposed for corruption and killed by the emperor Jiā Qìng 嘉庆.
[12] The *sānzuò dàshān* 三座大山 (three mountains) which were crossed on the revolutionary road are feudalism, imperialism, and bureaucratic capitalism.
[13] Shortly after the foundation of the P.R.C., the Chinese government introduced *liǎngdàn yīxīng* 两弹一星 (two bombs, one satellite), a long-term plan to produce long-range nuclear missiles and spacecraft; it became a symbol of technological and military progress.

(ii) A person's ability to think, speak and write is improved. Hence logic education can enhance the effects of education, both in schools and in society at large.

(iii) A person's ability to learn is improved. Only when we grasp the method of logical thinking can we choose what to learn and learn it efficiently. The learning of political theory is like this, but also science.

(iv) A person's creativity is improved. Creativity is the combination of logical thinking and "emotional thinking".[14] Emotional thinking provides new ideas. Logical thinking helps select the more feasible ones. Hence most successful theoretical creations start with both emotional thinking and logical thinking.

Related publications

Yīnmíng Jīngshén hé Xiàndài Shèhuì Fāzhǎn 因明精神和现代社会发展 (The Spirit of Yinming and the Development of Modern Society), in Zhang Zhongyi, et al eds., *Yinming Xinlun-Shoujie Guoji Yinming Xueshu Yantao Wencui*《因明新论 —首届国际因明学术研讨文粹》, Beijing: Zhongguo Zangxue Chubanshe, 2006.

---

[14] *gǎnxìngsīwéi* 感性思维 (emotional thinking), Chinese Marxist term for thinking determined by the senses or feelings, often contrasted with *lǐxìngsīwéi* 理性思维 (rational thinking).

Chapter 4

Liú Péiyù 刘培育

Chinese Academy of Social Sciences, Beijing

1. Why did you begin working on the history of logic in China?

I'll tell you in two parts. First: why logic?

I started to learn logic while studying philosophy as a postgraduate student at Jilin University from 1959 to 1964. One day, I remember, I had some doubts about a definition in the textbook, although I can't now say exactly what it was. My logic teacher, Du Xiushi[1] agreed with me immediately, telling the whole class that I was right and the textbook wrong. It encouraged me greatly and that day I became interested in logic. In September 1964, I left a beautiful small town along the Songhua River in the north-east of China for the capital city of Beijing, where everyone was yearning to be. I first enrolled as a logic major in the Chinese Academy of Sciences, supervised by Jin Yuelin[2] and after graduating I found a teaching job in the same place.

So, for the second part, why the history of Chinese logic?

To tell the truth, at first I had no plans to study the history of Chinese logic. I clearly remember that Zhou Liquan[3] was asked by my supervisor to talk with me, only six days after I arrived at the Academy. "It is clear that you'll want to focus on the philosophy of logic or philosophical logic",

---

[1] Dù Xiùshí 杜岫石, 1923-2002, taught logic for many years at Jilin University and later Peking University.

[2] Jīn Yuèlín 金岳霖, 1895-1984, philosopher and logician, studied in Columbia University, whose *Luoji* is one of the earliest books on modern logic in Chinese; founder of the philosophy department at Tsinghua University.

[3] Zhōu Lǐquán 周礼全, 1921-2008, philosopher and fellow of the Chinese Academy of Social Sciences; pioneer of *yǔyánluóji*.

he said, adding that my five years of studying philosophy had given me a solid grounding and that my examination script in epistemology suggested I had a lot to say. At that time, I knew little about logic, and so in preparing for my graduate studies, I followed my teacher's advice.

It was later that I changed to study the history of Chinese logic. Now I think this was caused by two factors: one was the two years of the Four Clean-ups,[4] and the other was the ten years of the Great Proletarian Cultural Revolution. In 1967, the Ministry of Education issued a document saying that we were "considered" to have graduated but at that time I knew almost nothing about the philosophy of logic.

By the time the Cultural Revolution ended and professional life resumed, it was already 1978. When the Sixth Five-year Plan was being drawn up, all logicians in China considered the history of Chinese logic to be one of the most important research directions. In fact, even in 1956, in the research plan made by the Institute of Philosophy of the Academy, it was already considered an area of research concentration. *A History of Chinese Logical Thought* by Wang Dianji and *A Study of Logic in the Mojing* by Shen Youding were about to be published, and these two distinguished gentlemen, needing someone to help them, let me assist in organising their manuscripts.[5] It was while working on this project that I became interested in the history of Chinese logic. Thereafter, from the late 1970s to the early 2000s, it has been the focus of my research.

2. What is the best way to define your area in terms of historical period, textual sources, methodology or other factors?

It took me some time to find my way in the history of Chinese logic but after studying the contributions of my senior colleagues in the field, in the late 1970s and early 1980s, I developed the following ideas.

Logic itself studies the forms and rules of thought, especially forms of inference. But the history of Chinese logical thought concerns a diverse array of topics: the rules and forms of thinking involved in *míngbiàn*[6] and its methods of argumentation; the relationship between logical thought and language; dialectical thought; and the introduction and influence of Indian and western logic in China.

There were two special features of my approach at that time. One is that I defined "the history of Chinese logic" to have broad scope, as described in my article "A Brief Discussion of the History of Logical

---

[4] *sìqīng* 四清, the socialist education campaign in rural areas, 1963-1965.
[5] *Zhōngguó Luóji Sīxiǎngshǐ* 《中国逻辑思想史》 (A History of Chinese Logical Thought) by Wang Dianji, Shanghai: Shanghai Renmin Chubanshe, 1979, and *Mòjīng de Luójixué* 《墨经的逻辑学》 (A Study of Logic in the Mojing) by Shen Youding, Beijing: Zhongguo Shehuikexue Chubanshe, 1980.
[6] *míngbiàn* 名辩 (names and argument), topic of *míngbiànxué*.

Thought in China". This was a deliberate choice so as to include the relationship between logical thinking and language, dialectical thought, epistemology, and fragmentary logical thoughts scattered in texts whose principal concern is some other topic. In fact, I often called it the "history of Chinese logical thought" instead of the "history of Chinese logic". My main reason was that research in the field had only just started and it was better to begin by searching for relevant historical material without too many restrictions.

The other is that, in the 1980s, I took "ancient Chinese logic" to be the same as *míngbiànxué*,[7] which was already established in the pre-Qin period. In the book *The History of Pre-Qin Logic*, on page 305, I said that the greatest contribution of pre-Qin logic was the appearance of ancient logical systems, especially those expressed in the *mòbiàn*[8] and Xun Zi's *Zhengming* in the 4th to 3rd centuries B.C.E.

In the 1990s, scholars who study the history of Chinese logic reflected on their work to date, and my view subsequently changed in two ways. Firstly, I now distinguish between "ancient Chinese logic" and *míngbiànxué*, as described in my article "The Theory of Name and Argumentation and Ancient Chinese Logic". Although its core is logic, *míngbiànxué* is also concerned with epistemology, fallacies and paradoxes, and has a close connections to politics and ethics; its concerns are broader than the merely logical. Secondly, I now think that the history of Chinese logic should be confined to logical topics: the logical part of *míngbiànxué*, the logical part of *Zhouyi*, and then *yīnmíng* and the development of western logic in China. In my opinion, the most characteristically Chinese logic is that of *míngbiànxué*, which is closer to "informal logic" or "critical thinking", having inference by analogy as the main reasoning method.

3. What is your favourite example of logical acumen by an early Chinese thinker?

In the *Mojing* and Xun Zi's *Zhengming*, there are many such examples. In the *Mojing*, we find

《墨子·經說上》：小故，有之不必然，無之必不然。體也，若有端。大故，有之必{然}，無{之必不}然，若見之成見也。(A1)

When there is a *xiǎogù*, something is not necessarily so; when there is not, something is necessarily not so. It is a part - like a point. When there is a *dàgù*, something is necessarily so; when there is not, something is necessarily not so. Like seeing something complete seeing.

---

[7] *míngbiànxué* 名辯學 (study of names and argument), combination of *míngxué* 名學 and *biànxué* 辯學 used by modern scholars to refer to discussions of logical thought in ancient China.
[8] *mòbiàn* 墨辯 (Mohist disputation), later Mohist theory of *biàn* 辯 (disputation).

So a *xiǎogù* is a necessary but not sufficient condition: when the antecedent occurs, the consequent may not also occur, but when the antecedent does not occur, the consequent certainly doesn't occur. A *dàgù* is a sufficient condition: when the antecedent occurs, the consequent must also occur. Many of the school of *míngbiàn* distinguished between necessary and sufficient conditions, and were able to describe the difference in ordinary language. Yet western traditional logic talks only about sufficient conditions, not necessary conditions, which is to say that the two kinds of condition were not distinguished. In the whole history of logic, it was logicians in China who first proposed hypothetical propositions about necessary conditions, and also the corresponding inferences. The above passage from the *Mojing* is one example of this.

There is a famous story in *Hanfeizi* that elegantly expresses the Law of Non-contradiction:

《韓非子·難一》：楚人有鬻盾与矛者，誉之曰："吾盾之坚，莫能陷也"。又誉其矛曰："吾矛之利，于物无不陷也"。或曰："以子之矛陷子之盾，何如？"其人弗能应也 。

Once there was a man of Chu selling shields and halberds. In praising his shields he said, "My shields are so solid that nothing can penetrate them." Again, in praising his halberds, he said, "My halberds are so sharp that they can penetrate anything." In response to his words somebody asked, "How about using your halberds to pierce through your shields?" To this the man could not give any reply.

This is the very famous *máodùnzhīshuō* 矛盾之说 (explanation of contradictions).[9] Han Fei cleverly uses a story to give a clear account of the central aspects of the Law of Non-contradiction, and its application to relational propositions. It is a valuable contribution to logic.

Moreover, in the *Yinci* we find the following story:

《呂氏春秋·淫辭》：空雄之遇，秦、趙相與約約曰："自今以來，秦之所欲為，趙助之；趙之所欲為，秦助之 。"居無幾何，秦興兵攻魏，趙欲救之 。秦王不說，使人讓趙王曰："約曰'秦之所欲為，趙助之；趙之所欲為，秦助之'。今秦欲攻魏，而趙因欲救之，此非約也 。"趙王以告平原君 。平原君以告公孫龍 。公孫龍曰："亦可以發使而讓秦王曰：'趙欲救之，今秦王獨不助趙，此非約也 。'"

At the meeting at Kongxiong, Qin and Zhao joined together in a treaty which said, "From this time forward, Zhao will support Qin in whatever Qin desires to do, and Qin will support Zhao in whatever Zhao desires to do." Shortly thereafter, Qin raised an army to attack Wei, and Zhao wished to rescue the latter. The king of Qin was displeased and sent a man to reprimand the king of Zhao. "Our treaty says, 'Zhao will support Qin in whatever Qin desires to do, and Qin will support Zhao in whatever Zhao desires to do.' Qin now desires to attack Wei, and Zhao on account of this wishes to assist Wei. This is contrary to our treaty." The king of Zhao reported this to the Lord of Pingyuan, who told Gongsun Long. Gongsun Long said, "You too may send

---

[9]The Chinese word *máodùn* 矛盾 (contradiction) literally means "spear" (or "halberd" in Liao's translation) and "shield" and is derived from this story.

out an emissary to reprimand the king of Qin, saying 'It is Zhao's desire to assist Wei, but now the king of Qin alone refuses to support Zhao. This is contrary to our treaty.' "[10]

Gongsun Long was a logician. He noticed the symmetry of the two clauses of the treaty, showing that the two parties had equal standing in their arrangement. So he advises the king of Zhao that he can use a very similar argument to criticise the king of Qin for breaking their agreement. From this story we learn that when you refute someone you cannot make use of reasoning that has the same effect on both sides. The *yīnmíng* fallacy of *pínghéng lǐyóu* 平衡理由 (balanced reason) is very similar to this. The above three examples differ in their degree of abstraction, with the second more concrete than the first, and the third more concrete still. It is a common practice of Chinese people to use the specific to illustrate the general, and here we can see the general logical principle behind the details of the concrete examples.

4. In your opinion what is the most difficult or problematic aspect of studying logical thought in China?

For the last 30 years, research in this field has been fruitful. In the 1980s, in order to investigate logical ideas in ancient China and to summarise the results of the last 70 years of the twentieth century, Chinese scholars complied two multi-volume works: *A Source Book for the History of Logic in China*[11] and *The History of Logic in China*[12]. We have also published two textbooks, the first of their kind. And again in the 1980s, we went on to explore further aspects of *míngbiànxué*, especially the idea of *tuīlèi*[13] from the perspective of modern logic, semantics, pragmatics, semiotics and critical thinking. In addition, some scholars have analysed the logical thinking of the *Zhouyi*, traditional Chinese medical science and ancient Chinese science. The abundance of material has attracted the interest of scholars who had not previously studied the history of logic in China, and also some foreign scholars.

Based on the current status of our field, I think we should pay special attention to the following two issues.

First, we need to develop a comprehensive picture of *míngbiànxué*, correctly evaluating its logic, and interpreting it in relation to the characteristic ways of thinking of Chinese people. It is a branch of ancient

---

[10]translated by John Knoblock and Jeffrey Riegel, *The Annals of Lü Buwei: A Complete Translation and Study*, Stanford University Press, 2000, p.457.

[11]*Zhōngguó Luójishǐ Zīliàoxuǎn* 《中国逻辑史资料选》(A Source Book for the History of Logic in China) edited by Li Kuangwu, Zhou Yunzhi, et al, 5 vols., Lanzhou: Gansu Renmin Chubanshe, 1985-91.

[12]*Zhōngguó Luójishǐ* 《中国逻辑史》(The History of Logic in China), edited by Li Kuangwu, 5 vols., Lanzhou: Gansu Renmin Chubanshe, 1987-89.

[13]*tuīlèi* 推類 (kind-based inference), the central Mohist conception of inference, also known as *lèituī* 類推 (kind-based inference).

Chinese learning with a distinctive character and forms a self-contained system. Together with western logic and Indian *hetuvidyā*, it is one of the three origins of logic, of equal value to the others.

The scarcity and obscurity of original material is the biggest problem for those who study *míngbiànxué*. Most research to date has been mere comparison with related ancient literature about western logic. We really need to go further to expose the true nature of this logical thought and explain it in its own terms. Until now, this kind of work has been very rare.

Second, in order to produce a thorough comparison of the three origins of logic across the world, we need a proper evaluation of their similarities and differences. Introduced into China in the Han dynasty, Indian *hetuvidyā* became Chinese *yīnmíng*, which flourished in the Tang dynasty and then gradually split into two branches. Western logic was introduced at the end of the Ming dynasty, and at the beginning of 20th century it became highly valued by many scholars, who called it "the rule of all rules and the knowledge of all knowledge."[14] The three traditions all developed and competed with each other within China, something that has not happened elsewhere.

In the last century, scholars have made some progress in making these comparisons, but they should go further. The biggest difficulty is that they need to be familiar with all three traditions of logic; and such scholars are very few.

5. Which other areas of study could benefit from a better understanding of Chinese logic, or vice versa?

From my research experience, the history of logic in China is deeply related to argumentation, linguistics, mathematics, the history of Chinese philosophy and the history of ideas in China. Its central concern, *míngbiànxué*, is a generalisation of the practice of argumentation that emerged against the background of the Warring States period and the Contention of the Hundred Schools.[15] So a study of the history of argumentation in China is bound to be helped by a history of logic, and vice versa.

There is also a close relationship between the history of Chinese logic and the history of Chinese language. *Mingbianxue* was deeply influenced by the ancient Chinese language, which was both its means of expression and a source of problems. Its conceptual framework is *míngcíshuōbiàn*,[16]

---

[14] in Chinese: 一切法之法，一切学之学, quoted as the translation of Bacon's dictum by Yán Fù 嚴複, 1854-1921, scholar and translator of western books, include *Mule Mingxue* and *Mingxue Qianshuo*.

[15] *bǎijiā zhēngmíng* 百家爭鳴 (contention of the hundred schools) is the period of great philosophical activity in ancient China from 500 to 200 B.C.E.

[16] *míngcíshuōbiàn* 名辭說辯 (logico-linguistic categories), literally "name, phrase, explanation, disputation", a sequence of categories discussed in the *Mojing* and *Xunzi*.

whose ingredients have both logical and linguistic significance: *míng* is both "name" and "concept"; *cí* is both "sentence" and "proposition".[17] For this reason, logicians and linguists interested in ancient China and can learn from each other's work.

Logic and mathematics are also naturally related. Research into their histories shows that they have much in common, and consequently, logicians and mathematicians are paying more and more attention to each other's work, especially in recent years.

There is a similar trend of relating the history of Chinese logic to the history of Chinese philosophy. On the one hand, their common interest in ancient epistemology encourages a dialogue between the two fields, although from different perspectives. Both need to refer to each other's results. In the 1950s research in logic depended more on research in the history of philosophy, but in the last 20 years, logical studies have assisted research in Chinese philosophy, thanks to logical insights into ancient Chinese epistemology. On the other hand, both logic and philosophy face issues of legitimacy, the structure of their subjects, and the cultural background of their development, and so they cannot avoid referring to each other.

Related publications

Zhōngguó Luóji Sīxiǎngshǐ Lùnlüè 中国逻辑思想史论略 (A Brief Discussion of the History of Logical Thought in China), in Zhou Yunzhi, Sun Zhongyuan, and Dong Zhitie, eds., *Zhōngguó Luójishǐ Yánjiū* 《中国逻辑史研究》(Studies in the History of Logic in China), Beijing: Zhongguo Shehuikexue Chubanshe, 1982.

(Co-ed Zhou Yunzhi), *Xiānqín Luójishǐ* 《先秦逻辑史》(The History of Pre-Qin Logic), Beijing: Zhongguo Shehuikexue Chubanshe, 1984.

Míngbiànxué yǔ Zhōngguó Gǔdài Luóji 名辩学与中国古代逻辑 (The Theory of Name and Argumentation and Ancient Chinese Logic), *Zhexueyanjiu* 哲学研究, supplementary issue, 1998.

---

[17] For other discussions of *míngcíshuōbiàn*, see Dong Zhitie, p. 10.

Chapter 5

Shěn Jiànyīng 沈剑英

East China Normal Univeristy, Shanghai

---

1. Why did you begin working on the history of logic in China?

Originally, I dedicated myself to creative writing and the study of literature, favouring classical Chinese literature especially from the pre-Qin period. But my dream was destroyed by the Cultural Revolution. I had to tear up two of my manuscripts, and after that I decided to part from my dear literature. Having gone through all kinds of suffering, I was finally able to teach again. With such painful experiences in the past, I wanted to change my subject and so started teaching logic, an area that causes less trouble politically. Although my reason for studying logic was just to play it safe, I gradually developed great interest in history of Chinese logic. Studying this subject was relatively easy for me as I always enjoyed pre-Qin literature, and had a good understanding of pre-Qin philosophy. After some time, I became aware of the work of scholars such as Zhang Taiyan[1] who compared western traditional logic with Mohist logic using the terminology of *yīnmíng*,[2] the Chinese interpretation of Indian *hetuvidyā* (theory of reason). In his *Guogulunheng* Zhang Taiyan states:

> The way of *biàn*[3] is first to see the point, then to clarify its foundations, making the connection by choosing examples which make things plain. In

---

[1] Zhāng Tàiyán 章太炎, 1868-1936, philologist, philosopher, journalist and revolutionary; author of *Guogulunheng*.
[2] *yīnmíng* 因明 (*hetuvidyā*, theory of reason), style of reasoning originating in India and introduced to China in the 7th century, also known as "Buddhist logic", divided into an ancient phase including the *Nyāyasūtra* and a new phase from Dignāga and onwards; the sanskrit term "hetuvidyā" is reserved for the later phase.
[3] *biàn* 辩 (disputation), also interpreted as "distinction-drawing", one of the Mohist *míngcíshuōbiàn*.

yīnmíng these are called *zōng* 宗 (pakṣa, thesis), *yīn* 因 (hetu, reason) and *yù* 喻 (dṛṣṭānta, example). In India, *zōng* comes first, then *yīn*, then *yù*. In the far West, the *yùtǐ* 喻體 (dṛṣṭāntakāya, example-statement) comes first, then the *yīn*, then the *zōng*. This is similar to inference by *trayāvayava*.[4] The *Mojing* uses *yīn* to give reasons, the claim comes later: first *yīn*, then *yùtǐ*, then *zōng*, which is quite different from India and the far West. The *zōng* of the Mohists and those from the far west, always comes after the *yùtǐ*, leaving no room for a *dṛṣṭāntāśraya* (example-base, *yùyī* 喻依), and so are at a disadvantage compared to of those using the rules of *yīnmíng*.

That Zhang Taiyan thought so highly of *yīnmíng* aroused my interest, and I wasted no time in borrowing some books on the subject, including Kuiji's *Yinmingdashu*.[5] But I wouldn't say it's easy reading. Even the abridgement *Yinmingdashu Shanzhu*[6] is hard, and when I had a question, I had no one to ask, because of the tensions between people due to the Cultural Revolution. So in studying I had many problems and only myself to solve them. The positive side of such hardship was to deepen my understanding of the subject, and when I came to know that *yīnmíng* was virtually extinct in China, I resolved to revive it.

I became more and more fascinated by *yīnmíng* since there was plenty to get involved in: elucidating its doctrinal aspects, collating and annotating the literature, studying the history of how Indian *hetuvidyā* spread to China, translating important texts, etc. These tasks awaited us; there was so much to do! Facing such a glorious landscape, which attracted me deeply, I began by taking small steps and eventually moved deep into the territory. From the gateway of the pre-Qin *míngxué*,[7] I had arrived unwittingly in the grand palace of *hetuvidyā*, where I began my research on Chinese Buddhist logic, one of the most important parts of history of Chinese logic. The book *History of Chinese Buddhist Logic* that I edited over ten years ago, reflects only the initial stages of research in this subject; in fact, I would like to re-edit and improve it.

2. What is the best way to define your area in terms of historical period, textual sources, methodology or other factors?

There are several aspects to my research:

---

[4] *trayāvayava* (form of three branches, *sānzhīlùnshì* 三支論式), *yīnmíng* term for the form of argumentation proposed by Dignāga as an improvement of the *wǔzhīzuòfǎ* 五支作法 (*pañcāvayava*, five-membered argument), composed of *zōng* 宗 (pakṣa, thesis), *yīn* 因 (hetu, reason) and *yù* 喻 (dṛṣṭānta, example).
[5] Kuijī 窺基, 632–682, student of Xuan Zang and author of *Yinmingdashu*. *Yīnmíngdàshū* 《因明大疏》 (Great Exegesis of *Yinming*), by Kuiji, an influential commentary on the *Ruzhenglilun*.
[6] *Yīnmíngdàshū Shānzhù* 《因明大疏删注》 (Great Exegesis of *Yinming*: Abridged with Commentary), by Xiong Shili, first published at Shangwu Yinshuguan in 1929, later published at Shanghai Shudian Chubanshe in 2008.
[7] *míngxué* 名學 (study of names), term for "logic" dating from 1895 (Yan Fu).

(1) Textual study, the basis of all research. In terms of methodology, I have four kinds.

Firstly, philology. The Indian *hetuvidyā* texts are very difficult to understand, and need philological methods to clarify the structure and interpretation of words and phrases in the text. For example, at the end of the 1980s, when I was teaching Dignāga[8] in graduate course, there had been very few studies of his *Nyāyamukha*[9] because its content is just too difficult. But this is a fundamental work of *hetuvidyā*, and so I gave an interpretation of it from the perspective of philology.

Secondly, textual emendation. For example, I have corrected the text of *Ruzhenglilun Wenguishu*,[10] restoring it to its original size composed in three volumes, based on the Dunhuang manuscripts and the edition of *Ruzhenglilun Wenguishu* published by the Cheen Institute of Inner Learning in 1933. This work also required verification based on historical documents, used to determine the time when it was spread within China and Japan and the time when it was lost. This work is described in my article "The Interpretation of the *Hetuvidyānyāyadvāraśāstra*".

Thirdly, combining philological and theoretical perspective. For example, when examining the *Ruzhenglilun Luechao* and *Ruzhenglilun Houshu* by Jingyan, I used both an analysis of both the language and theoretical content of the texts to evaluate their strengths, weaknesses and errors.[11] This study was very difficult and it took me a long time to finish. A report of this work is given in my *A Study on Hetuvidyā Manuscripts in Dunhuang*.

Fourthly, translation and comparative studies. The *Zhenglijing*[12] is the fundamental scripture of the *Nyāya* school, and the eighth chapter in the third part of *Zheluo Jiabenji*[13] is the oldest text in history of Indian logic. Yet it had not yet been translated into Chinese. At the beginning of the 1980s, I made a start on this project, annotating the text following the *Zhenglishu*.[14] In the mid-1990s, I completed my translation and provided an interpretation based on important texts of ancient Indian logic, such as *Fangbianxinlun*,[15] *Zhenglijing*, *Zhenglishu* and *Rushilun*.[16] I also conducted a

---

[8] Dignāga (Chén Nà 陳那), c. 480 – c.540, Indian scholar and Buddhist logician, pioneer of *hetuvidyā*.
[9] *Nyāyamukha* (Gateway to Logic, Zhènglǐménlùn《正理門論》), translation by Xuan Zang in 649 of Dignāga's primary text on *hetuvidyā*.
[10] *Rùzhènglǐlùn Wénguǐshū*《入正理論文軌疏》(Wen Gui's Commentary on the Nyāyapraveśa), also known as the Zhuāngyánshū 莊嚴疏, named after Wen Gui's temple.
[11] *Rùzhènglǐlùn Luèchāo*《入正理論略抄》(Commentary on the Nyāyapraveśa), by Jingyan. *Rùzhènglǐlùn Hòushū*《入正理論後疏》(Commentary on the Final Part of the Nyāyapraveśa), by Jingyan. Jìngyǎn 淨眼, a student of Xuan Zang.
[12] *Zhènglǐjīng*《正理經》Nyāyasūtra (Aphorisms on Correct Principles), ancient philosophical text composed in 2nd century B.C.E. by Akṣapāda Gautama of the Nyāya school, containing the theory of *wǔzhīzuòfǎ* (five-membered argument).
[13] *Zhēluó Jiābĕnjí*《遮羅迦本集》Charakasamhitā (Compendium of Charaka), ancient Indian medical text with a chapter on logic.
[14] *Zhènglǐshū*《正理疏》(Commentary on Nyāya Sūtra), by Vātsyāyana.
[15] *Fāngbiànxīnlùn*《方便心論》Upāyakauśalyahṛdaya śāstra (On the Heart of Skilful Means), 5th century translation of an Indian text controversially attributed to Nāgārjuna.
[16] *Rúshílùn*《如實論》Tarkaśāstra (On Reasoning), translation by Zhen Di of a text about

comparative study, relating it to different logical theories and the historical development of ancient Indian logic. This work has been re-edited and collected in my recent published book *Essays on Buddhist Logic*.

(2) Principles of *hetuvidyā*. Throughout my 40 years of doing research, this has always been an important topic for me. My early work, completed in the 1970s, is published in my book, *Studies of Hetuvidyā*, but I also published many articles, such as a study of *wùnán* (erroneous refutation) and *duòfù* (falling into failure), both of which had scarcely been touched by other scholars. In recent years I have focussed on the issue of whether the rule of *trairūpya* can be used to avoid the thirty-three fallacies of *hetuvidyā*. In my article, "On the axioms, rules and fallacies of *hetuvidyā*" I used formal logic to study this and related issues, proposing that the main axiom should be the inseparability of *hetu* and *pakṣa*, as was repeatedly emphasised by Dignāga, and that *trairūpya* is a syntactic rule for the formation of the *trayāvayava*. *Hetuvidya* is a logic for argumentation which involves syntax, semantics and pragmatics, and so the the *trayāvayava* should not only be governed by syntactic rules, but also by pragmatic and semantic rules. Yet Dignāga does not give any details except for a few references, scattered throughout his works. But I was able to extract some explicit rules from a close analysis of his text, and thereby categorise all three types of fallacy in *hetuvidyā*: syntactic, semantic and pragmatic. These three kinds of fallacy are not completely distinct, because some fallacies contain more than one aspect, e.g. semantic and pragmatic. They are not separated either, for one fallacy may contain the other fallacy as well, and could be the intersection of the two types of fallacy. The articles are also included in my *Essays on Buddhist Logic*.

(3) The history of Chinese Buddhist logic. This massive undertaking, begun in the mid-1980s after writing some contributions to the *History of China Logic*, was completed by my graduate students and published as *History of Chinese Buddhist Logic* in 2001. I wrote the introduction and the part on *hetuvidyā* in the Tang dynasty, as well as planning and editing of the whole book. Of course, this is an initial study, and we hope that a more comprehensive book on the subject will come into existence in the near future.

3. What is your favourite example of logical acumen by an early Chinese thinker?

Among early Chinese thinkers, the discussion of *báimǎfēimǎ*[17] by Gongsun Long is a significant albeit controversial topic. We read that "the purpose of this *biàn* is to regulate the relationship between *míng* and *shí* and to educate the people."[18]. We can see that it is a heartfelt and

---

argumentation by Vasubandhu.
[17] *báimǎfēimǎ* 白馬非馬 (white horse not horse), thesis defended by Gongsun Long.
[18] 《公孫龍子·跡府》欲推是辯，以正名實而化天下焉 。

purposeful discourse, not mere trickery. So at the time, more than a few dialecticians agreed with Gongsun Long and became his disciples. But criticism from members of the various schools was also not uncommon. He was mocked by Zhuang Zi as having "the heart of a decorator, the ideas of a simpleton, the mouth of one capable of victory, but the mind of one incapable of dressing himself."[19] And the Later Mohists were even more comprehensively negative about his doctrines. Up until the present day, there have been many theorists whose views of his doctrines were clearly prejudiced, judging them with mere "common sense". In fact, his theory more properly belongs to analytic philosophy of language and logic. Some scholars believe that Gongsun Long used linguistic analysis to break through the traditional point of view, setting up an advanced metaphysics or ontology, by which he constructed a rich philosophical theory in terms of language itself. In Gongsun Long's thought one can find the seeds of many ideas from modern and contemporary analytic philosophy. I agree with such a view and so regard Gongsun Long, among all early Chinese thinkers, as having considerable logical acumen.

4. In your opinion what is the most difficult or problematic aspect of studying logical thought in China?

The most difficult thing is that Chinese logic lacks one main continuous line of development unlike the traditional logic in the West before the 19th century. Indian logic is the history of the integration of *nyāya* and Buddhist *hetuvidyā*. In China, *míngbiànxué*[20] was the most glorious part of the history of Chinese logic, but it died after the Qin period, lacking any followers. Well, there was one person, the hermit Lu Sheng[21] in the West Jin period, who was determined to revive *míngbiànxué* after a five hundred year lapse. He annotated and compiled Mohist works in a vain attempt to revitalise Mohist logic. The situation was so bad that even the original texts of Mohist logic no longer existed. Fortunately, the chapter on hermits in the *Jinshu*[22] included Lu Sheng's introduction to his annotation on the from which we are able to know his thoughts on logic and what he tried to do to revive Mohism. It was unfortunate that *míngbiànxué* was ignored at that time, even though the scholars of the Wei and Jin periods were constantly engaged in debate; it should have been a perfect context for the revival of logic. But perhaps what happened is not so surprising: the intellectual big shots of the time were too busy ridiculing

---

[19] 《庄子·天下》：飾人之心，易人之意，能勝人之口，不能服人之心 。
[20] *míngbiànxué* 名辯學 (study of names and argument), combination of *míngxué* 名學 and *biànxué* 辯學 used by modern scholars to refer to discussions of logical thought in ancient China.
[21] Lǔ Shèng 魯勝, scholar of Jin period, known for his *Mobianzhuxu* in the *Jinshu*; he tried but failed to revive an interest in Mohist logic.
[22] *Jinshū* 《晉書》 (Book of Jin), official record of the Jin dynasty compiled in 648, containing the *Mobianzhuxu*.

each other to pay attention to logic. And then, since *míngbiànxué* did not become the major tradition, its scattered thoughts were too sparse to form a systematic theory, and it wasn't until much later that *hetuvidyā* and, later still, western logic came to China to fill the space.

Aside from this troubled history, there are serious problems in contemporary scholarship. Some scholars today do not give adequate attention to the classics and rush to make false claims that distort the original meaning and create theoretical chaos. Some scholars totally reject the existence of relevant research by others, without argument, in order to show that their own results are unprecedented. All of this just shows how these scholars lack rigorous scholarly training. In reality, it takes a long time and enormous patience for one to understand the classics; one needs to sit down, read and study. One shows very little respect for scholarship by rushing to conclusions, misinterpreting classic literature and by denying previous work. Scholars should come up with their own views only if they can provide enough evidence to sustain their arguments. Unfortunately, this is not the present situation.

5. Which other areas of study could benefit from a better understanding of Chinese logic, or vice versa?

The history of Chinese logic is closely related to and can therefore be expected to enrich and deepen the history of Chinese thought, the history of Chinese philosophy, the history of Chinese Buddhism, and Tibetology. For example, the introduction of *hetuvidyā* to China involved two phases, corresponding to the old and the new versions of Indian logic, and there is also the introduction of *hetuvidyā* to Tibet. Relating the history of these events requires an understanding of Chinese logic, which thereby contributes to the wider concerns of history and philosophy. And in the opposite direction, of course, even our initial investigation into history of Chinese logic has both drawn materials from and is framed in terms of the history of Chinese thought, philosophy, Buddhism and Tibetology.

We have even sought historical materials from the history of Chinese literature such as the *liánzhūtǐ*,[23] which appeared after the Han dynasty. This is a genre of short, beautifully written essays, each having a profound meaning. They were originally composed to be presented to the emperor, so as to make suggestions and offer advice in subtle ways. The literati of later eras imitated and expanded the style. Now these essays, although only as a matter a literary style, are also a form of argumentation, using intricate analogies to manifest their hidden conclusions, revealing deeper meanings with words and sentences strung like beads on a thread. The constraint of criticising and offering advice within a fixed style makes

---

[23] *liánzhūtǐ* 連珠體 (genre of thread beads), literary genre appearing after the Han dynasty, in which argumentation is disguised by means of various conventional devices within a fixed form.

these essays very different from other lyrical, narrative and chanting prose. No one ever developed an explicit systematic theory of *liánzhūtǐ* as logical demonstrations, but its writers consciously used logical methods in their compositions. This phenomenon should be given more attention by those studying the history of Chinese logic.

Related publications

Yīnmíngxué Yánjiū《因明学研究》(Studies on Hetuvidyā), Beijing: Zhongguo Dabaike Quanshu Chubanshe, 1985, Tainan: Zhizhe Chubanshe, 1992.

Yīnmíng Zhènglǐménlùn Yìjiě《因明正理门论译解》(The Interpretation of the *Hetuvidyānyāyadvārasāstra*), *Buddhist Logic*, Beijing: Kaiming Chubanshe, 1992, Taipei: Shangding Wenhua Chubanshe, 1994.

Zhōngguó Fójiāo Luójíshǐ《中国佛教逻辑史》(History of Chinese Buddhist Logic), Shanghai: Huadong Shifan Daxue Chubanshe, 2001.

Dūnhuáng Yīnmíng Wénxiàn Yánjiū《敦煌因明文献研究》(A Study of Hetuvidyā Manuscripts in Dunhuang), Shanghai: Guji Chunbanshe, 2008.

Yīnmíng Lùnwénjí《因明论文集》(Essays on Buddhist Logic), Lanzhou: Gansu Minzu Chubansh, 2011.

Fójiāo Luójí Yánjiū《佛教逻辑研究》(A Study of Buddhist Logic), Shanghai: Guji Chunbanshe, 2013.

Chapter 6
Sūn Zhōngyuán 孙中原

Renmin University of China, Beijing

---

1. Why did you begin working on the history of logic in China?

I began by wanting to explore such fundamental questions as: Did logic exist in ancient China? What is its nature? Is it essentially same as, or essentially different from western logic? Can we say that different ethnic groups have different logics? Or is it that, despite what is shared between Chinese and western logic (generality, common features), they have essential differences (particularity, individual features)? And so on. I have probed such questions for several decades.

From 1956 to 1964, I studied logic and the history of logic, attended courses by famous logicians and read many of the important books from ancient and modern times. From 1956 to 1958, this was as an undergraduate in the Department of Philosophy at Renmin University of China. Then from 1958 to 1961, at the Advanced Communist Party School, I took a number of postgraduate courses in logic. From 1961 to 1964, I studied with the Logical Research group of the Chinese Academy of Social Science, where I specialised in ancient Chinese literature and the history of Chinese logic, supervised by professors Wang Dianji and Shen Youding.

In 1974, UNESCO produced the following classification of subjects: mathematics, logic, physics, chemistry, astronomy, geography and biology. These are the fundamental and universal divisions of human knowledge, and the second is logic. The logic that comes from the west is a tool for thinking that is shared by all people, without limitations of geography, ethnicity, race, colour, national origin, economics, politics, language, culture and art, psychology, customs, history or any of the other ways in which we differ.

The modernisation of China and the continuing trend of the Chinese people's integration into the world depends on us mastering western logic and scientific knowledge of the other fundamental subjects, which have already become fully integrated within the Chinese national education system, and are now an integral part of Chinese culture, the national spirit and the knowledge of Chinese people.

Western logic is a well-ordered, developed, and refined system. From ancient Greece to now, it has evolved for more than two thousand years. In terms of order, development, and refinement, ancient Chinese logic was far inferior. Flourishing in the Warring States period, from the 5th to the 3rd century B.C.E., a time of lively debate, it was not superseded by a more advanced system for two thousand years, from the Han to the Qing dynasties. It was not until the 20th century, stimulated by the arrival of western logic, that Chinese scholars began a re-examination of their own tradition.

Recently, with modernisation and globalisation, it was inevitable that research on logic in China should adopt a western focus with ancient Chinese logic as only a subsidiary interest. Even in re-examining ancient Chinese logic, one must use the methods and tools that have been developed for thousands of years in the West and are now universal. To deny, to reject or to try to remain somehow outside their scope is today absurd.

A poem from *Shijing*[1] says that the stones on other hills can be used to work jade.[2] Marx said that human anatomy contains a key to the anatomy of the ape. Likewise, western logic, systematic, developed, and refined as it is, can be taken to provide the correct perspective and methods for the study of ancient Chinese logic. We *can* do this; we *should* do it; and it is quite reasonable to do so. And by doing so, we will not only provide a modern scientific explanation of ancient Chinese logic but also illuminate its development, nature, value and meaning, as well as reconstruct it in modern terms, so as to provide a "mirror" for our modern minds.

In the *Zhengming*, Xun Zi said that all human beings have the same nature, the same organs of understanding (eyes, ears, nose, tongues, body and brain).[3] Likewise, when facing the same world, all people must have the same logic, just as we have the same scientific knowledge of the other fundamental subjects.

Then, by using the shared methodology of logic to provide a scientific explanation of ancient Chinese logic, we can obtain a modern theory that is essentially consistent with the logic we all share. Anything that diminishes this should be excluded from consideration.

---

[1] *Shījīng*《詩經》Shih-ching (Book of Odes), oldest existing collection of Chinese poetry comprising 305 works dating from the early Zhou (11th to 7th centuries B.C.E.) and part of the literary canon for all Chinese scholars even in pre-Qin times.

[2] 《詩经·小雅·鶴鳴》：他山之石，可以攻玉 。

[3] 《荀子·正名》：凡同類同情者，其天官之意物也同 。

Just as I claim that western logic is shared by all humans across the world, and the essence of both ancient Chinese and western logic are the same, I reject the view that "different ethnic groups have different logics" which contradicts the basic historical facts concerning both the peoples of the world and the development of logic.[4] It is as absurd as saying "different ethnic groups have different mathematics, physics, chemistry, astronomy, geography and biology."

I likewise reject the view that "despite what is shared between Chinese and western logic (generality, common features), they have essential differences (particularity, individual features)", which is really just to say the same but in a way that is easily confused with and made to seem more appealing by the principle that generality and particularity are unified.[5] The differences between western and Chinese logic are not "essential" but rather differences in representation. Variation in geography, time, language, culture, even the differences between individual scholars and schools of thought, inevitably produce different representations of logic. Ancient Chinese logic was represented in the ancient Chinese language. It did not use formal symbols as logical variables, did not have logical formulas, and did not use western logical terms such as the Law of Identity, the Law of Contradiction, the Law of Excluded Middle, and so on.

The correct view of this variation can be summarised as *yìyuán duōbiǎo* 一元多表 (one origin, many manifestations). Here *yuán* 元 (origin) means basis, root, and essence. And *biǎo* 表 (manifestation) means description, expression, and representation. The logic of humanity is essentially the same everywhere, but the representations of it by individual scholars are different.

Think of the consequences of taking seriously that "different ethnic groups have different mathematics, physics, chemistry, astronomy, geography and biology" and "despite what is shared between these Chinese and western disciplines, they have essential differences." If we applied these ideas to industrial practice, we would end up with useless mechanical equipment, which would have to be discarded.

The doctrines "different ethnic groups have different logics" and "despite what is shared between Chinese and western logic (generality, common features), they have essential differences (particularity, individual features)" are therefore both false. We must not be undiscriminating; we must not lack attention! This view is the result of long-term and painstaking research in logic and the history of logic.

---

[4] Such views are held by other scholars in China, notably Cui Qingtian (Chapter 1) and Wang Kexi (Chapter 7).

[5] *gòngxìng hé gèxìng tǒngyī* 共性和个性统一 (generality and particularity are unified) is a principle of Marxist Dialectical Logic. For this view, see Cui Qingtian on page 5 and Zhai Jincheng on page 76.

2. What is the best way to define your area in terms of historical period, textual sources, methodology or other factors?

I think the best way to define the area is with a combination of these factors.

We can divide the history of ancient Chinese logic into three periods: the period of inception (from the 5th to the 3rd century B.C.E.), a dormant period (from the 2nd B.C.E. to the 19th century) and a period of rediscovery (from the 20th century to the present).

The main textual sources for ancient Chinese logic are the *Mojing*, Xun Zi's *Zhengming*, and Gongsun Long's *Mingshilun*. The *Mojing*, composed between the 5th and 3rd centuries B.C.E., reflects the development from the application of logic to argumentation and object logic to theoretical logic and meta-logic. Xun Zi's *Zhengming* and Gongsun Long's *Mingshilun*, completed in the 3rd century B.C.E., express the logical conclusions of the Confucian school and School of Names, respectively.

My methodology is to compare ancient to modern and Chinese to western, using the tools of western logic and modern linguistics, in order to produce a modern meta-study of the classical works of ancient Chinese logic, to reconstruct it in modern terms and to demonstrate its compatibility with western logic. These are the mission, purpose and characteristics of modern research in the history of Chinese logic.

David Hilbert, the German mathematician and logician, initiated the study of metamathematics. He called the theory of whatever topic is being studied an "object theory" and the theory of that object theory, a "meta theory". Alfred Tarski, the American logician, originally from Poland, proposed that there is a hierarchy of languages. He called the language being discussed "object language" and the language used to discuss it, "meta-language". The word "meta" means "afterwards", "beyond", "as a whole". Scholars from Hong Kong and Taiwan have translated it as *hòushè* 后设 (establish after) and *diànhòu* 殿后 (set after). I translate it as *yuán* 元 (first, primary, basic).

The division of logic into object logic and meta-logic is a general methodology that can also be used to study ancient Chinese logic, and which helps to explain its properties, function and value, and how to reconstruct it in modern terms.Hence, the *yuányánjiū* 元研究 (meta-study) of ancient Chinese logic, of which there have been two high points: one in the pre-Qin period and one in modern times, as shown in Table 6.1.

	pre-Qin	modern
investigators	pre-Qin scholars	modern scholars
object of investigation	application of logic to the theory of ancient Chinese argumentation and object logic	ancient Chinese logic (Mohist biànxué, Xunzi's and Gongsun Long's míngxué)
language	ancient Chinese language	modern language
form	ancient Chinese logic (Mohist biànxué, Xunzi's and Gongsun Long's míngxué)	reconstruction of ancient Chinese logic
properties	the first meta-study of Chinese logic	the second meta-study of Chinese logic
function	to provide a logical method for ancient people	to provide a logical method for modern people
evaluation	hard to understand and apply without modification	easy to understand and apply, after modification

Table 6.1: Two high points in the meta-study of ancient Chinese logic.

3. What is your favourite example of logical acumen by an early Chinese thinker?

The Mohists' reasoning form named as *tuī* 推 in the *Xiaoqu*, lies behind my favourite examples. It corresponds to the western principle of *reductio ad absurdum*, involving a process of abstraction and generalisation from the application of logic to argumentation and object logic to theoretical logic and meta-logic.

The *Xiaoqu* appeared in the 3rd century B.C.E., about two hundred years after Mo Zi. During that period, the Hundred Schools each argued for their own doctrines and refuted those of their opponents. In order to make their arguments more convincing, Mo Zi vividly revealed that the absurd and irrational arguments of his opponents were self-contradictory, using all kinds of metaphors, in a very creative way.

《墨子·公孟》：教人學而執有命，是猶命人包而去其冠也 。... 執無鬼而學祭禮，是猶無客而學客禮，無魚而爲魚罟（ 網 ）也 。

> Asking someone to study while holding the doctrine of fatalism is like asking a someone to wrap his head in cloth while telling him to take off his hat. ... To maintain there are no ghosts while learning the ceremony for ancestral worship, is like learning how to be polite to guests when there are no guests, or making nets for fishing when there are no fish.

Teacher Mozi criticised those who attack another state, saying:

《墨子·非攻》：小爲非，則知而非之，大爲非攻國，則不知非，從而譽之，謂之義 。

A small wrong is committed, and people know that they should condemn it; but when a great wrong is committed, such as attacking a state, people do not know that they should condemn it. On the contrary, they praise it and call it justice.

The doctrines criticised here are clearly self-contradictory. In the same text, we also find some simple illustrative examples: "When a man sees only a little black, he says it is black; but when he sees a lot of black, he says it is white. When a man tastes a little bitterness, he says it is bitter; but when he tastes a lot of bitterness, he says it is sweet."[6]

Mo Zi uses his opponents' self-contradictions, absurdities and irrationalities, in order to refute them. This is the method of reductio ad absurdum. But as well using this method in practice, he was the first to isolate the concept of *bèi* 誖 (self-contradictory) from arguments such as these. He uses this term explicitly in the following passages:

《墨子・耕柱》：世俗之君子，貧而謂之富則怒，無義而謂之有義則喜，豈不悖哉？

A gentleman may get angry when he is poor but you call him rich; yet when he is immoral but you call him moral, he feels happy. Isn't this *bèi*?

《墨子・貴義》：世之君子，使之為壹犬壹彘之宰，不能則辭之。使為壹國之相，不能而為之。豈不悖哉？

If sent to kill a dog or pig as a butcher, a gentleman may decline the request for his inability to kill a dog or a pig as a butcher; yet when he is sent to hold the post of premier of a country, he would accept the post even if he is not competent. Isn't this *bèi*?

Likewise, in the *Mojing*, written two hundred years later, the followers of Mo Zi show their proficiency in applying the concept *bèi* to refute many of their philosophical opponents from the Hundred Schools. A good example of this is

《墨子・經下》：以言為盡誖，誖，說在其言。(B71)

The statement "all statements are *bèi*" is *bèi* because "all statements are *bèi*" is itself a statement. Explained by: the statement itself.[7]

They further explain that "*bèi* is the state of being untenable. If one's statements are tenable, they are non-*bèi* statements; if one's statements are untenable, yet one holds them to be correct, then one is certainly incorrect."[8] This shows a profound understanding of the origin of paradox, similar to that found in other early logical traditions and so confirms the universality of Mohist logic and the common subject matter of Chinese and western logics.[9]

---

[6]《墨子・非攻》：少見黑曰黑，多見黑曰白。少嘗苦曰苦，多嘗苦曰甘。
[7] This passage is also a favourite of Chad Hansen, p. 130, and Chris Fraser, p. 118, with a slightly different interpretation of *bèi* as "perverse".
[8]《墨子・經說下》：誖，不可也﹒(出)*{之} 人之言可，是不誖，則是有可也。之人之言不可，以當必不(審)*{當}。(B71)
[9] *Yīnmíng Zhènglǐ Ménlùn* 因明正理門論 (Nyāyamukha), translated by Xuan Zang, Dinnāga cites "all sayings are but false" as an example of a self-contradictory thesis. Aristotle

tradition	paradox
Mohist logic	all statements are *bèi*
Indian logic	all statements are false
western logic	all statements are false all Cretans are always liars what I say is false

Table 6.2: Semantic paradoxes in China and the West.

Mo Zi uses a number of technical terms for his *reductio* arguments: a failure of *zhīlèi* 知類 (understanding kinds) and *zhī xiǎo bù zhī dà* 知小不知大 "knowing the small not the great" or *míng xiǎo bù míng dà* 明小不明大 "understanding the small, not the great". These terms are used explicitly to note his opponents' contradictions.

> Teacher Mozi criticised Gongshu Ban. Gongshu said, "I am an honest man. I do not kill people," but at the same time he was building a kind of ladder to attack the State of Song, which helped his lord kill many common people. So Mo Zi criticises Gongshu: "When you said you did not want to kill, you meant you did not want to kill a few, but not that you would not kill many. This cannot be called *zhīlèi*."[10]

> Teacher Mozi says, in little things such as making a coat, killing an ox or a sheep, repairing a shabby bow and arrow, and so on, people know well that they should esteem the virtuous and hire the capable for doing business. However, when the disorder of the country and the danger of the society are concerned, they do not know that they should esteem the virtuous and hire the capable for government. Mo Zi criticises those who *zhī xiǎo bù zhī dà*.[11]

The universality of Mo Zi's methods are shown by their impact on the style of argument employed by other philosophers of the time, such as Meng Zi, Zhuang Zi, Gongsun Long, and Lü Buwei, all of whom used similar *reductio* style arguments.

In the *Xiaoqu*, the Mohists explicitly discuss the *reductio* method as a general means of arguing against those who object to Mo Zi's doctrines: "The latter propositions are the same as the former. Still, the people of the world do not think it wrong to hold the former, yet they condemn Mohists as wrong for holding the latter."[12] They also present a general account of the method using ancient Chinese as meta-language:

---

criticises Cratylus's statement, qtall propositions are false, saying, "He who says everything is false makes himself also false." Elsewhere, he says: "If everything is false it will not be true to say even this." See Aristotle's Metaphysics, Vol. 7 of *the Collected Works of Aristotle*, eds by Miao Litian, Zhongguo Renmin Daxue Chubanshe, 1993, p. 109 and p. 252. Earlier, Epimenides, a Cretan, was reported as saying "All Cretans are always liars." And this has been studied in more recent times as in the form: "what I say is false". See Table 6.2 for a summary.

[10] 《墨子・公輸》載墨子引公輸盤說"吾義固不殺人",卻幫楚國造雲梯,殺更多百姓,墨子批評他"義不殺少而殺眾,不可謂知類"。

[11] 《墨子・尚賢》載墨子批評殺牛羊、制衣裳、醫病馬、修危弓等小事,知道尚賢使能,而到治國大事,卻不知道尚賢使能,是"明小不明大"。

[12] 《墨子・小取》:此與彼同類,世有彼而不自非也,墨者有此而非之。(NO 15)

tradition	term	main point	alternate term
Mohist biànxué	tuī	what is present in your case should not be rejected in his, and what is absent from yours should not be demanded of his.	not knowing the categories (bù zhī lèi) knowing the small but not the great (zhī xiǎo bù zhī dà) understanding the small but not the great (míng xiǎo bùmíng dà)
western logic	dialectic	the method of exposing one's opponents' contradictions to defeat them in debate	reductio ad absurdum, reductio ad impossibile

Table 6.3: *Reductio* in China and the West

《墨子·小取》：推也者，以其所不取之，同于其所取者，予之也 。

> When you use the same premises that he accepts in order to convince him of a conclusion that he does not accept, it is called *tuī* 推 (inferring).[13]

That is to say, what is present in your case should not be rejected in his, and what is absent from yours should not be demanded of his.

This tells us that *tuī* is a method of using analogy for *reductio ad absurdum* with the following structure: my opponent accepts that proposition, but does not accept this proposition, so I will prove that "this one and that one are the same kind"[14]. If my opponent still does not accept *cǐ*, he will fall into *bèi*. Using this method, logic forces the opponent to accept *cǐ* because *bèi* is unacceptable.

We can also see this as the endorsement of two rules: "accept according to category and propose according to category"[15] and "do not refuse to others what you accept for yourself; do not propose to others what you reject for yourself"[16] In western logic, the latter is just the law of non-contradiction, which was the first explicit law to be proposed. Similarly, reductio ad absurdum, which can be seen as an application of this law, is the earliest method of argumentation, at the core of dialectics (Greek: *dialektikos*) and logic, as can be seen by its central place in the history of logic. In ancient Greece, it was proficiently applied by many philosophers, including Pythagoras, Zeno, Socrates and Plato. It is the original meaning of "*tarka*", the Sanskrit word for logic, and it was an important part of the *Minglitan*, China's first exposure to western logic. A comparison between the Chinese and western conceptions of *reductio* is shown in Table 6.3.

---

[13] (NO 11) See also the discussion of this passage by Yang Wujin, p. 68.
[14] 《墨子·小取》：此與彼同類 。(NO 15)
[15] 《墨子·小取》：以類取，以類予 。
[16] 《墨子·小取》：有諸己不非諸人，無諸己不求諸人 。

4. In your opinion what is the most difficult or problematic aspect of studying logical thought in China?

I think the greatest problems are with finding the correct interpretation of ancient literature and adopting the correct methodology for making comparisons between Chinese and western logic.

In thinking about the difficulties, I am reminded of how, in comparing logic to other subjects, Hegel said it is "work which, belonging to the modern world, is confronted by a profounder principle, a more difficult subject matter, and a material richer in compass"[17] The most significant materials for the history of logic in China are from ancient China. The works of Mohism, including the *Mojing*, were composed during the Warring States period, and then transmitted over more than two thousand years from the Qin and Han dynasties to the Qing dynasty. During this period, aside from a brief commentary by Lu Sheng[18] in the Jin period, almost no one understood them properly, no one cited them, interpreted them or developed their thought, and no one produced a logical system more advanced than theirs. In the late Ming dynasty, Li Zhizao,[19] the translator of the *Minglitan*, and in the late Qing dynasty Sun Yirang,[20] who edited the *Mojing*, did not really understand Mohist biànxué, not because of the ancient language of the Mohist texts but because they lacked a proper understanding of logic, not having been exposed to the western scientific methodology of using logic as a tool.

Sun Yirang held that the *Mozi* is the most difficult to read among all the works of pre-Qin philosophers and that the *Mojing* is its most difficult part. Scholars have translated the ancient text into modern Chinese many times; even so, it is very difficult to understand. Sun had a rough idea that the *Mojing* had logical content, but without understanding what kind of logic it was, writing the following in a letter to Liang Qichao in 1897:

> There must be a deep and ingenious meaning in the *Mojing*, and scholars have much to probe...I suspect that it contains subtle and profound statements, as are found in the theories of western logicians, such as Aristotle's deduction and Francis Bacon's induction, as well as the Indian *hetuvidyā*. It is unfortunate that the work has an ambiguous and elliptical nature, which has prevented scholars from gaining a clear understanding.[21]

---

[17] Hegel 1969, p. 42
[18] Lǔ Shèng 鲁胜, scholar of Jin period, known for his *Mobianzhuxu* in the *Jinshu*; he tried but failed to revive an interest in Mohist logic.
[19] Lǐ Zhīzǎo 李之藻, 1564-1630, translator of the *Minglitan* with Francisco Furtado.
[20] Sūn Yírǎng 孫詒讓, 1848-1908, influential editor and commentator on the *Mojing*, author of *Mozixiangu*.
[21] *Yǔ Liángzhuórú Lùn Mòzǐshū* 《与梁卓如论墨子书》(Discussing the Mo Zi with Liang Zhuoru), in the Collection of Sun Yirang's Works with a Chinese title《籀廎述林》, appeared in 1916, 8 years after Sun passed away. This book can be found in the library of Renmin University of China.

Huang Shaoji, remarked that the *Mojing* contained "many technical terms" and "profound ideas of the *míngjiā*". And Yan Fu, the Chinese translator of William S. Jevons' *Primer of Logic* also states that he was sure that logic existed as an academic study in China before the Qin dynasty. Yet they too failed to understand Mohist logic in a profound way. To decipher this material, we need to understand not only the special style and grammar of the original but also how to analyse it using modern language and logical tools. This is therefore the primary difficulty of research in Chinese logic.

A further problem concerns the use of correct methodology for comparative research. "Method" is a general term for direction, path, means, tools and procedures. The essential goal of research methodology in the history of Chinese logic is to make the topic of the research clear and to determine the direction, purpose and aim of the research, i.e., what to do and why.

We must be clear about how to produce research, that is to say, we must understand the path, the means, the tools and the procedures. On the basis of deciphering the original works of Chinese logic, we must choose appropriate methods to analyse the materials correctly. This is the second main difficulty of our work.

5. Which other areas of study could benefit from a better understanding of Chinese logic, or vice versa?

The history of Chinese logic is a part of logic, the history of philosophy, intellectual history, and cultural history more generally. Research in the history of Chinese logic and related subjects, such as logic, philosophy, the history of Chinese philosophy, intellectual history, cultural history, philosophy of science and so on, inevitably influence each other. Researchers in one area can benefit from the results of research and methods in the other areas, as has been shown by many important works of the past hundred years.

My "meta-study" of ancient Chinese logic is inspired by Hilbert's meta-mathematics program and Tarski's hierarchy of languages. Studies of the history of Chinese logic have also benefitted from the history of Chinese philosophy, intellectual history and cultural history, and, in the other direction, progress in the history of Chinese logic will enrich teaching and research in those areas. This is my personal experience from many years of research.

In particular, my own work has been greatly inspired by ideas from the philosophy of science about the origins and social function of academic research. The Chinese poet Li Bai once said "Everything and everybody is born to be useful for the world"[22]. Ancient Chinese logic was not created without reason, and it will not disappear without trace. It conforms to an

---
[22] 天生我材必有用

inexorable law of formation and development, and functions to adapt to the needs of society.

Today, we should use modern language and the logical methods developed in the West to study the history of Chinese logic, and to reconstruct ancient Chinese logic in modern terms. By exploiting the compatibility of Chinese and western logic we can convert ancient Chinese logic into a modern form of knowledge that is easy to understand and apply, so that it continues to play an important and positive role in serving humanity.

Related publications

Zhōngguó Luójíshǐ《中国逻辑史》(History of Chinese Logic), Beijing: Zhongguo Renmin Daxue Chubanshe,1987.

Mòxué yǔ Xiàndài Wénhuà《墨学与现代文化》(The Theory of Mohism and Modern Culture), Beijing: Zhongguo Guangbo Dianshi Chubanshe, 1998.

ZhūzǐBǎijiā de Luójí Zhìhuì《诸子百家的逻辑智慧》(Logical Wisdom of the Pre-Qin Philosophers), Beijing: Zhongguo Jixie Gongye Chubanshe, 2004.

Zhōngguó Luójí Yánjiū《中国逻辑研究》(Research on Chinese Logic), Beijing: Shangwu Yinshuguan, 2006.

Mòzǐ jí qí Hòuxué《墨子及其后学》(Mozi and His Academic Successors), Beijing: Zhongguo Guoji Guangbo Chubanshe, 2011 (new edition).

Chapter 7

Wáng Kèxǐ 王克喜

Nanjing University

---

1. Why did you begin working on the history of logic in China?

My studying the history of Chinese logic was an accident. While I was doing a master's degree in linguistic logic, I read a book called *Language and Logic in Ancient China* by Chad Hansen, which contained the following passage:

> The assumptions that are implicit in classical thought about language fall into four categories: (1) Assumptions about the function of language, that is, what is the language for?; (2) Assumptions about the way in which language relates to the world, that is, what model of reality informs the account of the function of language?; (3) Assumptions about the origin and status of language, that is, how do languages come to be and what kind of knowledge do we have when we know how to use them?; and (4) Miscellaneous contrasts in assumptions about the relation between language and mental or abstract objects–thoughts, meanings, universals, classes, and the like.[1]

Comparing Chinese with English, Hansen asked how language affects the appearance and development of logic.

> Our conclusion is simply that it should not be taken as unreasonable or lacking in philosophical depth that Chinese thinkers never developed theories of abstract entities like ideas, concepts, or universals. These kinds of theories, either in ontology, semantics, philosophy of mind, or theory of knowledge (epistemology), are motivated and stimulated by features of language which divide the Chinese family of language from the Indo-European family. Since philosophical questions are generated out of our ordinary ways of speaking and writing, we can expect that the different forms in which philosophical question are posed will push theorization in different directions. It is not

---

[1] Chad Hansen, *Language and Logic in Ancient China*, The University of Michigan Press, 1983, p. 57-58

that abstract theories are impossible for Chinese but that they are not necessary.[2]

I was also attracted by some views of Zhang Dongsun,[3] that were criticised by Hansen in this book. Since different languages have different functional aspects, Zhang thought that Aristotle's logic could not be the only one. He said "the grammatical differences between Latin, French, English and German are not sufficient to give them deductive rules different from those of Aristotle. This is because they belong to the same language family. If we try to apply Aristotelian logic to the thinking of Chinese people, we will find it unsuitable because Aristotelian logic is based on the structure of western languages." Hansen's criticised this as follows:

> Chang's observations do little to justify or clarify the special logic retort.[4] It is not clear why the application of Aristotelian logic to Chinese thought is inappropriate. All the propositional forms (A, E, I, O) are expressible in classical Chinese. Some inferences licensed in Chinese cannot be put in the form of an Aristotelian syllogism, but that does not provide any contrast with western languages. In fact, some of the most important of Aristotle's own reasoning cannot be cast in syllogistic form.[5]

Hence, there are some important questions we have to confront when we study the history of Chinese logic.

A. Is there only one logic? If so, on what is it based?

B. What was the role of language in the origins of logic? How did it affect the development of logic? In particular, what is the role of ancient Chinese in the origins of Chinese logic? If language can affect people's actual thinking, why doesn't it also affect logic, which is a generalisation of that thinking?

C. Does the idea of "generality and particularity" apply to logic? In his book, *The philosophy of Language*, Martinich said that contemporary philosophy of language is all based on English, and that he hopes to see the results of taking Chinese as an alternative. Can't we apply the same idea to logic?

D. Is the logic that was influenced by ancient Chinese language a Chinese version of Aristotelean logic, or does it have its own unique style? If China has its own logic, what is it like? Can we construct a research paradigm for the history of Chinese logic with Chinese characteristics?

E. It is well known that language, as one important element of culture, can affect logic. But are there other cultural elements that also affect logic?

---

[2] Ibid., p.53
[3] Zhāng Dōngsūn 張東蓀, 1886-1975, philosopher and government official who studied in Japan in the 1900s, known for the view that different cultures have different logics.
[4] Here "Chang" refers to Zhang Dongsun. The "special logic retort" is an objection to Hansen's methodology of using standards of consistency, coherence and rationality to interpret ancient Chinese texts. It is the claim that ancient Chinese thinkers were using a quite different logic than "our" logic, making Hansen's methodology inappropriate.
[5] Ibid., p.17

Interested in these questions, I started my research on the history of Chinese logic, and after studying with Cui Qingtian at Nankai University, I have pursued them ever since.

2. What is the best way to define your area in terms of historical period, textual sources, methodology or other factors?

The history of Chinese logic is literally the study of the birth and development of Chinese logic.

As to the concept of logic itself, I have a broad view. There is no one logic nor is its development linear. Firstly, from a diachronic perspective, we can see the development from Artistole, the Stoic and Megarian schools, through Bacon's inductive logic, to Leibniz, Frege and Whitehead, and then to today's "modern logic" including paraconsistent and informal logic. This shows that the development of logic never stops. "Logic is its history and the history of logic is logic itself" as was said by Dumitriu in his four-volume *History of Logic*. If we take the criterion for being "logic" from a single part of the development of logic, we will get too narrow a view. Likewise, we should not use today's logic to identify "logic" in the past.[6]

Secondly, from a synchronic perspective, we should recognise the diversity of the development of logic in China, India and the west. As the view that there are three origins of logic is accepted more widely, it is natural for us to focus on the status of Chinese logic.

Studies of Chinese logic requires a study of those features in common to Chinese, Indian and western logic. There are four main aspects. The first is the foundation of logic as a science, its basic theory, such as first-order predicate logic, which can be studied from the comfort of the ivory tower. The second is to study logic's applications to philosophy, natural science and social science, such as the use of logic in linguistics. The third is methodology. And the last is the history of logic. These last three are extensions of the first but they have a greater connection to real life and can both enliven and energise our research.

The development of logic is not isolated in space and time. Different cultures can produce different logics, and so the logic of any one ethnic group must be intimately entangled with its culture. Language is a basic element of culture, so the study of how Chinese logic differs from the other two origins on the basis of Chinese language has become a priority. One of the most important questions is whether Chinese logic is based on Chinese language in the same way as Aristotle's logic is based on ancient Greek. Chinese language has many characteristics lacked by western languages. It is called a "process language" by western scholars. And the Chinese way of thinking influenced by language is called "corelative thinking"

---

[6] For discussions of the same issue, see also Gregor Paul and Sun Zhongyuan in this volume.

again by western scholars. We have traditionally studied language only by *xùngǔxué*[7]; there was no Chinese linguistics. So what then is our logic?

We believe that the history of Chinese logic is just the study of the history of logic in China, which has three parts: the introduction and evolution of western logic in China (such as the *Minglitan* translation by Li Zhizao in the late Ming dynasty, the presentation of western logic in *Luojizhiyao* by Zhang Shizhao, and many more translations and studies of contemporary western logic), the introduction and evolution of Indian logic in China, and the development of Chinese logic itself, especially the characteristically Chinese style of logical inference that governs reasoning in the *Zhouyi*, *tuīlèi*[8] in the Mohist school, occult reasoning and astrological reasoning[9].

From a historical point of view, we can say that Chinese logic was dominant before the Qin and Han dynasties, after which Indian logic became important, with western logic arriving at the end of the Qing dynasty. The study of the history of Chinese logic must include all three, and is not restricted to the ancient Mohist *biànxué*.[10]

3. What is your favourite example of logical acumen by an early Chinese thinker?

In the history of Chinese logic, we can find many such examples. Here is a typical one from the *Zhanguoce Qicesi* :

《戰國策·齊策四》：齊人見田駢，曰："聞先生高議，設為不宦，而願為役。"田駢曰："子何聞之？"對曰："臣聞之鄰人之女。"田駢曰："何謂也？"對曰："臣鄰人之女，設為不嫁，行年三十而有七子。不嫁則不嫁，然嫁過畢矣！今先生設為不宦，訾養祿鍾，徒百人。不宦則然矣，而富過畢也！"田子辭。

A man from Qi who went to meet a scholar named Tian Bing, saying "I heard that you don't want to be an official because of your high regard for righteousness. I am willing to become your loyal retainer, to do whatever you ask." Tian Bing asked him, "How do you know this?" He answered, "I learned it from my neighbour's daughter." "What does this mean?" said Tian Bing. "She is thirty years old and does not want to marry, but she already has seven sons. Although she is not married, she has more than many women who are. Now, you are not an official, but you get a large government salary. Although you are not an official, you are richer than those who are." After hearing this, Tian Bing was ashamed and ran away.

---

[7] *xùngǔxué* 訓詁學 (critical interpretation of antiquity), late Ming early Qing dynasty movement concerned with establishing objective knowledge about ancient texts.
[8] *tuīlèi* 推類 (kind-based inference), the central Mohist conception of inference, also known as *lèituī* 類推 (kind-based inference).
[9] *fāngshù tuīyǎn* 方術推演 (occult reasoning) and *zhànxīngshù* 占星術 (astrological reasoning)
[10] *biànxué* 辯學 (study of disputation), used as a translation for "logic" in the later 19th by Joseph Edkins and early in the 20th century by Wang Guowei.

This example shows the typical characteristics of the ancient Chinese method of corelative thinking. Pointing out a person's shortcomings to his face is difficult because he will find it humiliating. And learning to say one thing when you mean another is something that requires serious study. Isn't it worth our reflecting on how our ancestors used *yūhuí* 迂回 (roundabout) and analogical ways to scold one another?

Not only is this way of criticising others "soft on the surface and hard at the core, pointing at a mulberry tree to scold the japonica", but it is also like "planting a stick to see the shadow; half the effort, double the gain!"[11]

4. In your opinion what is the most difficult or problematic aspect of studying logical thought in China?

After Liang Qichao's pioneering studies of the history of Chinese logic there have been more and more explorations. However, from the very beginning, research in this area was based on the assumption that "logic's name came from Europe but logical principles apply everywhere"[12] that although the nature of language is specific to different ethnic groups, the nature of logic is just that of rationality, which is universal, applying to all of humankind. We have given enough emphasis to the generality of logic but we have ignored its individual origins and development, apparently believing that Aristotle's logical system is suitable for all of humankind and that the languages and ways of thinking of different ethnic groups have a universal nature, with common principles and standards. Even Zhang Shizhao in *Luojizhiyao* realised the mismatch between western logic and the available means to express it in Chinese, pointing out that

> Chinese language frequently includes pairs of opposites, like *yàohài* 要害 (advantage/disadvantage), which Yan Shigu[13] explained as an advantage for me and a disadvantage for my enemy, so including both sides. Extending this: by saying *lì hài* 利害 (benefit/harm), we do not mean *lì* 利 (benefit), by saying *huǎnjí* 缓急 (slow/fast) we do not mean *huǎn* 缓 (slow), and by saying *zǎowǎn* 早晚 (early/late) we do not mean late. Each of these expressions combines two opposite meanings which both contradict and support each other. There are innumerable examples like these.[14]

Yet there is nothing with this flavour in our contemporary logic textbooks. As the formality of logical research has increased, so has its distance from traditional studies of Chinese language and the practice of thinking and speaking by Chinese. The feeling of this research is of something quite independent of Chinese culture.

---

[11] 柔中带刚，指桑骂槐; 立竿见影，事半功倍
[12] 《邏輯指要》：邏輯之名，起於歐洲，而邏輯之理，存乎天壤 。
[13] Yán Shīgǔ 顏師古, 581-645, Confucian scholar, philologist and historian.
[14] Zhāng Shìzhāo 章士钊, *Luójizhǐyào*《邏輯指要》(Outline of Logic), first written in 1917 by Zhang Shizhao, officially published at the Chongqing Zhongxin Yinshuguan in 1943; a new edition was published by Sanlian Shudian in 1959, p.18

Consequently, some scholars have adopted the perspective of cultural hermeneutics to examine the distinction between genuine comparisons and merely superficial analogies within studies of the history of Chinese logic.[15] By deeply reflecting on those comparisons that followed the work of Liang Qichao, they argued from many angles that Chinese ancient logic is not Aristotle's logic and that Mo Zi is not Aristotle. This created a huge wave in the field, resulting not only in vigorous debate but also more confusion, specifically about the following issues:

A. If Chinese ancient logic is not Aristotelean, what is it? Whether we call it *míngxué*[16] or *míngbiànxué*[17] or even *míngcíshuōbiàn*[18], in the end our studies of the ancient system of Chinese logic are still based on a comparison to Aristotle's logic. So what is the special character of Chinese logic? Scholars have investigated logical thought in the *Zhouyi*, in traditional Chinese medicine, in *sizhu*,[19] in *liuren*,[20] in ancient argumentation, and many other areas. There is an important issue here: that of how to reconstruct a system for expressing the content of Chinese logical thought. This has the most urgent priority, and is also the most difficult task we face. Without it, one might say that research in the history of Chinese logic has not really started. We have a long way to go and there are many difficulties.

B. Perspectives on the history of Chinese logic. We need a *change* of perspective. Some scholars do not believe in the existence of logic in ancient China, even adopting a post-modern point of view. Others use modern logic, lacking a historical perspective, and identifying logic as something that does not change over time.[21] This fits neither the history of the development of logic, nor the properties of logic itself.

C. Methodology for the history of Chinese logic. We need to *update* our methods. Our approach so far has been to extract logical thought from pre-Qin texts. We have not yet made much use of methodologies relating logic to psychology and pragmatics.

---

[15] These scholars include Cui Qingtian (Chapter 1) and the present author.

[16] *míngxué* 名學 (study of names), term for "logic" dating from 1895 (Yan Fu).

[17] *míngbiànxué* 名辯學 (study of names and argument), combination of *míngxué* 名學 and *biànxué* 辯學 used by modern scholars to refer to discussions of logical thought in ancient China.

[18] *míngcíshuōbiàn* 名辭說辯 (logico-linguistic categories), literally "name, phrase, explanation, disputation", a sequence of categories discussed in the *Mojing* and *Xunzi*.

[19] *sìzhù* 四柱 (four pillars) is a system based on the idea that a person's fate is determined by fours pairs of *tiangan dizhi* characters for the year, the month, the day and the moment the person was born. *tiāngān dìzhī* 天干地支 (heavenly stem earthly branch) is an ancient system of numerals used throughout Chinese history for measuring time, navigation, and numerous other symbolic purposes.

[20] *liùrén* 六壬 (six nine) is another system for making predictions, based on the numerals *rén zǐ*、*rén yín*、*rén chén*、*rén wǔ*、*rén shēn*、*rén xū* 壬子、壬寅、壬辰、壬午、壬申、壬戌 which have special significance, due to the association of *rén* 壬 (the 9th heavenly stem) with water. These are combined with calendrical information in very complex calculations.

[21] For a view of this kind, see Sun Zhongyuan, Chapter 6.

D. Philology for the history of Chinese logic. Many philological concerns arise when interpreting ancient texts from the perspective of western logic, ignoring the issue of whether there is anything like western logic in Chinese culture. For example, *yī zhōu yī bù zhōu* 一周一不周 (sometimes all sometimes not all). in *Mozi* has been taken to be about the distinction between universal and particular categorical propositions, and the phrase *bù kě liǎng bù kě* 不可两不可 (not admissible both not admissible) has been emended to *bù liǎng kě liǎng bù kě* 不两可两不可 (not both admissible both not admissible) so as to fit the interpretation of this as Law of the Excluded Middle.[22] The relationship between conditionals (found in the text) and conditional reasoning is not clear; and that between disjunctions and disjunctive reasoning is thoroughly entangled. Chen Yingque once said "Those who comment on Mozi today will emend the old texts and characters according to their whim, without any guiding principles, as if they were dice players who could call sixes every time."[23] This situation is unbelievable!

5. Which other areas of study could benefit from a better understanding of Chinese logic, or vice versa?

Historical research on Chinese language can benefit from research on Chinese logic and vice versa. The history of Chinese language always starts from research on *míng* 名 (name), a major topic in Chinese logic, which also provides many examples.

Reflecting on the development of Chinese culture in modern times, we see that both logic and linguistics were imported from outside of China. As with logic, there were no systematic studies of grammar in ancient China. In the words of the contemporary scholar Pan Wenguo: "Traditional scholarship rarely touches grammar; serious modern studies started from *Mashiwentong* in 1898"[24] After Ma Jianzhong's *Mashiwentong*,[25] Chinese grammarians went through a period of merely imitating the West but then, realising the important role of general rules, went on to make good use of western linguistic theory as a framework for explaining real Chinese language practice. Although in the meandering course they took, there were occasional hints of westernisation or eurocentrism, research on grammar, which was of incidental interest in ancient China, took root

---

[22] See also the discussion of this passage by Dong Zhitie on p. 11

[23] Chén Yínquè 陳寅恪, 冯友兰中国哲学史上册审查报告 (A Review on Feng Youlan's History of Chinese Philosophy Volume I), in Liú Mèngxī 刘梦溪 ed., 《中国现代学术经典·陈寅恪卷》(Volume of Chen Yinque of the Academic Classics of Modern China), Shijiazhuang: Hebei Jiaoyu Chubanshe, 1996. p.389

[24] Pān Wénguó 潘文国, 比较汉英语语法研究史的启示 (Revelation of the Comparison between the Syntactical Studies of Chinese and English), Yuyan Jiaoxue yu Yanjiu 语言教学与研究, Issue 2-3, 1996.

[25] *Mǎshìwéntōng*《馬氏文通》(Grammar of Mr. Ma), the first systematic work on Chinese grammar, edited by Ma Jianzhong and published by Shangwu Yinshuguan in 1898.

in the soil of language practice and became the absolute core of linguistic research.

Again, as Pan said, "Under the influence of de Saussure, Bloomfield and Chomsky, Chinese linguistics has become increasingly formal, and increasingly distant from traditional studies." There are some who complain that "this is the fault of *Mashiwentong*" and others who take research on common properties of Chinese and western languages to be the most urgent task for Chinese linguistics. We should think about whether this trend is positive or negative. Nonetheless, since *Mashiwentong*, Chinese linguists and grammarians, such as Wang Li, Lü Shuxiang, Li Jinxi, Zhao Yuanren, Chen Chengze have made good use of western linguistic systems and frameworks, while focussing on the actual practice of Chinese. By bringing linguistics closer to language practice, they have established a "linguistics with Chinese characteristics." With our own independent analysis and thought about what is specific to Chinese, we have been able to find aspects of our language that are very different from western languages, especially English and Latin. By emphasising both commonalities and those features that are distinctively Chinese, the study of Chinese language is gradually maturing.

Unlike research in linguistics, from the very beginning, research in logic was based on the assumption that "logic's name came from Europe but logical principles apply everywhere," and so ignores the possibility of logic with different special features. As the contemporary scholar Ju Shier says:

> Although there are different opinions, many logicians, including the author of this book, have discussed various uses of the term "logic". Among them, the most influential is Scholz, a German historian of western logic. In his book, *A Brief History of Logic*[26] logic is divided into six sorts. The first is classical logic, the formal logic originating from Aristotle...The second is the so-called "extended" formal logic of the *Port-Royal Logic* (1662) and Lambert (1764), who added methodology, semantics and epistemology to Aristotle's system. The third sort is the series of tools that are used to acquire scientific knowledge in a general sense. The fourth is inductive or probabilistic logic... The fifth is speculative logic, represented by Hegel and Kant. For Hegel, logic is a science of the truth "in itself and for itself" of *Die Idee* (The Idea), and is mainly concerned with metaphysical and epistemological issues. Kant mainly studied the epistemological content of judgements. The sixth sort is the modern style of formal deductive logic, started by Frege and Russell, including classical mathematical logic and its extensions, such as modal logic and non-classical logic.[27]

Aristotle's system of logic, which is the heart of what is taught today as *pǔtōngluójí*,[28] was based on his deep studies of the ancient Greek language.

---

[26] Translated by Zhāng Jiālóng 张家龙 as 《简明逻辑史》, Shangwu Yinshuguan, 1977

[27] Jū Shíér 鞠实儿, 《简明逻辑学》序言 (Preface of Logic: A Very Short Introduction), Yilin Chubanshe, 2010.

[28] *pǔtōngluójí* 普通逻辑 (common logic), syllabus for logic instruction in most Chinese universities, derived from the Russian education system, and including basic logic laws, concepts, judgements, inference, and argumentation, and occasionally induction but no

In *Catégories de pensée et catégories de langues* (1958), the French scholar Benveniste gave a convincing analysis and proof that the names of Aristotle's categories are actually those of linguistic categories. This led the English linguist A. Lance to believe that Aristotle took the terminology for logic from grammar, rather than the other way around. Aristotle's logical system was established against the backdrop of western culture, and took shape through his analysis of western language. Bearing the imprint of both place and culture, we can definitely say it is a product of western culture and civilisation.

Scholars who study western logic have also reflected on the relationship between logic and language. Strawson has stated that "...many of the features of the use of ordinary speech which are sufficiently general to deserve consideration under the title 'The Logic of Language' are necessarily omitted from consideration under the narrower title of 'Formal Logic'."[29] And also: "Side by side with formal logic, and overlapping it, we have another study: the study of the logical features of ordinary speech... What we shall not find in our results is that character of elegance and system which belongs to the constructions of formal logic. It is none the less true that the logic of ordinary speech provides a field of intellectual study unsurpassed in richness, complexity, and the power to absorb."[30]

Bocheński, a famous mathematical logician, has related comments about the role of formalism. In recalling Łukasiewicz, he gives us a perfect example:

> Łukasiewicz is a genius. His papers are so perfect that they cannot be modified. One night, I went to meet him. He sat in front of the typewriter and typed a logic proof. When he saw me, he showed me the theorem he had just finished typing. It was like this: CCCCCKCACCNKNKCCCPPPPP...usw He shouted at me: "How beautiful! Obviously, it is valid!" At that time I thought about the word "obvious" and found it was obvious that the validity of CCCCCKCACCNKNKCCCP... was not obvious![31]

Even for Bocheński, a famous mathematical logician, the validity of this expression in a highly formalised artificial language was not obvious; it is much less obvious to ordinary people. He goes on to tell us to "remember that formal systems are always abstract. You mustn't look at them as real. You shouldn't think that formal method is the only method. On the contrary, you should use it together with other methods."[32]

---

discussion of probability or mathematical logic. *pǔtōngluójí* syllabus for logic instruction in most Chinese universities, derived from the Russian education system, and including basic logic laws, concepts, judgements, inference, and argumentation, and occasionally induction but no discussion of probability or mathematical logic

[29] P. F. Strawson, "Two Kinds of logics", Ch.8 Part III of *Introduction to Logical Theory*, 1952, p. 215-216

[30] Ibid., p.231 and p.232.

[31] Quoted in Wáng Lù 王路, *Yígè Luójixuéjiā de Huíyì* "一个逻辑学家的回忆" (A Memorial to a Logician), *Zhéxuéyìcóng* 哲学译丛, 1987 (1).

[32] Tóng Shìjùn 童世骏 et al tranlators, *Dāngdài Sīwéi Fāngfǎ* 《当代思维方法》, Shanghai Renmin Chubanshe, 1987, p. 46, which is a translation of Bocheński, *Die zeitgenössischen Denkmethoden*, 1954.

Related publications

Gǔdài Hànyǔ yǔ Zhōngguó Gǔdài Luójí 《古代汉语与中国古代逻辑》 (Ancient Chinese Language and Chinese Logic), Tianjin: Tianjin Renmin Chubanshe, 2000.

Chapter 8

Yáng Wǔjīn 杨武金

Renmin University of China, Beijing

1. Why did you begin working on the history of logic in China?

Chinese *míngbiànxué*,[1] Indian *hetuvidyā* and western logic are the three origins of logic. The first two didn't develop well for various reasons and only western logic made significant progress. I was motivated to study the history of Chinese logic by the following issues.

The first is the Needham[2] problem: why the modern scientific revolution didn't happen in China. China, which led the world in terms of scientific progress before the early Ming dynasty, was one of the world's four great civilisations. But why did it later fall behind? There may be economic and political reasons, but I have always believed that the more fundamental cause was cultural.

Albert Einstein once said that the development of western science was based on two great achievements: the invention by Greek philosophers of systems of formal logic (as in Euclid's geometry) and the discovery in the Renaissance that one can find out causal relationships by systematic experiment.[3] Furthermore, in modern times, the enormous progress

---

[1] *míngbiànxué* 名辯學 (study of names and argument), combination of *míngxué* 名學 and *biànxué* 辯學 used by modern scholars to refer to discussions of logical thought in ancient China.

[2] Joseph Needham (Lǐ Yuēsè 李约瑟), 1900-1995, British biochemist and sinologist noted for his work on the history of science in China in particular as the main editor of *Science and Civilisation in China*, 27 volumes, Cambridge University Press, 1954-2008.

[3] Xǔ Liángyīng 许良英, Lǐ Bǎohéng 李宝恒, Zhào Zhōnglì 赵中立, et al., translators and editors, 《爱因斯坦文集》(Collected Works of Einstein), Vol. 1, Shanghai: Shangwu Yinshuguan, 1976, p. 574.

of western science has benefited from the development of an inductive method, and inductive logic. Science and logic are closely connected. For example, development of ancient Chinese medicine, astronomy, and agriculture was closely linked with the pre-Qin development of *míngbiànxué*. Writings on ancient science are deeply influenced by the spirit of logic, in the form of *míngbiànxué*. There was no study of logic in China after the Qin and Han dynasties, and that is the most important reason why the modern scientific revolution did not happen in China.

The second issue to motivate me is that of the legitimacy of Chinese logic: whether there really was logic in ancient China. Among Chinese scholars, there are sharply contrasting views on this matter. My opponents maintain that China had no logic, or even "logical thought", and that "the history of Chinese logic" is just a fantasy. But in my opinion, the existence Chinese logical thought has clearly been demonstrated. The key questions for me are rather: What kind of logical thought? What were the principal logical problems? And how far did the research go?

There are some academics who say that China has *míngxué* (study of names) and *biànxué* (study of disputation) but no "logic", and similarly that there were *jīngxué* (study of the classics), *xuánxué* (neo-Daoism), *fóxué* (Buddhism), *dàoxué* (Daoism), *rúxué* (Confucianism), *lǐxué* (neo-Confucianism), *xīnxué* (study of mind), *xīnxué* (new studies) but no "philosophy".

From my point of view, to understand these issues more clearly, it is necessary to distinguish the matter of "legitimacy" from that of "reasonableness". Regarding "reasonableness", some say that it is just "unreasonable" to use western logic to explain Chinese logic, that they are fundamentally different, so much so that one should not even use the term "Chinese logic". They say that Chinese logic cannot be clearly explained using the concepts of either traditional or modern western logic, that Chinese logic is completely different from western logic, that we need a totally new definition of "logic" and that only under such a definition can Chinese logic be studied.

On the "legitimacy" issue, there are some who say that one should define logic based on existing common opinion about what is essential to logic, and then see what kind of logic (or logical thought) existed in ancient China. Since logic itself is framed in terms of the traditional and modern concepts of western logic, I believe that it is appropriate to use these to interpret Chinese thought.

2. What is the best way to define your area in terms of historical period, textual sources, methodology or other factors?

We need combine all of these things to define the history of Chinese logic.

The most important period of history for Chinese logic is the pre-Qin period. From the Han dynasty on, logic was studied in China only sporadically. Of course, later on, both Indian *hetuvidyā* and, in modern times, western logic were introduced and then studied in China. At that time, pre-Qin logic was used as an aid to the digestion and absorption of this foreign logic, but it was never really developed further in its own right. For this reason, I believe that the history of Chinese logic should be concerned mainly with the pre-Qin period.

The textual sources in which one can find the development of Chinese logic are those containing the logical thoughts of the Hundred Schools of the pre-Qin period: the Confucians, the Mohists, the Daoists, the legalists, the School of Names, and so forth. The most well-known logical works are Xun Zi's *Zhengming*, the *Mojing* and Gongsun Long's *Baimalun*. Another important reference is Lu Sheng's *Mobianzhuxu* from the Jin period.

From a methodological point of view, I strongly believe that the history of Chinese logic should be the history of the development of logic in China, and not the fabrication of a specifically Chinese logic, fundamentally different from that of the west. Of course, the issues that concern a history of Chinese logic may be different from those of western logic. For example, western logic values reasoning and proof, while Chinese logic emphasizes more on argumentation and refutation; western logic pays more attention to deduction and induction, while Chinese logic pays more attention to analogical reasoning; western logic is concerned with the study of propositions and inference, while Chinese logic focusses on the study of concepts and relations between them.

Through my research, I have come to believe that at the level of "object-theory", Chinese logic should be regarded as what we now call "informal logic" or critical thinking, whereas, at the level of "meta-theory" it is about logical theory and logical laws. In other words, in Chinese history, there was little if any development of formal logic, as such, but the reflections on the way logic works, the Chinese "meta-logic" can be compared with the theories and ways of thinking of formal logic. I have written about this situation in my book *Studies of the Logic of the Mohist Canons* and my article "Object-logic and Meta-logic in Mohist Logic".[4]

3. What is your favourite example of logical acumen by an early Chinese thinker?

Many examples show that the logical skill of early Chinese thinkers is no less than that of western thinkers. Among them, Mo Zi is the best, as can be seen his debate with Gongshu Pan,[5] who had made siege engines for the King of Chu to attack the state of Song. Mo Zi wanted to prevent the war and said "I've been insulted by a northerner. Please help me kill him." Gongshu Pan replied, "My sense of righteousness prevents me from killing

---

[4] See also discussion on object theory and meta-theory by Sun Zhongyuan on p. 46.
[5] Gōngshū Pān 公输盘, 507–440 B.C.E., carpenter, engineer, and inventor, a contemporary of Mo Zi, and the patron saint of Chinese builders and contractors, also known as Lǔ Bān 鲁班.

people." And Mo Zi retorted: "But you have made siege engines to help Chu attack Song. Aren't you going to kill a large number of people?"[6]

Here Mo Zi cleverly employs the method known in the west as *reductio ad absurdum* but which he called *tuī* 推 (inferring). Mo Zi's *Xiaoqu* gives an explicit definition: "*tuī* is to contrast what your opponent accepts with what he does not accept, and so refute him."[7] More specifically, the argument is a good illustration of the importance to Mohist logic of *tuīlèi* 推類 (kind-based inference), which following the principle of "inference from sameness of kind".[8] My refutation of you depends on the fact that what we said is of the same kind. The key here is the concept of *zhīlèi* 知類 (understanding kinds), which means knowing differences and similarities among kinds; someone who is not *zhīlèi* is someone who doesn't know the distinctions between kinds, which is just to say he is irrational. Mo Zi often criticises those views that are not *zhīlèi*, such as "knowing the small witch but not the great witch" and "those who run fifty paces laughing at those who ran a hundred pace"[9]. Likewise, as Mo Zi points out, by having a "sense of righteousness" that prevents him from killing one person but allows him to kill many people, Gongshu Pan shows that he was not *zhīlèi*.

4. In your opinion what is the most difficult or problematic aspect of studying logical thought in China?

The most difficult problem is how to integrate ideas from modern (western) logic with studies in the history of Chinese logic in a way that is both authentic and intellectually fruitful. We need a scientifically rigorous understanding of how to conduct comparative research in Chinese and western logic. This is the problem I have thought most about.

In the first place, this problem concerns the exegesis of those early Chinese texts that are of relevance to logic. All ancient literature is extremely remote in terms of both time and culture, and our difficulties in grasping the thoughts of the ancients are further confounded by extensive physical damage or loss of the documents themselves. But another significant aspect of the problem is the nature of logic itself. We cannot avoid deciding how to distinguish between what is and what is not "logic". And after making this distinction, we must strictly comply with it when conducting our research.

---

[6] See discussion of the same story by Sun Zhongyuan on p. 49.
[7] 《墨子·小取》：推也者，以其所不取之，同於其所取者，予之也。(NO 11)
See also the discussion of this passage by Sun Zhongyuan, p. 50.
[8] *tónglèixiāngtuī* 同類相推 (inference from sameness of kind), inference from different kinds is inappropriate, e.g. concerning the length of a piece of wood and the night 《墨子·經說下》：木與夜孰長 (B6).
[9] *zhī xiǎo wū ér bú zhī dà wū* 知小巫而不知大巫 and *wǔ shí bù xiào bǎi bù* 五十步笑百步. These are modern phrases referring to the fallacy of not reasoning according to kind, i.e. responding in different ways to what are essential the same things.

I believe that this problem requires Chinese and western scholars to combine their research, to learn from each other and to engage in a common effort to make progress in the history of Chinese logic. western logic is familiar to many western scholars, who are therefore better able to use modern logical methods, while Chinese scholars are more familiar with the relevant literature and textual material. If Chinese and western scholars are able to study the history of Chinese logic together, we will more easily find the gaps and flaws in each other's research and so advance the field more rapidly. I sincerely believe that Liu Fenrong of Tsinghua University will play an important role in this kind of collaborative research.

In my book *Studies of the Logic of the Mohist Canons*, I argued that modern scholars from Liang Qichao, Hu Shi, and Shen Youding onwards, all made greater progress in the study of Mohist logic, the more they learned about western logic. Improvement in the study of the history of Chinese logic comes from deeper understanding of western logic and a mastery of modern logical methods, and so the comparative study of Chinese and western logic will undoubtedly benefit from collaborative research between Chinese and western scholars.

5. Which other areas of study could benefit from a better understanding of Chinese logic, or vice versa?

Research in the history of Chinese logic can provide a new perspective on issues in the history of Chinese philosophy, by a close study of philosophical argumentation. Unfortunately, many historians of Chinese logic often lack an understanding of modern western logic, making it difficult for them to analyse the arguments of pre-Qin thinkers, especially the Mohists and the School of Names, who are the most logically sophisticated. Scholars who also have a knowledge of western and modern logic can therefore obtain a deeper understanding of Chinese philosophical thought.

Study of the history of Chinese logic can also inspire research in modern logic and "linguistic logic".[10] In particular, the study of analogical reasoning has been thorough, systematic and profound, and so can provide much material of interest to modern logicians. For example, in *Mozi*, we find " A white horse is a horse. To ride a white horse is to ride a horse"[11] But we also find "A robber is a person. Many robbers are not many people. Not being a robber isn't not being a person. ...Loving a robber is not loving a person. ... Killing a robber is not killing a person."[12] The former is classified as *shì'érrán* 是而然 (there being this and it is so) the latter as *shì'érbùrán* 是而不然 (there being this and it is not so).[13] Knowing how to understand

---

[10] *yǔyán luójí* 语言逻辑 (linguistic logic) is the term used in China for formal approaches to the syntax, semantics and pragmatics of natural language.

[11] 《墨子·小取》：白馬，馬也。乘白馬，乘馬也。(NO 14)

[12] 《墨子·小取》：盜人，人也。多盜，非多人也。無盜，非無人也。... 愛盜，非愛人也。... 殺盜，非殺人也。(NO 15)

[13] Such examples are also discussed by Yiu-ming Fung, p. 124 and Thierry Lucas, p. 183.

these distinctions may contribute to research in both modern logic and linguistic logic.

In the opposite direction, I think I have already emphasised that research in the history of Chinese logic can benefit from western traditional and modern logic, but other areas are relevant, including linguistics, semiotics, the history of Chinese philosophy and the history of science.

Our historical research required the study of many texts written in ancient Chinese, which can be translated and interpreted in many different ways. Deciding between them is enhanced by a good understanding of linguistics and semiotics. In the *Mojing Zhengdu*,[14] researchers on both sides of the Taiwan Straits achieved some significant results concerning textual interpretation and analysis, aided considerably by the expertise of Wang Zanyuan concerning ancient bronze inscriptions and his profound understanding of linguistics.

Logical thought in China is only one part of Chinese culture, and so cannot be understood fully without a grasp of the many other aspects, especially the history of philosophy and the history of ideas. Science is also part of culture, and we can see the application of ideas and methods from logic in the early history of science in China.

Yet despite the importance of these other areas, comparison between Chinese and western logic is a fundamental. I have made some attempts to contribute to this in my book and articles that are appended at the end of this interview. It is my firm view that modern logic can be used as an important tool in the history of Chinese logic, with great methodological significance.

Related publications

Mòjīng Luójí Yánjiū 《墨经逻辑研究》(Studies of the Logic of the Mohist Canons), Beijing: Zhongguo Shehuikexue Chubanshe, 2004.

Mòjiā Luójí de Duìxiàngluójí hé Yuánluójí 墨家逻辑的对象逻辑和元逻辑 (Object-logic and Meta-logic in Mohist Logic), in *Philosopher* 哲学家, edited by Feng Jun 冯俊, Beijing: Renmin Chubanshe, 2006.

Zhōngxī Luójí Bǐjiào Yánjiū Zhuāntí 中西邏輯比較研究專題 (Topics in Comparative Studies for Chinese and Western Logic), *Zhexue yu Wenhua* 哲學與文化, Vol. 435, August, 2010.

Zhōngxī Luójí Bǐjiào Yánjiū de Yìyì 、*Yuánzé hé Jīběnnèiróng* 中西逻辑比较研究的意义、原则和基本内容 (Significance, Principles and Basic Content of the Comparative Study of Chinese and Western Logic), *Bijie Xueyuan Xuebao* 毕节学院学报, Vol. 7, 2010.

---

[14] *Mòjīng Zhèngdú*《墨經正讀》(Correct Reading of the Mohist Canons), edited by Tainwan scholar Wang Zanyuan, published by Shanghai Tushuguan and Shanghai Kexue Jishu Wenxian Chubanshe in 2011.

Chapter 9
Zhái Jǐnchéng 翟锦程

Nankai University, Tianjin

1. Why did you begin working on the history of logic in China?

For me to become involved with research on the history of Chinese logic was both accidental and inevitable.

In 1986, I began work on my undergraduate dissertation. Comparative cultural studies between China and the west were very important at the time, so I began to write a comparative study of Mohist and Aristotelian epistemology. My adviser, Cui Qingtian[1] told me that there was also a lot of work to do in comparing Mohist and Aristotelian logic. From then on, I was curious to see how this field would develop.

After graduation, I began a two-year post-graduate degree with a major in logic at Nankai University, in the Philosophy Department. I learned about the logical thought of the ancients in Greece, India and China, which gave me some understanding of the history of both western and Chinese logic. I wrote my Master's thesis in 1990 on studies in comparative logic from a methodological point of view.

From 1988, I started to teach courses on the history of western logic, philosophy of culture, and so on. During that time, Fang Keli[2] encouraged me to apply for a doctoral degree in the history of Chinese logic, and in 1993, I began under the supervision of Wen Gongyi[3] and Cui Qingtian.

---
[1] Cuī Qīngtián 崔清田, 1936-, scholar of the history of Chinese logic and professor at Nankai University.
[2] Fāng Kèlì 方克立, 1938-, scholar of Chinese philosophy and professor at Nankai University and the Chinese Academy of Social Sciences.
[3] Wēn Gōngyí 温公颐, 1904-1996, philosopher and professor at Nankai University who wrote extensively on the history of Chinese logic.

In 1994, I published "Study and Reflection on Mingbianxue from the Perspective of Cultural Development", my first paper on Chinese logic.

I have found that there are many issues in our field that require deep reflection from the perspectives of both cultural development and logical analysis, especially the relationship between logic in general and Chinese logic in particular, the relationship between Chinese, Greek and Indian logic, and the relationship between logic, philosophy and culture.

The study of logical thought in China only began when western logic spread into China for the second time, just over 100 years ago. But there remain many questions about China's relationship to western logic: whether the introduction of this logic to China gave the whole picture of western logic, whether Chinese scholars at the time understood it properly, and then later, what kind of western logic was used to study Chinese logic, and so on. These all need to be reconsidered from the perspective of developments in contemporary logic.

2. What is the best way to define your area in terms of historical period, textual sources, methodology or other factors?

The history of logic is part of history. There are many textual sources. But using the correct methodology is very important. The issue of methodology is connected to the introduction and spread of western logic in China, which influenced Chinese scholars in three ways.

Firstly, at the epistemological level. By accepting and learning western logic, Chinese scholars were able to acquire western knowledge of natural and social science.

Secondly, at the methodological level. By learning western logic, Chinese scholars could apply deductive and inductive methods to understand both modern western systems of knowledge, but also as a tool to study traditional Chinese thinking.

Thirdly, at the conceptual level. The concepts of western logic had a deep influence on the modern reorganisation of academic subjects within China, especially within philosophy.

These three influences of western logic are also deeply embedded in our studies of Chinese logic.

At the epistemological level, there was a direct application of western logic to the study of logical thought in ancient Chinese, to produce a so-called "Chinese logic", simply by matching it to ideas that could be found in traditional western logic.

At the methodological level, which was comparative, the most influential scholars were Liang Qichao, Hu Shi and Zhang Shizhao.

Liang Qichao's *Zimozi Xueshuo*,[4] which includes a chapter on Mo Zi's

---

[4] *Zǐmòzǐ Xuéshuō*《子墨子學說》 (Doctrines of Mo Zi), by Liang Qichao, published in the biweekly periodical Xinmin Congbao in 1904.

logic, is the earliest account of the logical accomplishments of the Mohists. This and his later *Mòjiā zhī Lùnlǐxué jí Qítā Kēxué* [5] marked the beginning of research on Chinese logic. The first fully systematic study was Hu Shi's dissertation *The Development of the Logical Method in Ancient China*. From 1917, Zhang Shizhao began to teach the history of logic at Peking University, and finally published a book based on his lecture notes as *Luójizhǐyào*《邏輯指要》(Outline of Logic), in which he claimed that Chinese and western logic are parallel, like the two wheels of a barrow.

Finally, at the conceptual level, these studies differed, despite having the same topic and the same comparative method, mainly due to the different orientations of the three scholars. Liang introduced western logic using Mohist logic; Hu studied Chinese logic using western logic; whereas Zhang studied Chinese and western logic on an equal footing.

Modern interest in the history of logical thought in China has lasted about a century, and so coincides with both the development of modern logic in the west and the development of modern Chinese culture. As such, the study of Chinese logic should be based on both an understanding of the nature of logic itself and the relationship between Chinese logic and Chinese culture.

Since Chinese logic is a part of logical thought more generally, we should use logical concepts and methods to reveal its significant characteristics. One hundred years ago, the logic that Chinese scholars learned from the west and then applied to study Chinese logic, was very limited. It corresponded roughly to deduction and induction in traditional western logic, but was introduced into China mainly through Japanese translations, rather than the western originals. This traditional logic was based on a limited understanding of the nature of logic, without many of the subtleties familiar from modern logic. Today we have a better grasp of logical science, and can use its concepts to show that Chinese logic has the general character of logic.

Likewise, Chinese logic is both a product and an example of Chinese traditional culture, and as such, we can interpret its significance against a more general cultural background. By working within the framework of the development of Chinese culture and philosophy, we can interpret the cultural meaning of Chinese logic. This involves a study of its development, an analysis of its content and particular features and a discussion of its distinctive cultural aspects.

From the perspective of comparative studies, the development of Chinese logic can be viewed as an important part of the "world logic system",[6] parallel to Greek and Indian logic. We can discover their common features, analyse the special character of Chinese logic and so recognise

---

[5] *Mòjiā zhī Lùnlǐxué jí Qítā Kēxué* 墨家之論理學及其他科學 (Mohist Theories of Reason and Science), Ch. 7 of *Mòzǐxuéàn*《墨子學案》(Critical Survey of the *Mozi*)

[6] *shìjiè luóji tǐxì* 世界邏輯体系 (world logic system) is a term used by Chinese scholars for the unity of logical thought across the world, having its ancient origins in three places: Greece, India and China.

its contribution to the development of the world logic system. Further comparative research should be directed to the question of why Chinese logic is the only logic based on a non-Indo-European language.

3. What is your favourite example of logical acumen by an early Chinese thinker?

An interesting new area in the study in Chinese logic is that of *yìxué*,[7] which contains many such examples.[8] *Yìxué* is a vital part of Chinese traditional culture and thought, and an important influence on many fields of knowledge in ancient China, such as astronomy, architecture, mathematics, and medicine. One could say that it is the key to understanding the secrets of Chinese traditional culture.

The logic of *yìxué*, which is different from that of traditional *míngbiànxué*, contains many ideas and methods concerning *tuī* and *tuīlèi*, which are the main forms of reasoning in Chinese logic.[9] Its study is therefore essential for an accurate and complete understanding of Chinese logic.

Yixue is a system of divination, which is ancient but has survived more or less intact. The symbols for male (—) and female (--) are combined by certain special rules to produce one of 64 forms, after which there is some calculation and a conclusion about what will happen. This process is highly formal, with obvious logical characteristics. It has even been suggested that Leibniz was influenced by *yìxué* to create the system of binary numbers, in which "1" is equal to — and "0" is equal to --. This matter requires further research to establish whether or not it is really true. In the historical development of Chinese culture, the ideas and methods of *yìxué* were maintained for a long time, and so the study of its logic should be taken to be an important part of the study of Chinese logic.[10]

4. In your opinion what is the most difficult or problematic aspect of studying logical thought in China?

What is most difficult is to understand the nature of logic itself, and then to use this to delineate a history of Chinese logic. This issue has been a

---

[7] *yìxué* 易學 (study of the changes), study of the ancient divinatory text *Zhouyi* and the book containing its subsequent commentaries, *Yijing*.

[8] Logic in the *Zhouyi* has been discussed in Wen Gongyi, Cui Qingtian eds.,《中国逻辑史教程》(The Course of the History of Chinese Logic), Tianjin: Nankai Daxue Chubanshe, 2001 and Zhou Yunzhi ed.,《中国逻辑史》(The History of Chinese Logic), Taiyuan: Shanxi Jiaoyu Chubanshe, 2004, and then more systemically in Wu Kefeng《易学逻辑研究》(The Study on Logic in *I Ching*), Beijing: Renmin Chubanshe, 2005.

[9] *tuī* 推 (inferring), one of the *pìmóuyuántuī*, a method by which one uses one's opponents own ideas to refute him, sometimes associated with the method of *reductio ad absurdum*. *tuīlèi* 推類 (kind-based inference), the central Mohist conception of inference, also known as *lèituī* 類推 (kind-based inference).

[10] See also discussion on *yìxué* by Wang Kexi in this volume.

focus for many scholars in our field, who concentrate on what logic is, the place of logic in the history of thought, whether or not Chinese "logic" even exists, and if it does, what relationship it has to logic in general.

I think that to address these issues, we must use logical concepts, so as to study logical thought within the history of thought in general. And yet we must not examine Chinese logic through the distorting lenses of western and Indian logic; instead, we need a general characterisation of logic itself.

The main point of my 2007 paper "Using Logical Concepts to Investigate the Study of Chinese Logic" is that although each of the world logic systems (Chinese logic, Indian logic and Greek logic) have their own characteristics and processes of development, they share a common object of study in the idea of proof or argumentation. Logic is now a rigorously systematic scientific instrument, but in its initial development there was no strict system of proof. It is something that grew from nothing, from vague to clear, from fragmentary to complete, and from scattered to systematic—like the development of human thought in general.

I also identified three general logical features, which can help us to place Chinese logic within the three world systems.

A. Instrumentality. Logic, in general, is tool for establishing proof, and in the arguments between different philosophical schools of the pre-Qin period, Chinese logic certainly played this role.

B. Formality. Logic concerns the form of proof rather than its specific content. Lu Sheng commented that in ancient China, despite the opposing ideologies of the Confucian and Mohist schools, Mencius criticised Mo Zi using the same patterns and methods of reasoning employed by Mo Zi himself.[11] This suggests not only that Chinese logic is a general instrument of argument, but that the different schools used common patterns of reasoning; which is just to say that Chinese logic is to some degree formal.

C. Validity. For a proof to be accepted, its reasoning must follow certain rules. In *Xiaoqu* we find this principle articulated as *zhòngxiào* 中效 (match exemplar):

> 《墨子·小取》：效者，為之法也。所效者，所以為之法也。故中效，則是也；不中效，則非也。(NO 5)

> *Xiào* 效 is to make a standard for things, to be used to judge whether something is right or not. So what conforms to the standard is right and what does not conform is not right.

So we can say that *xiào* is the rule or standard by which one should verify an idea or an opinion.

---

[11] 《墨辯注序》：孟子非墨子，其辯言正辭則與墨同。

What we should properly call "Chinese logic" is that part of traditional Chinese thought concerned with proof or argumentation, which has the three properties of instrumentality, formality and validity. With this criterion, we find that there is indeed a Chinese logic, but one that is different from both Aristotelian and Indian logic. This situation is similar to that of Chinese traditional medicine when compared to western medicine. Despite different theoretical systems and methods of treatment, they have the same aim: to cure disease and make people more healthy.

5. Which other areas of study could benefit from a better understanding of Chinese logic, or vice versa?

The first decade of the 21st century has seen new trends in the study of Chinese logic, one of which is an emphasis on its place in the general history of thought. This both deepens our understanding of the interaction between logic and thought in general and enables us to see developments in Chinese logic against a wider background.[12]

Within Chinese history, the development of Chinese logic is in a constant state of change, influencing and influenced by contact with different areas of thought. We must therefore pay attention to the character of Chinese logic in different historical periods. Due to the varying influences and restrictions of particular social structures, logical thought at different times possesses different social and cultural characteristics. These result from differences in political, ethical, philosophical and legal thinking. Likewise, logical thought influenced social development through its role in the same areas of social activity.[13]

The latest developments in the philosophy of logic also bear on the study on Chinese logic. The first is "the plurality of logic", which in the words of the contemporary philosopher of language, Dale Jacquette, is "a vital key to understanding the nature of logic in contemporary philosophy and mathematics... The puzzle in a nutshell is to understand how it is that so many different kinds of formal systems can all deserve to be called logics."[14] As one of three world logic systems, Chinese logic illustrates logical plurality.

---

[12] Works that follow this trend are Zhāng Guógāng 张国刚 and Qiáo Zhìzhōng 乔治忠 eds., *Zhongguo Xueshushi* 《中国学术史》 (Intellectual History in China), Shanghai: Dongfang Chuban Zhongxin, 2002 [on *míngbiàn* and *mòbiàn*]; Huáng Jiàndé 黄见德 *Xīfāng Zhéxué Dōngjiānshǐ* 《西方哲学东渐史》(History of the Eastern Spread of Western Philosophy), Vol. 1, Beijing: Renmin Chubanshe, 2006 [on the influence of western logic in modern China]; various chapters of Zhū Dàwèi 朱大渭 *Zhōngguó Gǔdài Sīxiǎngshǐ* 《中国古代思想史》(History of Thought in Ancient China), 6 volumes, Nanning: Guangxi Renmin Chubanshe, 2006, [concerning Chinese logic]; Má Tiānxiáng 麻天祥 *Zhōngguó Jìndài Xuéshùshǐ* 《中国近代学术史》(History of the Modern Chinese Academy), Wuhan: Wuhan Daxue Chubanshe, 2007 [on the development of logic in modern China].

[13] For a contrasting view, see Sun Zhongyuan on page 76.

[14] Dale Jacquette, ed., *Philosophy of Logic*, Elsevier, 2006, Introduction, p. 2.

The second one is the existence of a "universal logic", which has been an issue in the philosophy of logic for nearly 20 years. Jacquette summarises the various positions as follows:[15]

A. There is a universal logic.
B. All of the various systems of logic that seems so disjoint today will eventually or can potentially be unified and integrated as a single super-system.
C. There is no universal logic, but there is a universal concept of logic that underlies one and all of the many different logical formalism that have been advanced.
D. There is a universal logic and a universal concept of logic, but we can never fully or confidently come to know what it is.
E. There is no universal logic or universal concept of logic, but something rather like a Later Wittgensteinian family resemblance among disparate logics.
F. There is no universal logic, universal or family resemblance concept of logic that can hope to incorporate all of the disparate systems of logic.

My own opinion is that "universal logic" is not a new logical system but rather those general features shared by all logics. We can use Leibniz's concept of "universal mathematics" and "universal language" to help with this issue. Despite their specific content, they show how we can think of there being a "general" or "universal" logic, which is just those general features characteristic of modern symbolic logic. Chinese logic is then a kind of logic which, like other logics, possesses the general features of logic.

The third relevant issue from the philosophy of logic is that of how logic is related to mathematics and natural science. In the west, these relationships are very close, as is shown by the history of western logic. Ancient China had its own mathematics and science, especially in the fields of astronomy, calendrical studies and architecture, suggesting that a proper study of the relationship between these sciences and Chinese logic is needed.

Taking "Chinese logic" to be that part of traditional Chinese thought concerned with proof and having the three general properties mentioned above, we find that there are other theories of Chinese logic besides the traditional míngbiànxué, including logical thought in yìxué and traditional Chinese mathematics. Further study of these is needed. There are also many interesting ideas in the later development of Chinese culture and thought after the Qin dynasty, which may well contain some as yet undiscovered logical thoughts.

---

[15] Ibid., pp. 5-6.

Related publications

Cóng Wénhuà Fāzhǎn Jiǎodù Yánjiū hé Rènshi Míngbiànxué 从文化发展角度研究和认识名辩学 (Study and Reflection on Mingbianxue from the Perspective of Cultural Development), *Zhexue Dongtai* 哲学动态 (1994 增刊), pp. 115-118.

Xiānqín Míngxué Yánjiū 《先秦名学研究》(A Study oF Pre-Qin Mingxue), Tianjin: Tianjin Guji Chubanshe, 2005.

(with Qiu Ya) *Jìnshínián Zhōngguó Luójishǐ Yánjiū de Zhǔyàotèdiǎn yǔ Qūshì* 近十年中国逻辑史研究的主要特点与趋势 (The Main Characteristics and Tends in the Study of Chinese Logic in Past Ten Years), *Zhexue Dongtai* 哲学动态, No. 10, 2010.

A New Interpretation of Reasoning Patterns in Mohist Logic, *Studies in Logic*, 4(3): 126–144, 2011.

The Importance and Research Methodology of Chinese Logic, in Clark Glymour, Wei Wang, Dag Westerståhl, eds., *Logic, Methodology and Philosophy of Science: Proceedings of the Thirteenth International Congress*, Vol. 2, London: King's College Publications, 2011.

Chapter 10

Zhèng Wěihóng 郑伟宏

Fudan University, Shanghai

1. Why did you begin working on history of Buddhist logic (*hetuvidyā*, 因明) in China?

This question is rather difficult to answer since my stepping on this road of no return was really quite accidental. But when I reflect on my career, I'm inclined to believe that there were three main factors that shaped my path: an initial radical shift in my intellectual interests, the kind and warm support of numerous colleagues, and, ultimately, a pressing desire to redress some very prevalent misunderstandings of Buddhist logic.

Thirty years ago, I could not have imagined that the rest of my life would be devoted to logic, nor that the reading of a huge number of ancient texts would occupy me on a daily basis. In 1965, I applied to study journalism at Fudan University, and only with reluctance accepted the place I was given as a student of philosophy. Shortly after graduation, I jumped at the chance to become an overseas correspondent for the People's Daily, which I took to be the supreme palace of journalism, and begun my training there. Yet for some reason, when I was invited to return to the university in 1978, I accepted. Perhaps the grass is always greener.

From then I taught formal logic and learned of the "great debate" of the 1950s and early 60s about the nature of formal logic and its relation to dialectics. Among my senior colleagues were representatives of both sides, and I benefitted greatly from their instruction. I was inspired to study Buddhist logic by Shicun,[1] which was the first publication on this subject after the Cultural Revolution. But for many years, I made little progress, lacking the courage to even begin. Finally, as a result of a conference at Fudan University organised by Zhu Zhikai, I was assigned to collect

---

[1] Shí Cūn 石村 *Yīnmíng Shùyào* 《因明述要》(A Summary of Hetuvidyā), Zhonghua Shuju, 1981.

materials on contemporary studies of Buddhist logic for the five-volumed compendium *The History of Chinese Logic*, edited by Zhou Yunzhi and others. This finally removed my hesitation and timidity.

In taking this bold step, I was influenced greatly by Zhou Gucheng at Fudan, whose famous slogan is "knowledge is acquired by no means but seizure"[2]. In his early years, he was denied promotion to professor because he was able to teach only Chinese history but not world history. By teaching himself, and with great effort and dedication, he published the book *World History*.[3] Besides, there is another saying, from another famous scholar at Fudan, that there were two types of scholars: those who pierce holes in sheets of steel and those who make holes in wood. Naturally, the latter made faster and better progress. His intention was to ridicule those who were afraid of potential difficulties in their research, picking the easy jobs and shirking the hard ones. But in spite of this, I was happy to be the second kind of scholar. After several years of academic research, I knew very well that it was enormously difficult to earn a living from modern western logic, so much so that a number of scholars had to leave their academic position because of a lack of publications. By contrast, Buddhist logic was unpopular and little known, and so publication was easier. As the saying goes, "to draw a ghost is easy, but to draw a person difficult"[4].

Today, looking back on those two decades, I find that everyone in the field of Buddhist logic, whether veteran or newcomer, can easily boast that they have solved some "millennium problem", or claim to be the world's leading authority. So, my choosing to earn a living from Buddhist logic stemmed not only from purely academic considerations, but also from my tendency to shirk the difficult and take the easy road, to "pinch the soft persimmon at first"[5]. In the somewhat less critical words of Zhang Peiheng,[6] the director of the Research Institute of Chinese Classics at Fudan, "in those fields few have touched, with a little effort, it is easy to produce results"[7].

In going from journalism to philosophy, and then to logic, I was increasingly distanced from the dream of my youth. In my thirties, I had begun to take Buddhist logic as my iron rice bowl and life-long support. All that was totally unexpected. That I could move straight into this work was not only due to the personal factors mentioned so far, but also thanks to a range of circumstances. As Buddhist doctrine states, there are no coincidences; everything has a cause. The most significant of these was my meeting Huang Shicun. Shicun was formerly a journalist and an accomplished writer. Long ago, he had written popular books about

---

[2] 学问是抓来的
[3] Zhōu Gǔchéng 周谷城 Shìjiè Tōngshǐ 《世界通史》(The World History), Shangwu Yin-shuguan, 1949.
[4] 画鬼容易画人难
[5] 拣软柿子捏 。The idea here is that people pinch the fruit to make it easier to eat.
[6] Zhāng Péihéng 章培恒, 1934-2011, worked at Fudan University in his life, had contributions in ancient Chinese literature.
[7] 在不大有人碰的领域，只要下功夫，就容易出成果 。

logic, including *Learning Logic from Chairman Mao's Works*.[8] He had read and appreciated a book of mine, and one day called me to his sickbed, solemnly presenting me with a collection of works on Buddhist logic, in the hope that I would study them in depth, and so advance our understanding of them. This collection was precious and had an unusual history. In the early 1960s, Dharma Master Yi Huan[9] was forced to leave his temple and return to normal life. Shicun helped him materially over a long period of time. They became friends in adversity, and it was from Dharma Master Yi Huan that Shicun received nearly 20 treatises on Buddhist logic, not only modern texts but also texts from the Tang dynasty, which he had collected over many years. The collection was so rich that no library in China could match it. It was only because of this remarkable gift that I was able to complete my editing of Buddhist texts on logic and the writing of a modern history of Buddhist logic. Other scholars working on the same topic had to give up because of the lack of research material, and work in this field became almost a one-man show.

In comparing my work on the relationship between Buddhist and western logic with that of my colleagues, it is clear that I have profited greatly from the intensive seminar on "the History of Buddhist, Chinese and western Logic" held in Spring 1985 and organised by the logic group at the Institute of Philosophy, Chinese Academy of Social Sciences. In particular, I was helped by Zhang Jialong's course on history of western logic and Zhuge Yintong's explanation of syllogism. Frankly, without a correct and accurate knowledge of western logic, one simply cannot do comparative studies of Buddhist logic. The errors in research conducted by those in China and abroad with an inaccurate understanding of syllogisms can be found everywhere.

Since Buddhist logic is far from being a popular topic, I could not have indulged in my studies without the support of my institute. For quite some time, Zhang Peiheng had paid great attention to cultivating and improving the level of logical thinking of researchers. As the vice director of the National Committee of the Collation of Ancient Books, he had been fully supporting of studies in Buddhist logic. Twenty years ago, it was he who personally invited me to his institute, and provided me with such excellent research conditions that I was glad to devote myself single-handedly and with endurance to research on this unpopular subject. Without his care, support, encouragement and supervision, I would have achieved almost nothing.

Twice, in 1987 and 1988 respectively, I visited the famous Buddhist scholar, Lü Cheng,[10] and learned by his side. He was a very distinguished scholar in both Buddhist philosophy and logic, and I derived a great deal of

---

[8] *Cóng Máozhǔxí Zùzuòzhōng Xuéluójí*, 《从毛主席著作中学逻辑》, Hebei Renmin Chubanshe, 1962.
[9] Yìhuàn Fǎshī 亦幻法师, 1903-1978, received an education in a Chinese monastery, and made a contribution to the study of Buddhism.
[10] Lǚ Chéng 吕澂, 1896-1989, scholar of Buddhist philosophy and logic, and fellow of the Chinese Academy of Social Sciences.

benefit from his explanations of certain significant theoretical problems. Huang Xinchuan[11] kindly provided me with a variety of works in English on Buddhist logic, including F. Th. Stcherbatsky's *Buddhist Logic* and Satis Chandra Vidyabhusana's *A History of Indian Logic*. Takemura Shōhō, the honorary president of Ryūkoku University in Japan, warmly presented me with one of his own works on Buddhist logic, *Studies in Buddhist Logic* and provided me with a photocopy of *A New Commentary on Nyāyamukha*, which was composed by a Japanese scholar in Chinese and published in 1845. The Indian Embassy in China also gave me a copy of *Buddhist Formal Logic* by R. S. Y. Chi, which was originally for display in a cultural exhibition. All these works were a significant help to me and my graduate students in our research.

My two articles, "On Trairūpya" and "A Comparison of Buddhist Trayāvayava and Logical Syllogism" became my essay for the seminar mentioned above. Although many specific points in these two articles are still valid today, they are influenced by the traditional erroneous account of Buddhist logic. When I went in depth, I found that the traditional account, which had prevailed for over half a century both in China and abroad, had a great loophole with respect to comparative studies of Buddhist and western logic. To fill this loophole then became the main purpose of my research for the rest of my career.

With the logical texts translated and handed down by the Tang dynasty monk Xuan Zang in my hands, I had stood in this somewhat cheerlessness position for more than two decades, publishing a series of monographs. In recent years, I found that the ideas admired and appreciated by most of the researchers on Chinese Buddhist logic in the last century in China were basically copied from those of F. Th. Stcherbatsky in the Soviet Union, Satis Chandra Vidyabhusana in India and Ōnishi Hajime in Japan. Zhou Wenying, the second president of the Society for the History of Chinese Logic, did confess that "when remarking on the structure of *trayāvayava* and on the *trairūpya*, I made certain mistakes", and "those ideas were of course not my own inventions, but were copied from the scholars preceding me. However, these ideas now seem to be incorrect."[12] This kind of confession reflected the straightforward academic character of that great scholar, who was of broad mind, and aroused in my heart a deep admiration. In addition, I found that two famous experts in Tibetan Buddhist logic, Dharma Master Fa Zun and Yang Huaqun,[13] erroneously interpreted Dharmakīrti's logic through Dignāga's wheel of nine reasons, the *Hetucakra-ḍamaru*, and then equated Dignāga's logic with that of Dharmakīrti's. Thus, they confused Dignāga's contribution with

---

[11] Huáng Xīnchuān 黄心川, 1928-, an expert in Indian philosophy and religion, and fellow of the Chinese Academy of Social Sciences.

[12] *Zhōuwényīng Xuéshùzhùzuò Zìxuǎnjí*《周文英学术著作自选集》(Self-selected Academic Writings of Zhou Wenying), Beijing: Renmin Chubanshe, 2002, p. 46

[13] Fǎzūn 法尊, 1902-1980, expert in the field of Tibetan Buddhism; Yáng Huàqún 杨化群, 1923-1994, well-known for his monograph *Zàngchuán Yīnmíngxué*《藏传因明学》(Tibetan Hetuvidyā), Lhasa: Xizang Renmin Chubanshe, 1990.

that of Dharmakīrti's. In regard to the above situation, I published a series of articles.

To look back, from the very beginning when I claimed to break with the tradition and asserted that Dignāga's logic was non-deductive,[14] I have been constantly criticised for "playing to the gallery" and "being showy without real worth". As a matter of fact, the growth of a theoretician needs the concern, care, encouragement and guidance from his supporters. To be criticised by the opposing views is also not necessarily bad, because the establishment of a correct thesis is bound to undergo attacks from a variety of opinions, while "the greenhouse flowers cannot afford heavy winds". For over twenty years, I have been doing research with my tail between my legs, and bearing in my mind the attitude that if there is any mistake, I will correct it, and if not, I will also warn myself about that possible mistake so as to guard myself against it. Each time when I set pen to paper, I will strive to make my discussion coherent, my argument well grounded and my thesis sufficiently justified so as to build my enterprise of Buddhist logic step by step without any uncertainty.

During these years, a group of young scholars specialising in Buddhist logic have been brought together around me. They are Zhang Lianshun of Guizhou University, who is adept in Buddhist epistemology and soteriology, my doctoral student Tang Mingjun, who is adept in comparative studies of Sanskrit and Chinese texts, my doctoral student Cheng Zhaoxia, who is familiar with both the ancient and contemporary Japanese scholarship on Buddhist logic, and the other doctoral student Dhamma Master Ānando, who comes from Thailand and is adept in the studies of the Pāli treatise Kathāvatthu. They have made sure progress on the basis of my own research. Buddhist logic has always been of little interest, so I hope my research team can scale new heights, and pass the torch of this rare discipline, generation by generation, making it more intelligible to a broader circle of learned man and woman.

2. What is the best way to define your area in terms of historical period, textual sources, methodology or other factors?

The main task of my research on Buddhist logic is to depict in an accurate manner Dignāga's and Dharmakīrti's respective systems of logic, and to discover the fundamental difference between these two summits of Indian Buddhist logic. This task is not only related to the correct discernment of different phases in the history of Buddhist logic but also to a careful examination of basic texts, especially the correct interpretation of Dignāga's *Gateway to Logic*,[15] which represents his early ideas about

---

[14]This is because of his requirement that the zōngyǒufǎ 宗有法 (*dharmin*, subject of the thesis) is excluded from the tóngpǐn 同品 (*sapakṣa*, similar instance) and yìpǐn 異品 (*vipakṣa*, dissimilar instance).

[15]*Gateway to Logic* Zhènglǐménlùn 《正理門論》 Nyāyamukha, translation by Xuan Zang in 649 of Dignāga's primary text on *hetuvidyā*.

Buddhist logic. This task also requires the application of many different methodologies: the holistic, the historical and the comparative methods. In addition, I also pay attention to results of comparative studies of Sanskrit, Chinese and Tibetan texts.

There are two main streams of Indian logic: the *nyāya* logic and Buddhist logic. The first system of Indian logic was set forth in the *Nyāyasūtra*, but the first deductive theory was developed as part of Buddhist logic. Dignāga laid the groundwork and Dharmakīrti finally transformed Indian logic from analogy to deduction, so reaching the level of western syllogism for the first time.

A fair number of important works on the history of Indian logic have made unfair remarks about Dignāga's and Dharmakīrti's contributions. Their expositions of Dignāga's and Dharmakīrti's systems of logic are also inaccurate but they have had a great influence on many Chinese studies of Buddhist philosophy and logic. Also, the new *hetuvidyā* system of logic, which is due to Buddhist theoreticians, is ignored in the context of Indian logic in general and Indian scholars pay little attention to the contribution of Buddhist logic to Indian logic. In sum, the ignorance of Dignāga's and Dharmakīrti's contributions is due to the fact that most scholars around the world cannot provide a clear account of the origin and development of deductive theory in the history of Indian logic. They erroneously state that there was already a universal premise in the "five-membered argument" of old *nyāya*, and hence that it is deductive.[16] For example, F. Th. Stcherbatsky gives the following argument:[17]

1) thesis: The mountain has fire.
2) reason: Because it has smoke.
3) example: As in the kitchen; wheresoever smoke, there also fire.
4) application: The mountain has smoke.
5) conclusion: The mountain has fire.

With line 3, the "example" (*dṛṣṭānta*) is taken to be a universal proposition, and so the argument is deductive; but this interpretation is wrong. The *dṛṣṭānta* should be just that "there is both smoke and fire in the kitchen", not "whatever is smoky is fiery" nor "where there is smoke, there is necessarily fire". However, if the five-membered argument of old *nyāya* were deductive reasoning, the contributions of Dignāga and Dharmakīrti would then be of trifling significance.

A rare exception to this tradition of misunderstanding, which is repeated by various Indian and Chinese scholars, is a remark by Tang Yongtong,[18] who presents the five-membered argument in a slightly but significantly different way, taking the *dṛṣṭānta* to be "as in a kitchen, you see the

---

[16] *wǔzhīzuòfǎ* 五支作法 (pañcāvayava, five-membered argument), *nyāya* term for a form of inference in five steps: *zōng* 宗 (pakṣa, thesis), *yīn* 因 (hetu, reason), *yù* 喻 (dṛṣṭānta, example), *hé* 合 (upanaya, application), *jié* 结 (nigamana, conclusion).
[17] F. Th. Stcherbatsky, *Buddhist Logic*, Vol. 1, New York: Dover Publications, Inc. 1962, p. 26.
[18] Tang Yongtong, *Yìndù Zhéxuéshǐluè* 《印度哲学史略》 (A Brief History of Indian Philosophy), Beijing: Zhonghua Shuju, 1998, p. 131.

smoke and the fire", which is not a universal proposition, so interpreting the argument to be not deductive but analogical.

The earliest record of the five-membered argument appeared in *Charakasamhitā*, a book on internal medicine compiled by the famous doctor Caraka in the early 2nd century on the basis of materials from the 5th century B.C.E. In *Charakasamhitā*, the definition of *dṛṣṭānta* in the five-membered argument is "drishtānta [sic!], verily, is that which effects an equality of apprehension among both the ignorant and the learned, and which illustrates the proposition to be established."[19] Here, *dṛṣṭānta* is taken to be an illustration and there is no judgement as such.

In order to know to what extent the old *hetuvidyā* was improved by Dignāga, we need to understand both the disadvantages of the old *hetuvidyā* and the advantages of the new one. In the old *hetuvidyā*, to justify the thesis "sound is non-eternal", an analogy is drawn between a sound and a jar (*yù* (example)). Since a jar is created and is non-eternal, so, being also created, a sound is also non-eternal. Yet in the same way we could argue that the sound is perceivable and flammable, because the jar has these properties.

However, this argument is totally absurd and so the five-membered argument is not reliable. If the analogy is made between the sound and the jar in *all* their aspects, then it is inevitable for an argument to be lost in absurdity. The old *hetuvidyā* cannot make any principled distinction that allows it to avoid such unreasonable analogies.

This is the first disadvantage of the old *hetuvidyā*. The second one is the infinite regress of the analogical process of giving a*dṛṣṭānta* (example). If the example of an argument is only an illustration, then it is necessary to explain the illustration itself. This requires another argument to justify, e.g., that the jar, being created, is non-eternal. But when the other argument is formulated, the example it contains must then also be justified. As a result, it is inevitable that the analogical argument of old *hetuvidyā* will be lost in infinite regress.

In order to remove these two disadvantages of old *hetuvidyā*, a new form of argument, the "three conditions for reason",[20] was proposed by Dignāga. In this form of argument, the *dṛṣṭānta*[21] has two parts: an example-statement[22] (*dṛṣṭāntakāya*), e.g. "whatever is created is non-eternal" and an example-base[23] (*dṛṣṭāntāśraya*), e.g. the jar. The *dṛṣṭāntakāya* expresses the connection between "being created" and "being non-eternal". This limits the scope of the comparison between jar and sound to the properties mentioned, and so avoids the problem of unreasonable

---

[19] K. M. Ganguli, *Charaka-Samhita translated into English*, Calcutta: Avinash Chandra Kaviratna 1890–1903, pp. 568-569.
[20] yīnsānxiàng 因三相 (*trairūpya*, three conditions for reason), *yīnmíng* principles for good reasoning, concerning the relation of the *yīn* (reason) to the *zōng* (thesis), *tóngpǐn* (similar instance) and *yìpǐn* (dissimilar instance) respectively.
[21] *dṛṣṭānta* (example, *yù* 喻)
[22] yùtǐ 喻體 (*dṛṣṭāntakāya*, example-statement), principle exemplified by *yù* (example).
[23] yùyī 喻依 (*dṛṣṭāntāśraya*, example-base), object used for *yù* (example).

analogies on the basis of irrelevant comparisons. Also, the universal form of "whatever is created is non-eternal" ensures that it applies to all other things that are created, including jars, lamps, lightning etc., but not sound (the subject of the thesis), which is excluded from consideration, so avoiding infinite regress.

In my view, the requirement of excluding the subject of the thesis from both the *tóngpǐn*[24] and *yìpǐn*[25] in Dignāga's new *hetuvidyā* is to avoid circular reasoning. In the case of the thesis "sound is non-eternal", the sound, the subject of the thesis, cannot be included in things both sides agree to be non-eternal, nor in things they agree to be eternal, because what is being disputed is whether the sound is eternal or not. In other words, the sound cannot be included in a *sapakṣa* (similar instance), nor in a *vipakṣa* (dissimilar instance). The exclusion is a general stipulation in Dignāga's system. Each case in the wheel of reasons should be in accord with it. Dignāga's new form of *trairūpya* (three conditions for reason) are based on his investigation in the context of *Hetucakra-ḍamaru* (On the Wheel of Reason). The principle expressed in the *dṛṣṭāntakāya* (example-statement) is grounded on the new form of the *trairūpya* (three conditions for reason). Hence, the stipulation of excluding the subject of the thesis from similar instance and dissimilar instance is valid for not only each case in the wheel and the three conditions for reason, but also for the principle expressed in the *dṛṣṭāntakāya* (example-statement), i.e. the invariable relation (*avinābhāva*). Therefore, the domain of the invariable relation "whatever is created is non-eternal" has to be restricted to things apart from the sound. The relation, strictly speaking, is neither all-inclusive, nor a universal proposition.

Although the reliability of argumentation in Dignāga's system is much improved, the form of argument is still not deductive. His reformation of old *hetuvidyā* is mainly based on his definition of the three conditions for reason in terms of a description of the extensional relations of the logical reason to the subject of the thesis, to similar instance, and to dissimilar instance. Likewise, Dharmakīrti's reformation of Dignāga's theory is based on his redefinition of the three conditions for reason from an ontological perspective. It was Dharmakīrti who finally brought Indian logic from analogical reasoning to deduction. However, Dignāga's three conditions for reason formulae as well as Vasubandhu's were misinterpreted by F. Th. Stcherbatsky and many other modern scholars to be the same as Dharmakīrti's. They failed to draw a clear distinction between different forms of three conditions for reason of different logicians in different

---

[24] *tóngpǐn* 同品 (*sapakṣa*, similar instance), *yīnmíng* term for things similar to the subject of the thesis in the sense that they possess the property attributed in the *zōng* (thesis); for a *tóngpǐn* to qualify as a *tóngyù* (positive example) it must also possess the property attributed in the *yīn* (reason).

[25] *yìpǐn* 異品 (*vipakṣa*, dissimilar instance), *yīnmíng* term for things dissimilar to the subject of the thesis in the sense that they do not possess the property attributed in the *zōng* (thesis); for a *yìpǐn* to qualify as a *yìyù* (negative example) it must also not possess the property attributed in the *yīn* (reason).

phases of Indian logic. In my view, the main concern of Dignāga's theory is how to define the extensional relation of the *hetu* (reason) to the *dharmin* (subject of the thesis), to *sapakṣa* (similar instance) and *vipakṣa* (dissimilar instance), while the main concern of Dharmakīrti is to find an intensional definition of *hetu* (reason). Such a difference in the starting point of logical theorisation is of principal and utmost significance insofar as a clear distinction between Dignāga and Dharmakīrti is concerned.

3. What is your favourite example of logical acumen by a Chinese Buddhist logician?

My answer is that Dharma Master Xuan Zang in the Tang dynasty is my favorite Buddhist logician because of his contribution to the preservation and improvement of Dignāga's new theory of *hetuvidyā* in China, which has left us some vital clues for the interpretation of Dignāga's system. Xuan Zang also preserved and systematically improved the Indian theory of "three types of reasoning" which at that time had been little explored. Furthermore, he applied this theory to practical argumentation and finally won a resounding victory in debate. As a researcher and inheritor of the Chinese tradition of Buddhist logic, I think it is my duty to carry forward to the international academic circle of Buddhist logic and epistemology the historical contribution of Xuan Zang and the Chinese tradition of Buddhist logic to the preservation and improvement of Dignāga's new theory of *hetuvidyā*. We should make the whole world know about this!

In the early 7th century, Xuan Zang went towards the west to seek the *dharma*. "He went through all the five disciplines, and his fame resounded through the history."[26] He was warmly received at the Nālandā temple[27] where he was taught *Yogācārabhūmi-śāstra* by the venerable Dharma Master Śīlabhadra,[28] who was then more than one hundred years old. During the almost five years he resided at the Nālandā temple, he studied Śīlabhadra's course in the *Yogācārabhūmi-śāstra* not once but three times, and studied the *Gateway to Logic* and the *Pramāṇasamuccaya*[29] two times respectively. He was selected as one of the ten masters being proficient in all the *Tripiṭaka*.[30] He was selected to be one of four monks representing the temple in debate when challenged by the rival Sāmitīya School.[31] King Śīlāditya, who was king of the whole of India, invited Xuan Zang to take part in a great debate on Buddhist philosophy, held

---

[26] 道贯五明, 声映千古
[27] Nālandā temple (Nàlàntuó Sì 那烂陀寺), a large Buddhist monastery in ancient Magadha (modern-day Bihar), India. It was a centre of learning from the 5th century to c.1200.
[28] Śīlabhadra (Jiè Xián 戒贤), 529-645, Buddhist monk and abbot of the Nālandā monastery, where he taught Xuán Zàng 玄奘.
[29] *Pramāṇasamuccaya* (Compendium on Means of Valid Cognition, Jíliàng《集量》), central text on logic and epistemology by Dignāga.
[30] *Tripiṭaka* (Three Baskets, Sānzàng《三藏》), a formal term for the earliest surviving canon of Buddhist scriptures also called the "Pāli Canon", containing the *Vinaya Piṭaka* (monastic regulations), *Sutta Piṭaka* (discourses of the Buddha) and *Abhidhamma Piṭaka* (philosophical commentary on the Buddha's teachings).
[31] Sāmitīya (Zhèngliángbù 正量部), a school of Buddhism in South India.

in Kanyākubja.³² In the debate, Xuan Zang set forth his argument for "argument for mere-consciousness".³³ When no one could shake any part of it, the name of Xuan Zang spread suddenly all over India. In fact, Xuan Zang's achievements in Buddhist logic are far greater than those of his Indian contemporaries.

First, Xuan Zang was an eminent student of Buddhist logic who was taught personally by almost all the authoritative scholars of his time. Second, the scope of his knowledge was comprehensive, including texts of both the old and the new *hetuvidyā*, such as Dignāga's early thoughts in the *Gateway to Logic* and his late thought in the *Compendium on Means of Valid Cognition*.³⁴ Third, Xuan Zang not only studied these works carefully, but also examined the theories they contain in detail, together with their origin and development. Fourth, Xuan Zang was also an eminent practitioner of Buddhist argumentation. He was not only well versed in the application of Buddhist logic but also dared to go beyond his teachers. He truly put his knowledge into practice, not only skilfully taking advantage of the existing logical theories but also extending them in new directions. As a result, he won many debates, including the highest level debate of his time, at the great feast of Pañcavārṣikamaha,³⁵ held once every five years.

Thus, we can see that Xuan Zang is not only one of the most important theorists, translators and pilgrims in the history of Chinese Buddhism but also a great Buddhist logician. By the time he had finished his study in India as a foreign student and returned to China, he had reached the highest level of Indian Buddhist logic, so that when he founded the Chinese tradition, in the first half of the 7th century, China was at the forefront of the world. This led to the preservation and development in China of the Indian system of demonstration and refutation, which was the central part of Dignāga's new theory of *hetuvidyā*. Moreover, Xuan Zang's interpretation of Dignāga's system is undoubtedly the most ancient one we know of. It is a faithful account that is in accord with the Nālandā tradition before Dharmakīrti.

4. In your opinion what is the most difficult or problematic aspect of studying logical thinking by Chinese Buddhists in the past?

It's to combine accurate knowledge of western formal logic with accurate knowledge of Buddhist logic. Whether this difficulty can be overcome in a satisfactory manner or not directly determines whether a proper comparative study of the Indian, Tibetan and Chinese traditions of Buddhist logic can be conducted.

---

³²Kanyākubja (Qǔnǚchéng 曲女城), in central India.
³³*wéishíbǐliàng* 唯识比量 (*vijñāptimātrānumāna*, argument for mere-consciousness), Xuan Zang's argument for the Yogācāra tenet that the object of vision is not separate from visual consciousness.
³⁴*Compendium on Means of Valid Cognition* Jíliàng《集量》Pramāṇasamuccaya, central text on logic and epistemology by Dignāga.
³⁵*wúzhē dàhuì* 无遮大会 (meeting open to all)

In fact, the perspective of formal logic reveals the heart of Dignāga's system of Buddhist logic, as presented in the *Gateway to Logic*. In recent years, scholars from the Tibetan tradition have made remarkable efforts in the comparative study of Buddhist logic and modern formal logic, but few have truly succeeded in using the methods of formal logic in their study. The mistakes made by Stcherbatsky in comparing Buddhist logic with western logic have left a black mark on the field, in both the Chinese and Tibetan traditions. Scholars from both these traditions should continue to improve their knowledge of formal logic.

Another problem concerns the study of Dharma Master Xuan Zang. Although recorded and highly revered within ancient Chinese and Japanese literature on Buddhist logic, the historical contribution of Xuan Zang to the whole tradition of Buddhist logic has been less well-known or even totally ignored until now, not only in Indian and western scholarship but also in traditional and modern Tibetan scholarship. The outstanding achievements of Xuan Zang were not mentioned even in passing in the seven treatises on Buddhist logic by Dharmakīrti, although these seven works were written after Xuan Zang's return from India. Moreover, they were completely omitted from both the *History of Buddhism in India* by Tibetan historian Tāranātha,[36] and *A History of Indian Logic* by the Indian historian S. C. Vidyabhusana,[37] the monumental *Buddhist Logic* of F.Th. Stcherbatsky, or *Indian Buddhism* by A. K. Warder.

Over the past century, most of the scholars from the Chinese tradition have also failed to present the historical contribution of Xuan Zang in an accurate and just manner. And until now, the scholars from the Tibetan tradition are still unfamiliar both with Xuan Zang's historical place in the development of Indian Buddhist logic, and with the history and literature of the Chinese tradition of Buddhist logic. Some scholars even refused to consider the historical achievements of not only Xuan Zang but also Dignāga, "the father of mediaeval logic" in classical India.

Furthermore, some scholars, notably Bao Seng,[38] completely reject the Chinese tradition of Buddhist logic, disregarding the literature on logic in the Tang dynasty. He claims that Dignāga's work was "newly born and therefore immature" and so the logical system learned by Xuan Zang, and then brought to China, was primitive and insufficiently developed. The whole Chinese tradition of Buddhist logic therefore was trivial and worthy of no serious consideration. Secondly, he asserts that in understanding Dignāga's system of Buddhist logic, Xuan Zang "must not have reached" the level of Dharmakīrti. By implication, Xuan Zang must have misunderstood the Buddhist logic of Dignāga. And thirdly, he proclaims that Xuan Zang's interpretation of the most important two concepts of Dignāga's system of logic, the *sapakṣa* (similar instance, *tóngpǐn* 同品) and

---

[36] *History of Buddhism in India* translated by Lama Chimpa and Alaka Chattopadhyaya, edited by Debiprasad Chattopadhyaya, Indian Institute of Advanced Study, 1970
[37] *A History of Indian Logic* Motilal Banarsidass Publishe, 1920
[38] Bǎo Sēng 宝僧, 1969-, scholar in Tibetan Buddhist logic.

vipakṣa (dissimilar instance, *yìpǐn* 異品), was incorrect in requiring them to exclude the subject in dispute, saying that Dharmakīrti and his followers had given no attention to such a "problem of no central significance".[39]

These criticisms result from not only a misidentification of Dignāga's system with that of Dharmakīrti, but also an evaluation of Dignāga's work *only* from the perspective of Dharmakīrti rather than by comparison with what came before. In fact, it is Dignāga's system of new *hetuvidyā* that saved Indian logical thinking from the fallacies of unreasonable analogy and infinite regress, as I explained before. Formulated in his system, the soundness of argument has been greatly improved, even if it is not entirely deductive. This is a considerable achievement, which by itself justifies Dignāga's title as "the father of mediaeval logic" in India.

As to the second criticism that Xuan Zang's understanding of Dignāga's thought was inferior to Dharmakīrti's, one doesn't knows where to begin to respond! The comparison is highly questionable just because Dharmakīrti aimed to go *beyond* Dignāga, proposing a new system of logic, whereas Xuan Zang aimed only to be a faithful interpreter. It is in this latter mission that the Chinese tradition founded by him is so valuable to us. And in interpreting rather than extending Dignāga's thought, Xuan Zang was at least as competent as Dharmakīrti. Again, the criticism stems from the mistake of thinking of Dignāga's system as merely an "immature" version of Dharmakīrti's.

A failure to understand the relationship between the logical systems of Dignāga and Dharmakīrti is also at the heart of the final criticism that Xuan Zang's requiring the *tóngpǐn* (similar instance) and *yìpǐn* (dissimilar instance) to exclude the subject in dispute was a misinterpretation of Dignāga and that Dharmakīrti had given no attention to such a "problem of no central significance". It is true, of course, that in Dharmakīrti's system there is no need for such a requirement, but the need for it in Dignāga's system, as noticed by Xuan Zang, is one of the essential features of Dignāga's system.

So, in studying the history of Buddhist logic in China, it is vital to make careful distinctions between the works of different Indian scholars, which are often missed by contemporary scholars. And this is a serious problem.

5. Which other areas of study could benefit from a better understanding of Buddhist logic in China, or vice versa?

Let us consider briefly the first half of the question, and then move to a detailed response to the second half. Firstly, a good understanding of Buddhist logical theories preserved within China will give us an alternative perspective on the historical development of Indian Buddhist logic. The

---

[39] The above views can be found in Bǎo Sēng 宝僧, On the Doctrine of Excluding the Subject in Dispute from Similar and Dissimilar Instances (论同品异品中除宗有法之说), in *Wúyuè Fójiào*《吴越佛教》(Wuyue Buddhism), Vol. 4, Beijing: Jiuzhou Chubanshe 2009, pp. 287-292.

comparative study of western and Buddhist logic in general will also benefit from such a perspective, in that it can help us to get out from under the shadow of the longstanding misunderstanding of Buddhist logic both in China and abroad. Secondly, the study of Buddhist logic in China will contribute substantially to the comparison and mutual understanding of Chinese and Tibetan culture, to the comparison of different traditions of logic across the world, to the development of a global view of logic and to the explanation of the origin and development of deductive theory in classical India. As such, the exploration of Buddhist logic in China should be a serious duty of Chinese scholars. Thirdly, the study of Buddhist logic in China also contributes to the study of the later phase of Buddhist philosophy, Indian philosophy, and to the comparative study of western and eastern philosophy in general. In this respect, the exploration of the philosophical foundations of the Buddhist tradition of logic, as well as an exposition of related problems in epistemology and in the philosophy of language from the perspective of Buddhist logic are blind spots of Chinese scholarship. Fourthly, research on Buddhist logic will also equip us with a better understanding of the history of world logic, the history of world Buddhism, the nature of logic and the theory of argumentation as well as the philosophy of Buddhism. Moreover, it will also benefit research in such fields as ethnology and Dunhuang studies.

As to the question of which areas of study could benefit research in Buddhist logic, my response relates to the methodology of studying Buddhist logic and methods for improving it. In my view, our basic methodology is to carry out philological analysis in the service of philosophical interpretation and philosophical interpretation on the basis of philological analysis. In the study of *hetuvidyā*, as a branch of the history of logic, our aim is to understand a number of theories of reasoning put forward by ancient Buddhist logicians on the basis of their transmitted works. Those texts, with their ancient commentaries, then constitute the philological base of our research. However, in order to make any progress, we inevitably encounter three sources of difficulty:

A. The original language versions of the texts on Buddhist logic, typically classical Sanskrit, if they exist at all, only exist as fragments quoted by later authors. This is especially so of the works of Dignāga. Although his magnum opus, the *Compendium on Means of Valid Cognition*, was translated into Tibetan, most other commentaries, especially those that pre-date Dharmakīrti, have been lost. Even their titles and authors are unknown. The indirect approach of interpreting Dignāga's system of logic based on later commentaries, has the disadvantage that those commentaries are deeply influenced by Dharmakīrti. The result, as described above, is that many scholars of the last century have interpreted Dignāga through the lens of Dharmakīrti, or even conflated the separate logical innovations of these two figures.

The Chinese tradition has the advantage that the doctrines of *hetuvidyā* preserved by Xuan Zang and his followers are based on the traditional interpretation of Dignāga from the Nālandā scholastic circle before Dharmakīrti. It is preserved in the Chinese translation of the *Gateway to Logic* and the *Primer on Logic* as well as in the Tang dynasty commentaries, which are mostly records of Xuan Zang's oral interpretation of Dignāga. Yet despite the importance of the Chinese tradition, it cannot represent the whole historical movement of Indian Buddhist logic. In the past, Chinese scholarship on Buddhist logic was limited by the texts available in Chinese, just as western scholarship was limited to a few Sanskrit texts, mainly those by Dharmakīrti and his commentators. Almost all the works on Buddhist logic after Dharmakīrti are preserved in Tibetan and Sanskrit. If we are unfamiliar with these two classical languages, and can only rely on the secondary literature in Chinese, we will be limited to a mere repetition of what has been said already, and so incapable of making a real contribution to research.

Furthermore, even for those works available in Chinese translation, comparison to the extant Sanskrit original or a parallel Tibetan translation is also necessary for a clear and accurate understanding of the Chinese translation itself. In fact, we should not confine ourselves merely to interpreting the opinions within the commentarial literature of the Tang dynasty, but rather search for the philological backgrounds for those opinions so as to trace their historical origins in classical India. In the last century, a series of philological studies by Lü Cheng have provided an excellent example of this kind of work. Of particular interest to me is to compare the Chinese tradition of *hetuvidyā* with the traditions preserved in the Sanskrit and Tibetan literature, so as to determine in which manner the Chinese tradition has, on one hand, preserved Dignāga's system of Buddhist logic, and on the other hand, developed it substantially.

B. In classical India, logic, dialectics and epistemology were presented as a whole but as historians of logic, we must extract those parts that are of relevance to logic. To do this requires a comparison with other approaches to logic, and any such comparison needs further justification. This is a particular case of the general problem of how to study ancient logic using the concepts of modern logic, and how to study eastern logic using the concepts of western logic.

C. The connection between *hetuvidyā* and Buddhist philosophy. Some scholars say that *hetuvidyā* needs to be understood in connection with Buddhist philosophical doctrines, at least insofar as is required to understand the examples of argumentation, almost all of which involve concepts of Buddhist philosophy. Some other scholars go on to say that by confining ourselves to logic, we cannot attain a true understanding of the Buddhist *hetuvidyā*, because it is essentially different from western ideas about logic. In my view, the main point of *hetuvidyā* is to judge in a general way whether or not an argument is good and to promote the soundness of arguments through a set of rules for formal debate. In this respect, Buddhist *hetuvidyā* has similar concerns to those of western logic. Even if we suppose that there may be some sort of essential difference, such a difference is only possible if the two approaches have at least some common concerns. Any difference can therefore be construed as a difference in approach to the same problem, which, I think, is the ground for a proper comparison between them, not against it. Moreover, to ask that we understand Buddhist philosophy before *hetuvidyā* is to ask that we understand the whole before understanding a part of it. To take it as merely an adjunct to *yogācāra*, as it is traditionally conceived, would require us to focus on such concepts as *pratyakṣa* (perception, *zhījué* 知觉) and *svasaṃvedana* (self-awareness, *zìwǒyìshí* 自我意识) and to miss the opportunity to study the great innovations in logic which are at least equally meaningful. This is not to deny that an epistemological or ontological perspective can also be useful in studying the logic.

Related publications

Lùn Yīnmíng de Tóng、*Yì Pǐn* 论因明的同、异品 (On Sapakṣa and Vipakṣa in Buddhist Logic), in *Luójìxué Lùnwénjí* 逻辑论文集 (Collected Papers on Logic), Shanghai: Baijia Chubanshe, 1988.

Chénnà Xīnyīnmíng shì Yǎnyì Tuīlǐ ma? 陈那新因明是演绎推理吗？ (Is Dignāga's New Hetuvidyā Theory of Deduction?), Nèimíng 内明, No. 3, 1990.

Fójiā Luójì Tōnglùn 《佛家逻辑通论》(A General Introduction to Buddhist Logic), Shanghai: Fudan Daxue Chubanshe, 1996.

Hànchuán Fójiào Yīnmíng Yánjiū 《汉传佛教因明研究》(Studies on Chinese Buddhist Hetuvidyā), Beijing: Zhonghua Shuju, 2007.

Yīnmíng Zhènglǐménlùn Zhíjiě 《因明正理门论直解》(A Modern Explanation of Dignāga's Nyāyamukha), Shanghai: Fudan Daxue Chubanshe 1999; revised edition, Beijing: Zhonghua Shuju, 2008.

Yīnmíngdàshū Jiàoshì、*Jīnyì*、*Yánjiū* 《因明大疏校释、今译、研究》 (The Great Commentary on Hetuvidyā: Critical Text with Notes, Modern Translation and Investigation), Shanghai: Fudan Daxue Chubanshe, 2010.

Chapter 11
Zhōu Shān 周山

East China Normal University, Shanghai

1. Why did you begin working on the history of logic in China?

My answer to this question goes back to 1970s. I had a chance to enter the Department of Philosophy at Fudan University in 1973 as a worker-peasant-soldier student to study "natural dialectics". For three years I majored in molecular genetics, under the supervision of Geng Zhencheng,[1] who was professor in the Department of Biology. After graduating, I published a popular science book on Darwin and his theory of evolution,[2] and this got me a chance to work as an assistant editor for the Journal of Natural Dialectics hosted by the Shanghai Revolutionary Committee. Two years later, the journal was closed when it was taken to be allied with the Gang of Four. I had to look for a new job. Bored with the endless political struggles, I wanted to find a place to start a more peaceful life. Logic, as a subject, has nothing to do with politics. As it happened, Fu Jizhong,[3] a colleague of mine and a very kind man, had been the head of the logic group of the institute of philosophy at the Shanghai Academy of Social Sciences before the Cultural Revolution, and so in 1978, I went with him to rebuild the institute. In this way, I started my study of logic.

Back in middle school, I was fascinated by ancient Chinese language and history. So after learning some logic (western traditional logic, modern logic and Russian dialectical logic), I was attracted to the history of

---
[1] Gěng Zhènchéng 庚镇城, biologist and professor at Fudan University.
[2] *Dá'ěrwén Jíqí Jìnhuàxuéshuō*《达尔文及其进化学说》, Shanghai: Shanghai Renmin Chubanshe, 1976.
[3] Fù Jìzhòng 傅季重, logician and fellow of the Shanghai Academy of Social Sciences.

Chinese logic as my research area. My choice was approved by Fu Jizhong. Just at that time, I received an invitation from Chinese Academy of Social Sciences, which said that the Association for the Study of the History of Chinese Logic was being established and the first workshop on the history of Chinese logic would be held in Guangzhou in December, 1980. I submitted a paper with the title "the history of science is an important object of the study of the history of logical thought."[4] As the youngest scholar invited to the workshop, my presentation was well received. And from then on, the study of the history of logic became a part of my academic life.

2. What is the best way to define your area in terms of historical period, textual sources, methodology or other factors?

One's method of doing research is clearly important. There is a Chinese saying that "gold appears when yellow sand is washed all away"[5], and this metaphor applies well to research in the history of Chinese logic. As we know, most ancient Chinese logicians, especially those who lived in the pre-Qin period, were famous thinkers, political figures, or educators. For example, Deng Xi, founder of the School of Names, was a great lawyer, who both taught law and gave advice on cases. Later, Hui Shi, also associated with the School of Names, was the prime minister of the state of Wei 魏 for more than ten years. Confucius was also a politician and educator. Later, Xun Zi, was a great thinker with whom the influential doctrine of "sage within, king without" originated.[6] Mo Zi was a politician of humble birth who advocated ideas of universal love and honouring the worthy. Even the works of the Later Mohists and those of Gongsun Long invariably contain things related to politics, economics and ethics.

In the 1950s and 60s, the contributions of our ancestors were evaluated through class analysis and classified as either materialistic or idealistic. Under such a scheme, Huishi's 10 theses were condemned as "reflecting the political thinking of a group of rulers struggling to maintain the boundaries of the six states." As Hou Wailu[7] said "it is merely a system of three components: one-sided analytic method, subjective idealism and relative eclecticism." Gongsun Long, considered even by scholars in ancient times to be "talking about names without objects," was labeled as a degenerate in the debate about names and argumentation. His statement that "material things are what is produced by Heaven and Earth" was

---

[4] *kēxuéshǐ shì luójí sīxiǎngshǐ yánjiū de zhòngyàoduìxiàng* 科学史是逻辑思想史研究的重要对象
[5] 淘尽黄沙始见金
[6] *nèishèngwàiwáng* 内聖外王 (sage within, king without), phrase from the *Zhuangzi* used by later Confucians as a term for the necessary separation of one's social role and the inner development of character.
[7] Hóu Wàilú 侯外庐, 1903-1987, historian of ideas and fellow of the Chinese Academy of Social Sciences.

thought to be "objective idealism". Yet, the content of the history of Chinese logic is just the origin and development of Chinese logical thought. It has nothing to do with class. So when we read the ancient thinkers, philosophers, politicians and educators, we should focus on what relates to forms and laws of thinking alone. And since the classics of logic, such as the *Mojing* and *Gongsunlongzi*, are purely concerned with issues of names and argumentation, there is no need to assess them using class analysis, ideas about political struggle, or the standards of idealism and materialism. That would cloud pure logical thought with obscurity, leading western scholars to conclude, quite wrongly, that there can be no logic in the tradition of "sage within, king without". In short, we need a sieve for the study of the history of Chinese logic by which we select only the logical thought of our ancestors. Class attributes, political tendencies, political thinking and opinions are washed out as sand; only logical thought remains as bright gold.

Identifying textual material is a big problem for the history of Chinese logic. Because of the prominence of Confucians throughout history, there is a good record of their early works and its transmission across the generations. The situation is much worse for other schools, especially concerning the authenticity of some texts. Take the *Daodejing* as an example. There are many places in which words of the text can also be found in *Xunzi*, and so scholars concluded that it was written or at least completed later, probably as a forgery from the Qin or Han Dynasties. In the 1970s, when the Guodian bamboo slips[8] were unearthed, several versions of the *Daodejing* became available, and the controversy ended. There are very few texts representing the School of Names and most are suspected to be fake, such as the *Dengxizi* and *Yinwenzi*. I disagree, and in the 1980s I wrote several papers to defend their authenticity, but it has proved very difficult to change the opinion of most scholars. We will have to wait for some day when these two books are also dug out of a tomb. These difficulties have had a very negative impact on the study of the history of Chinese logic.

3. What is your favourite example of logical acumen by an early Chinese thinker?

Looking at this question, the following story occurs to me:
《庄子·秋水》：莊子與惠子遊於濠梁之上。莊子曰："儵魚出遊從容，是魚樂也。"惠子曰："子非魚，安知魚之樂？"莊子曰："子非我，安知我不知魚之樂？"惠子曰："我非子，固不知子矣；子固非魚也，子之不知魚之樂全矣。"莊子曰："請循其本。子曰'汝安知魚樂'云者，既已知吾知之而問我，我知之濠上也。"

---

[8] *Guōdiànchǔjiǎn* 郭店楚簡 (Guodian bamboo slips), significant archeological find, unearthed in 1993 in Tomb no. 1 of the Guodian tombs in Jingmen, Hubei Province, and dated to the latter half of the Warring States period; they contained versions of as well as previously unseen philosophical texts.

Zhuang Zi was wandering with Hui Shi up above the Hao river, and remarked, "Those fishes are wandering about freely - that's the happiness of fishes." Hui Shi replied, "You're not a fish; how do you know the happiness of fish?" Zhuang Zi rejoined, "You are not me; how do you know that I don't know the happiness of fish?" Hui Shi said, "I'm not you, so I don't know you. You're not a fish, so you don't know the happiness of fish. Concluded!" Zhuang Zi replied, "Let's go back to the start when you said to me, 'How do you know the happiness of fish?' One who says this already knew I knew it. I knew it from up above the Hao."[9]

When Hui Shi heard Zhuang Zi infer the happiness of the fish from their swimming so freely, he immediately identified this as a violation of the principle that different kinds are not comparable: you are not a fish, so how can you know that the fish are happy? The logical reasoning that Hui Shi uses was common knowledge at that time. In the *Mojing* we find "different kinds are not comparable. Explained by measurement"[10] and "which is longer: a piece of wood or a night? which do you have more of: knowledge or grain?"[11] We cannot reason by analogy between different kinds when the standard of measurement is different.

Continuing from Zhuangzi's response "You are not me; how do you know that I don't know the fish are happy?" Huishi applies *lèituī* 類推 (kind-based inference) to go from "I am not you, so I don't know you" to "you're not a fish, so you don't know the fish are happy."

When confronted with the force of Huishi's logic, Zhuangzi makes several logical errors. The first is to take advantage of the multiple meanings of *ān* 安 (how/from where) to equivocate, turning a negative proposition into a positive one.[12] The second is to refute himself concerning what Hui Shi believes. First he says "you are not me, how do you know I don't know the fish are happy?" which presupposes Hui Shi believes he does *not* know the fish are happy. Then later he claims the opposite, that Hui Shi asked him the original question "already knew I knew it." So, from a logical perspective, we can see that Hui Shi was the winner.

Of course, Hui Shi and Zhuang Zi were the greatest thinkers in the middle part of the Warring States period, and so the story has implications for more than just logic. For example, that Zhuang Zi infers the fish are happy from their swimming freely, is related to his idea of "no difference between things", when "using the way to observe it" from which he derives "sky, earth and me are one."[13] It is also a concrete example of his principle of following nature and "forgetting each other in rivers and lakes."[14] But these rich implications should be ignored when we study its logic.

---

[9] See also the discussion of this passage by Chung-Ying Cheng, p. 154.
[10] 異類不吡，說在量。(B6)
[11] 木與夜孰長? 智與粟孰多? (B6)
[12] With the "how" meaning, *ān* expresses strong doubt: "how do you know?" implies "you don't know," a negative proposition. Zhuang Zi switches to the "from where" meaning, when he answers that he knows the fish are happy form up above the river, a positive proposition.
[13] 物无彼此; 以道观之; 天地与我为一。
[14] 相忘于江湖

In my view, Hui Shi, whose writings were said to have filled five carts, was one of the greatest thinker of the mid Warring States period, comparable to Zhuang Zi himself. That he was capable of more than just thinking about logic is shown by his serving as Prime Minister for more than ten years. Unfortunately — and what a terrible crime is it! — so many of his works have been lost. From what remains, we can see that he was a politician and natural scientist of the most logically sensitive kind, and the most outstanding logician of the whole pre-Qin period.

4. In your opinion what is the most difficult or problematic aspect of studying logical thought in China?

In my opinion, the biggest and most difficult problem in the history of Chinese logic is to determine what kind of logic it is.

When western logic was introduced into China in the late Ming dynasty, Li Zhizao adopted the pre-Qin term names and reasons for "logic" and translated traditional western logic in a volume called *Minglitan*.[15] In the late Qing dynasty, many aspects of western knowledge were introduced to China. Li Zhizao's term "*mínglǐ*" was then changed to *míngxué* 名學 (study of names) by Yan Fu when translating and editing two books of western logic. Soon after, the same term was used by Hu Shi in his *The Development of the Logical Method in Ancient China*, which was the first monograph written on the history of Chinese logic. Naturally, the early histories of logic in China compared western logic with Chinese *míngbiànxué*,[16] and the large number of early successes of this kind of research created an impression that western logic and the traditional logic of China are basically of the same kind. This created some unanticipated problems. Initially, some Chinese scholars who studied western logic concluded that there is no logic in the Chinese tradition. This was on the basis of definitions of "logic" taken from the West. Even a few historians of logic in China hastily proclaimed that the concept of logic didn't exist in ancient China. These traitors who "loved truth more than their teachers"[17] were eagerly welcomed by those studying western logic. Faced with this situation, other historians of logic in China searched and then found evidence of *bìrándìdéchū*[18] in early texts, so showing that ancient China had something that conformed to the western definition of logic. Yet clearly, these scholars also accepted the idea that there is no distinctively Chinese logic. Thinking that humanity has just one kind of logic, they sought to

---

[15] *Mínglǐtàn*《名理探》(Exploration of Names and Principles), translation by Li Zhizao and Francisco Furtado of *In universam dialecticam*, the Coimbra commentary on Aristotle, published in Hangzhou in the 1630s.

[16] *míngbiànxué* 名辯學 (study of names and argument), combination of *míngxué* 名學 and *biànxué* 辯學 used by modern scholars to refer to discussions of logical thought in ancient China.

[17] From 吾爱吾师，吾尤爱真理 (I love truth more than I love my teacher), which derives from a remark attributed to Aristotle in reference to his teacher Plato.

[18] *bìrándìdéchū* 必然地得出 (necessarily infer), modern term, taken by certain Chinese scholars as the hallmark of logic.

prove that this logic existed in ancient China. Digging for evidence in this way inevitably falls into the trap of "using the West to interpret China".[19]

In fact, there are many kinds of logic. Because of differences in cultural background, people from different geographical regions adopt different kinds of logic. In the West, where deductive thinking is prominent, special attention is given to the forms and rules of deductive reasoning. In China, analogical thinking is prominent because of the use of written characters, each of which is individually meaningful on the basis of its shape. And more attention is given to the forms and rules of analogical reasoning. For example, the ancient texts on divination and medicine, the *Zhouyi* and the *Huangdineijing* both contain of systems of analogical reasoning. When assessing traditional logical thought, we must be careful to consider which type of reasoning was prominent at that time and in that place. In my opinion, traditional logic in the West was of the deductive type, whereas traditional logic in China was of the analogical type. This is their biggest difference. If we take this to heart, research on the history of logic in China will have a clear direction and the field will follow a more normal track. Only then can we say to the world, with confidence, that there is logic in China.

Why do I say this is also the most difficult problem in the history of logic in China?

Firstly, the dominant theory of logic among researchers in china is "monism" (the view that there is only one logic). Consequently, some historians of logic in China think that their subject should be a history of formal logical thought in China. But if we fail to follow the development of logical thought in China itself, we cannot call this a history of logic in China, in any precise sense.

Secondly, there is currently no mature system of analogical reasoning that can serve as a standard for analogical logic. We can only follow the method of "using China to interpret China", analysing *lèi* 類 (kind) and the forms and principles of *lèituī* 類推 (kind-based inference) using our own traditional language. To understand and interpret traditional systems of analogical reasoning, some of which have been long regarded as the products of feudal superstition, requires expertise in *yìxué*,[20] study of Chinese medicine and even astronomy. Given the intellectual training of current researchers in the field, this is a important matter.

5. Which other areas of study could benefit from a better understanding of Chinese logic, or vice versa?

First are the history of Chinese philosophy and Chinese intellectual history more generally. Since the history of logic in China is intellectual

---

[19] yǐxī shìzhōng 以西释中, first expressed by Wang Guowei in his book 《哲学辨惑》 as "通西方哲学以治吾中国之哲学".
[20] yìxué 易學 (study of the changes), study of the ancient divinatory text *Zhouyi* and the book containing its subsequent commentaries, *Yijing*.

history and is part of the history of Chinese philosophy, these areas are deepened by specialist research in the history of logic in China. For example, for a long time, the *Zhouyi* was taken to be merely a "divination manual" and ignored, despite the text surviving intact from ancient times. After the mid Warring States period, when the most influential works of Chinese intellectual history and philosophy discussed the *Yizhuan*,[21] they paid little attention to the *Zhouyi*, giving the impression that the *Yizhuan* was developed earlier than the *Zhouyi*. This is to put the cart before the horse. Within the history of logic in China, the *Zhouyi* has been continuously used as a system of reasoning for thousands of years, serving as a text book for the analogical type of logic I referred to earlier. In the whole history of humanity it is the earliest symbolic system for analogical reasoning, with *yīn*, *yáng* and *yáo* as its primitive symbols.[22] The trigrams and hexagrams are its object language, the line statements provide its language of interpretation, and other languages are used to perform analogical reasoning.[23] In some textbooks of the history of logic in China, the *Zhouyi* is considered its origin and is discussed in the first chapter. Its prominence there is bound to have consequences for future studies of Chinese philosophical and intellectual history.

An example of this kind of influence is the view of Feng Youlan in the 1930s, who proposed a division within the School of Names. He attributed the doctrine unifying comparison to Hui Shi and that of separating hard from white[24] to Gongsun Long, and this was subsequently adopted by almost all textbooks of Chinese philosophy and intellectual history. Even in the treatment of other topics, such as the dialecticians' 21 theses,[25] most authors write in terms of this division. But further research on the history of logic has shown that the situation is quite different. Hui Shi and Gongsun Long both use *both* of the doctrines. And even in the *Mojing* we can find a lot of evidence for Later Mohist use of the related terms "distinguishing comparison" and "merging hard-white". Consequently,

---

[21] *Yìzhuàn*《易傳》(Narratives of the Changes), the ten lengthy texts that accompany the divination text *Zhouyi* in the *Yijing*, traditionally attributed to Confucius; also known as *Shiyi*.

[22] *yīn* 陰 (shady side), paired with *yáng* 陽 (sunny side). *yáng* 陽 (sunny side), one of the two aspects of the conception of the world as in constant change, paired with *yīn* 陰 (shady side), central to Chinese philosophical interpretations of the *Yijing*. *yáo* 爻 (line), line in the *bāguà* 八卦 (trigrams).

[23] *bāguà* 八卦 (trigrams), the 8 combinations of sequences of three *yáo* 爻 (line) each of which may be *yīn* or *yáng*, representing aspects of the natural world: sky, earth, wind, thunder, water, fire, mountain, marsh; the basis of the divinatory system *Zhouyi* and its interpretation as the *Yijing*. *liùshísìguà* 六十四卦 (hexagrams), 64 combinations of pairs of *bāguà*, each of which is given an interpretation in the *Zhouyi*. *guàyáocí* 卦爻辭 (line statements), interpretations given to the individual lines of the *bāguà*.

[24] *hétóngyì* 合同異 (unifying comparison), literally "unifying similarity and difference", paired with *biétóngyì* 別同異 (distinguishing comparison). *líjiānbái* 離堅白 (separating hard from white), view that qualities such as hardness and whiteness that pervade an object can nonetheless be "separated", attributed to Gongsun Long, opposite to the Mohist *yíngjiānbái* 盈堅白.

[25] *biànzhě èrshíyīshì* 辯者二十一事 (dialecticians' 21 theses), the 21 propositions held by various *biànzhě*, mentioned in the *Tianxia* chapter of *Zhuangzi*.

the proposed division of the school between *hétóngyì* and *líjiānbái* did not exist, and this conclusion will be of use to those compiling future editions of books on Chinese philosophy and intellectual history.

Finally, there are some connections between logic and traditional science, in the understanding of both classical texts and traditional practice. For example, we have analysed analogical reasoning in traditional Chinese medicine, based on the *Huangdineijing*, summarising its methods, patterns and rules of analogical inference, and proposing improvements. This research not only helps us read and understand the classics of Chinese medicine, but can also provide some methodological guidance for Chinese doctors in their medical practice.

Related publications

Zhōngguó Luójíshǐlùn 《中国逻辑史论》(On the History of Chinese Logic), Shenyang: Liaoning Jiaoyu Chubanshe, 1988.

Zhōuyì Wénhuàlùn 《周易文化论》(On the Culture of the *Zhouyi*), Shanghai: Shanghai Shehuikexue Chubanshe, 1994.

Zhōuyì Jiědú 《周易解读》(Interpreting the *Zhouyi*), Shanghai: Shanghai Cishu Chubanshe, 2011.

Chapter 12

Zhōu Yúnzhī 周云之

Chinese Academy of Social Sciences, Beijing

---

1. Why did you begin working on the history of logic in China?

I began to study the history of logic in China after the Chinese Cultural Revolution. Before that, I had only attended an ordinary (traditional) formal logic course when I was a freshman of the Department of Philosophy of Peking University, taking classes twice a week. It was only in 1976, when the Institute of Philosophy at the Chinese Academy of Social Sciences started working again, that I was appointed to its Logic Section. There I attended lectures by Shen Youding, a senior figure in the field of both mathematical logic and the history of logic in China. The lectures fascinated me, especially the many controversies about Gongsun Long and the *Mojing*, which were new to me. There were still many fundamental questions: Is there any logical thought in ancient China at all? What on earth were those texts about? If there was logical thought, how sophisticated was it? Can ancient Chinese logic be considered alongside other world traditions as one of the origins of logical thought? Was there was any subsequent development of logical thought in China? And so on. These questions were not limited merely to differences of the opinions of certain ancient thinkers but concerned fundamental issues about the importance of the study of Chinese logic and its establishment as a discipline.

It was during the time of these lectures that Zhou Liquan had a serious talk with me. He was the main person in charge of the Logic Section. He told me that Shen Youding and Wang Dianji were then the only experts in the history of logic in China, both of them were old and neither had a potential successor. By undertaking research in this area, he told me, I would be of service to the field of logic, the Logic Section, and myself. As a beginner, he thought, it would be a good place for me to start.

These two experts had both written monographs and papers, which provided me with excellent material and insights, although their academic points of views were quite different. All the same, I felt that the discipline was weak in many respects. There was not enough original material, insufficient annotations, and a lack of able researchers. After serious thought I decided to spend the rest of the year on this subject.

Shen Youding's lectures were of greatest value, giving me a starting point for my research, and a set of priorities and methods. And that's is how I came to begin with the logical thought of Gongsun Long, and in particular, the *Baimalun*.[1] After that, I devoted myself to reading, understanding and annotating the *Mojing*, striving to find its true meaning and the real significance of Mohist logic.

This was the start of my academic career. My first paper was "Gongsun Long's logical thought about *míng*", which received recognition and praise from Zhang Dainian.[2] My first major research project was on behalf of The Association of the History of Logic,[3] selecting and editing material for *A Source Book for the History of Logic in China*, consisting of five volumes, six books, and 2 million words altogether. I also wrote a four monographs and co-edited or participated in many other works on the subject.

2. What is the best way to define your area in terms of historical period, textual sources, methodology or other factors?

Speaking from my own experience in conducting research over the last few decades, I would think that the most important factor is methodology and that two methodological principles stand out as being the most essential.

The first is that in analysing and evaluating ancient Chinese thought about logic, we should use the scientific theories of modern logics.

In any historical science there is, of course, an issue about how to formulate appropriate standards for evaluating the contributions of our ancestors. Yet there is no doubt that to evaluate the thinking of the past scientifically we have to use today's science.

For instance, in chemistry, we can only accurately assess the history of such ideas as phlogiston and alchemy by using our current scientific knowledge; in physics, we can properly evaluate the contribution and weaknesses of ancient atomism, only using today's atomic theory. And in philosophy, we can correctly evaluate the contribution of each

---

[1] *Báimǎlùn*《白馬論》(White Horse Discourse)
[2] Zhāng Dàinián 张岱年, 1909-2004, influential scholar of Chinese philosophy and fellow of the Chinese Academy of Social Science.
[3] *Zhōngguóluójíshǐ Yánjiùhuì* 中国逻辑史研究会 (The Association of the History of Logic), founded in 1980 in Guangzhou.

philosopher's thought, only using the best scientific theory of dialectical materialism.

So which logical system or theory provides a basis and criterion for evaluating the history of Chinese logic? We must recognise that the theory and systems of logic established by western countries are more scientific, rigorous and complete, and so only with them can we evaluate ancient Chinese ideas about logic scientifically. In any case, we surely cannot do so with an imprecise, inaccurate and incomplete knowledge of logic. Nor can we evaluate the development of pre-Qin logic using only the standards of pre-Qin thinkers. In fact, the greater our grasp of modern scientific logical theory, the better our understanding of how to decide what in Chinese history can be studied as logic, and how to evaluate it. Answers to general questions about logic will influence even what counts as the history of logic. For example: is the Principle of Sufficient Reason to be taken as a basic law of logic? What is the relationship between dialectical contradiction and logical contradiction? Must traditional logic learn from mathematical logic?

To understand the situation in China, you need to know that some problems, which have been clearly solved in traditional western logic, are still the subject of confusion and controversy here, such as whether logic cares about the truth of propositions, whether it is a specific independent discipline, whether Law of the Excluded Middle should indicate which propositions are true and which are false, and so on.

Not all introductions to logic published in China are entirely accurate and learning the history of logic from popular literature is not only inadequate but can lead to serious errors. For example, some people recognise that the Mohist theory of *biàn* 辯 (disputation) contains the idea that in a pair of contradictory propositions, "there must be one that is false and one that is true"[4]. Clearly, that "there must a false proposition"[5] is a matter of the Law of Non-contradiction,[6] and that "there must be one true proposition"[7] is a matter of the Law of the Excluded Middle. But in summarising Mohist logic, it is sometimes said only that the Mohists discovered the Law of the Excluded Middle, which is defined by some popular publications merely as "there must be one that is false and one that is true".

How is it possible for Chinese scholars with this level of logical knowledge to analyse and evaluate ancient ideas about logic in a scientific way? Either we eventually master not only traditional western logic but also the basics of mathematical logic, or it will be impossible to improve our research into the history of Chinese logic in any significant way.

Of course, by saying this, I don't mean that we should require the

---

[4] *bìyǒuyījiǎ hé bìyǒuyīzhēn* 必有一假和必有一真

[5] *bìyǒuyījiǎ* 必有一假

[6] *bùmáodùnlǜ* 不矛盾律 (Law of Non-contradiction), translation of the western concept, considered as one of the basic laws of logic according to *Putong Luoji*.

[7] *bìyǒuyīzhēn* 必有一真

ancients to have met our modern standards, nor that we should rigidly apply today's ideas about logical form when interpreting their thoughts, nor even that we should use today's terminology merely to replace that of the ancients. Instead, we should respect history, maintaining the character of the original thought by refraining from those interpretations that impose contemporary ideas without genuine understanding and an over-simplistic identification of concepts.

I will give just a couple of examples. In the pre-Qin period there was no word for "concept" as such; instead the word *míng* 名 was used for this purpose in some contexts. So when we discuss pre-Qin logical thinking, we should continue to use *míng* as a term for "concept" and related logical thinking about concepts. But we must note that *míng* also meant "word", and that this indicates the inadequacies of logical thought in the pre-Qin period. It's also generally acknowledged that the pre-Qin term *dámíng* 達名 meant "unrestricted", and the Mohist term *lèimíng* 類名 meant "classifying". This comparative analysis not only reveals the scientific content of *dámíng* and *lèimíng* in logic but is also historically correct. We should not and need not simply replace the ancient words by their modern equivalent.[8]

In summary, research into the history of logic in China must respect both history and science, and correctly combine them. It is not right simply to make comparisons nor is it right simply to oppose the making of comparisons.

The second methodological principle I consider to be essential is that we carefully consider the historical authenticity and accuracy of our materials. Clearly, the exegetical work of annotation and translation of ancient materials involves application of the scientific method of argumentation. So this method is used both to categorise correct reasoning (i.e. formal logic) and to analyse basic historical materials. Yet, concerning these ancient sources, we must also consider matters of authenticity and accuracy that go beyond merely formal logic. For example, at the beginning of the *Mojing* we find:

《墨子·經說上》小故，有之不必然，無之必不然也。體也，若有端。大故，有之必無然，若見之所見也。

Xiǎogù 小故 (minor cause), having it, it is not necessarily the case; without it, it is necessarily not the case. *Tǐ* 体 (body/unit) is like having ends. *Dàgù* 大故 (major cause), having it, it is necessarily not the case, like what appears is what is seen.

Here there is clearly one word missing from "若有端 (like having ends)". I follow Wu Feibai in amending this to "若尺有端 (like a measuring stick having ends)". The measuring stick is related to is ends as whole to parts, which is a necessary condition. In addition it is hard to interpret "有之必無然 (having it, it is necessarily not the case)" and so I follow Sun Yirang

---

[8]Contrast/compare with other discussions on *míng* as names/concept, e.g. Dan Robins, Jane Geaney in this volume.

in amending it to "有之必然，无之必不然 (having it, it is necessarily the case; lacking it, it is necessarily not the case)". Corrections to the text of this kind are a necessarily starting point for research, and each one requires detailed argument and evidence. This approach is shown by even the titles of my books: *A Study of Gongsun Longzi's Theory of the Rectification of Names - Correction, Translation, Analysis and Evaluation* and *Notes, Translation and Study on Mohist Cannons: Logic of Mohist Cannons*. Each puts the annotation of the original text first, followed by its translation and analysis, and only then the study of the logical thought it contains. I believe that although there are many inaccuracies in my annotation, translation and subsequent research, this way of approaching the history of logic in China is correct and essential.

3. What is your favourite example of logical acumen by an early Chinese thinker?

Firstly, the *Mojing* introduces the central idea of using *shuō* 說 (reasoning/explanation) to bring out *gù* (reasons/causes), so as to explain inferential knowledge as distinct from other kinds of knowledge. It is only by inference that we can come to understand the unknown from what is known, and a theory of inference lies at the heart of both western logic and the logic of the *Mojing*. Traditional western logic is concerned with the forms of such inferences, expressed in terms of concepts and propositions, which correspond in the logic of the *Mojing* to *míng* and *cí*. Elsewhere in the *Mozi*, we find a proposal for a conception of inference in which "the future is known on the basis of the past"[9] and we are told that "explaining the relationship between what is so and what is not yet so is a matter of inference"[10] Then *shuō* is defined as "the means by which one makes plain"[11] and further described as *yǐshuōchūgù*. So for the Mohists, inference concerns *mínggù* 明故 (clarifying reasons) and *chūgù* 出故 (bringing out reasons). They also introduce the concept of *shuōzhī* 說知 (*shuō* knowledge), which is knowledge that is obtained by deductive inference from what is known to what is unknown. For example, the *Mojing* entry for *wénzhī* (testimonial knowledge) explains:

《墨子·經說下》：在外者所不{知是在室者所} 知也 。或曰："在室者之色若是其色"，是所不智若所智也 。(猶白) 若白者必白 。今也智其色之若白也，故智其白也 。...外，親(智)*{知} 也 。室中，說(智)*{知} 也 。(B70)

What someone outside doesn't know is what someone inside does know. Someone says "The colour of what is in the room is like the colour of this." This is that what you don't know is like what you do know....What is like white is necessarily white. Now you know its colour is like white, so you know it's white. ...What is outside you *qīnzhī* 親知 (know from experience); what is in the room you *shuōzhī* 說知 (know by inference).

---

[9] 《墨子·非攻》：以往知來，以見知隱 。
[10] 《墨子·經下》：在諸其所然未 者\然，說在於是推之 。(B16)
[11] 《墨子·經上》：說，所以明也 。(A72)

If, outside the door of a room, we already *qīnzhī* 親知 (know from experience) that the outside is white, and we *wénzhī* 聞知 (know by testimony) that the inside wall of the room is similar to the outside, we can infer that the inside is also white. Thus *shuōzhī* is different from both *wénzhī* and *qīnzhī*; it is knowledge that is inferred from these other kinds of knowledge taken as premises.

Secondly, also in the *Mojing*, we find a discussion of the evaluative criteria for an inference or argument: "For a proposition to arise, there must be three things"[12] The three things are *gù* 故 (reason/cause), *lǐ* 理 (principle) and *lèi* 類 (kind).

> 《墨子·大取》：{夫辭} 以故生，以理長，以類行也者。立辭而不明於其所生，妄也。今人非道無所行，唯有強股肱而不明於道，其困也，可立而待也。夫辭以類行者也，立辭而不明於其類，則必困矣。(NO 10)

> Propositions arise from *gù*, grow according to *lǐ*, and proceed according to *lèi*. It is stupid to hold a proposition[13] without being clear about how it arises. Now a person cannot proceed if he lack a path. Even with strong limbs, if he lacks a clear understanding of the path, he'll have problems. A proposition is something that proceeds according to *lèi*. To hold a proposition without being clear about its *lèi*, necessarily leads to problems.

If any of *gù*, *lǐ* or *lèi* is absent, there are three corresponding kinds of mistake: "the reasons have not been noticed", "the principles are not clear" and "the kind is not known".[14]

Concerning *gù* (reason/cause), as already mentioned, the Mohists distinguish between *dàgù* (major cause) and *xiǎogù* (minor cause), on the basis of a distinction between necessary and sufficient conditions. Inferences concerning *gù* are related to the hypothetical syllogisms of traditional western logic.

Concerning *lǐ* (principle), we read, again in the *Mojing*:

> 《墨子·經說下》：論誹(誹)之可不可（以）*{之} 理，{理} 之可誹，雖多誹，其誹是也。其理不可誹，雖少誹，非也。(B78)

> In discussing the *lǐ* of whether or not a rejection is admissible, if by *lǐ* the rejection is admissible, even if much is rejected, it is correct (to reject). But if by *lǐ* the rejection is inadmissible, even if little is rejected, it is incorrect (to reject).

The *lǐ* are the principles that govern the objects and events of the world, also known as "objective regularity". So the passage states that whether the criticism of a proposition (in a debate) is correct or not, lies not in how many sentences are used to express it but in whether they accord with objective regularity. As one of the three requirements for a proposition to hold, *lǐ* is the connection between the *gù* and the inferred proposition, roughly like the major premise in deductive reasoning. For example, the

---

[12] 《墨子·大取》：三物必具然後，{辭} 足以生。(EC 2)
[13] *lìcí* 立辭 (hold a proposition), within the context of a debate, the proposition is defendable: to hold a proposition without being clear about how it arises is stupid 《墨子·大取》：立辭而不明於其所生(忘)*{妄} 也。
[14] 不察故, 不明理, 不知類

gù for holding that the ground is wet is that it is raining today. In this case, the *lǐ* is that whenever it is raining, the ground is wet, which can be expressed as having the form $p \to q$.

Concerning *lèi* (kind), the Mohists think that only by understanding the differences between *lèi* can we make the similarities and difference between *gù* and *lǐ* really clear. Consequently, both deductive and inductive reasoning cannot avoid "clarifying *lèi*" and "noticing *lèi*". [15]In the we read that "if they are similar, they are of the same *lèi*"[16] and "if they are not similar, they are not of the same *lèi*"[17]. For *lèi* to play its role in the inference, we must provide an example of something of the same *lèi*, so as to clarify the relationship between the *gù* and *lǐ*. From this it can be seen that in order for one to hold a proposition, one needs three things: *gù* (roughly, "minor premise"), *lǐ* (roughly, "major premise") and *lèi* (something of the same kind, as an example).

Thirdly, the three terms *gù*, *lǐ* and *lèi* together constitute a *sānwùlùnshì* 三物論式 (form of three things), similar to Artistotle's syllogism and the Indian *trayāvayava*. This is the highest accomplishment of ancient research in logic, with great theoretical value, and is the most important embodiment of logical thought in ancient China. The following example is found in the *Mojing* (B25):

《墨子·經下》：(負)*{貞}而不撓，說在勝。
《墨子·經說下》：衡木(如)*{加}重焉而不撓，極勝重也。{左}右校交繩，無加焉而撓，極不勝重也。

> Bearing something heavy, it does not bend. Explained by *lèi*.
> A horizontal beam: when you add weight to it, it doesn't bend, so it can carry heavy weights. A rope hanging between two posts: even without adding weight, it bends, so it cannot carry heavy weights.

The analysis of this passage as a *sānwùlùnshì* and the corresponding syllogism and *trayāvayava* are shown in Figure 12.1. One main difference is that in Aristotle's syllogism, there is no *lèi* or *dṛṣṭāntāśraya*, which are illustrations or examples, characteristic of practical debate. The order is also different. Syllogisms emphasise the major premise, whereas *sānwùlùnshì* and *trayāvayava* put more emphasis on *gù* or *hetu*, respectively. We have to admit that unlike the deductive formal system of syllogisms, and the fixed format of *sānzhīlùnshì*, both of which were developed extensively, the Mohist *sānwùlùnshì*, has only a brief theoretical description and a few applications. Yet by giving a general form to inferences from the general to the specific, it shows significant scientific insight.

In addition to the above, ancient Chinese logical thought also contains a rich semantic theory, covering a range of topics. Together these constitute a body of theoretic work that lies at the foundation of the Chinese tradition in logic, which should therefore be considered as one of the three origins of logic in the world.

---

[15] 明類 and 察類
[16] 《墨子·經說上》：有以同，類同也。(A86)
[17] 《墨子·經說上》：不有同，不類也。(A87)

	sānwùlùnshì
cí	Bearing something heavy, it does not bend.
gù	It can bear heavy things.
lǐ	Everything that can bear heavy things, necessarily doesn't bend (omitted).
lèi	Similarity: a horizontal beam. When you add weight to it, it doesn't bend, so it can carry heavy weights. Difference: a rope hanging between two posts. Even without adding weight, it bends, so it cannot carry heavy weights.
	syllogism
Thesis	This thing that bears heavy things, does not bend.
Major Premise	Everything that can bear heavy things, necessarily doesn't bend.
Minor Premise	This thing can bear heavy things.
Conclusion	This thing that bears heavy things, does not bend.
	trayāvayava
pakṣa	Bearing something heavy, it does not bend.
hetu	It can bear heavy things.
sādharmyadṛṣṭānta	dṛṣṭāntakāya What can bear heavy weights does not bend, dṛṣṭāntāśraya e.g., a horizontal beam.
vaidharmyadṛṣṭānta	dṛṣṭāntakāya What bends without something added is unable to bear heavy weights, dṛṣṭāntāśraya e.g., a rope hanging between two posts.

Figure 12.1: Three-term inferences in China, Greece and India.

4. In your opinion what is the most difficult or problematic aspect of studying logical thought in China?

As I mentioned before, the study of the history of Chinese logic requires both the correct application of ideas from modern logic and also the correct annotation and translation of ancient texts. The greatest difficulties we face are related to these two goals.

Firstly, we must realise that a proper application of scientific method to the study of ancient texts requires not only that we identify correct forms of inference but also that the resulting arguments are consistent with the original text and the ideas of the ancients as illustrated in other texts of the period. For example, in the *Baimalun* we must decide whether to take the infamous phrase *báimǎfēimǎ* 白馬非馬 (white horse not horse) as a serious proposition or as a piece of mischievous sophistry. Any answer to this question must be based on a careful annotation and analysis of the original text and not merely on whatever ambiguities or analogies occur to the analyst when trying to make sense of it. In my Study of Gongsun Long's theory of *zhèngmíng*, I discuss this problem in detail, but as a quick summary, we can say that Gongsun Long identified both an extensional and an intensional difference between *báimǎ* (white horse) and *mǎ* (horse). This is on the basis of a careful translation of certain passages. The extensional difference is shown by the passage "When seeking a horse, yellow and black horses will do; when seeking a white horse, yellow and black horses will not do."[18] Here yellow and black horses are listed as included among *mǎ* (horse) but not among *báimǎ* (white horse). The intensional difference is shown by the passage "Having a horse is different from having a yellow horse; there is a difference between yellow horse and horse"[19] and "A horse must have colour, so there are white horses."[20] Here *bái* (white) is shown to be part of the intension of *báimǎ* but not of *mǎ*. Thus we see that Gongsun Long's *fēi* (not) of *báimǎfēimǎ* should be understood as meaning that *báimǎ* and *mǎ* are not identical, not that they are completely different, and that he was thereby illustrating an important logical insight. Unfortunately, many scholars take the *Baimalun* to be mere sophistry, without any attention to the evidence of the text; it is even categorised this way by logic textbooks of the 1980s. Of course, *fēi* usually means just "is not", and there are many examples of this usage, but there are also examples, both from ancient and modern Chinese, of it meaning "different from" or "not included in". So to decide which is the correct interpretation, one can neither rely only on philology nor only on logic; a sensitivity to the exercise of reason in the text itself is needed. Such considerations are not only important for understanding the work

---
[18] 《公孫龍子·白馬論》：求马，黄、黑马皆可致；求白马，黄、黑马不可致 。
[19] 《公孫龍子·白馬論》：以有馬為異有黃馬，是異黃馬於馬也 。
[20] 《公孫龍子·白馬論》：馬固有色，故有白馬 。

of Gongsun Long but also the more extensive logical investigations of the *Mojing*.

Secondly, we must lean to apply the methods of modern logic to the history of Chinese logic. Admittedly, the logic of ancient China is expressed entirely in ordinary language, without the use of any formal symbols, and so there are closer parallels with the traditional logic of the West. But when it comes to an understanding of logic, it is undeniable that modern logic is much purer, more stringent and accurate as a tool for formalising theories of reason and argument. Unfortunately, many contemporary scholars of the history of logic in China are unfamiliar with these tools. Some even deny that there was an ancient Chinese logic, if logic is understood in the modern sense. I think it is very important for us to learn how to use these tools properly in the analysis of ancient texts and hope that in the future more scholars, especially the young ones, will do so. Fortunately, some scholars have already made some progress using advanced methods of modern logic in the analysis of reasoning in the *Mojing*, especially concerning *móu*.[21] Some Chinese historians have also made use of propositional logical forms in their analyses. In my last monograph *History of Chinese Logic*, I used not only propositional logic but also predicate logic in my analyses of the *Baimalun*, *móu* inference in the *Mojing* and the account of *máodùn*[22] in *Hanfeizi*. This was the first time that predicate logic had been used in a monograph-length study. My purpose was, in the Chinese idiom, "to throw a brick to lead to jade",[23] namely to promote and initiate more historians of logic, especially young scholars, to use modern logical methods to analyse and demonstrate scientific thinking in the ancient Chinese texts. Despite this progress, there is still a lack of innovation in the field and I look forward to much more work of this kind in the future.

5. Which other areas of study could benefit from a better understanding of Chinese logic, or vice versa?

Firstly, the ancient texts that contain so much evidence of logical thought are also studied as part of the history of Chinese philosophy, which is a much richer and more mature field that the history of logic. Within philosophy there is considerable discussion of logic-related topics, for example, *zhèngmíng*, in such thinkers as Confucius, Gongsun Long and Xun Zi, the logical theories of the Mohists and the account of contradiction in *Hanfeizi*. Although different philosophers have different or even opposite evaluations of the merits of these ideas, their discussions are essential

---

[21] *móu* 侔 (parallelizing), one of the *pìmóuyuántuī*, "comparing propositions and letting all proceed"《墨子・小取》: 比辭而俱行也.
[22] *máodùn* 矛盾 (contradiction), literally "spear" and "shield", with the meaning of contradiction deriving from a story in *Hanfeizi*.
[23] pāozhuānyǐnyù 抛砖引玉

sources for scholars of the history of Chinese logic, who should first read and absorb the relevant philosophical studies both to properly orient their own research and to learn valuable lessons about how to interpret these difficult texts. Of course, in doing this, we must not blindly restate their arguments and conclusion. Instead, we should regard them simply as an important reference when, from the vantage point of modern logic, we produce our own scientific assessment of ancient Chinese logical thought.

When studying the ancient thought about *míngbiàn*, I first looked through over 100 history books. From them, I learned how Chinese scholars used the terms *"míngxué"*, *"biànxué"* and *"míngbiànxué"* and the relation between them. To reveal the common system of scientific thinking, I then proposed to categorise *zhèngmíng* as *míngxué*, the study of inference and argument as *biànxué* and the combination as *míngbiànxué*. Although my *On Names and Argumentation* contains only preliminary results and has many inadequacies, it was the subject of book reviews in both American and Taiwanese journals, and has gained some acceptance from scholars in China and Taiwan. It was also awarded first prize in the Outstanding Achievement Award of the Chinese Academy of Social Sciences for retired personnel. This personal example shows that research into the history of ancient Chinese thought and philosophy play an active role in promoting the study of the history of Chinese logic.

Conversely, research on the history of logic has an impact on our comprehension of ancient philosophy and the history of ideas. Misunderstandings of arguments in the ancient texts are common, and the role of inference and proof is underestimated. The more sober and scientifically oriented approach of historians of logic can and should play a more significant role in future studies of Chinese philosophy. For example, although some scholars, including Feng Youlan, correctly recognised *báimǎfēimǎ* as an instance of "generality and particularity"[24], they did not manage to uncover the more profound level of logical thinking contained in the text, such as the role of extension and intension in distinguishing *báimǎ* from *mǎ* and the proper understanding of *fēi*.

That my analyses and proofs have already had a positive impact on the study of the history of ideas and the history of logic was most clearly illustrated when in a meeting about the writing of the *Chinese Encyclopedia of Philosophy* volume on Chinese philosophy, the editor Zhang Dainian declared "Comrade Zhou Yunzhi will be in charge of logical thought and philosophy in *Gongsunlongzi*." This shows that my ideas about Gongsun Long's thinking in general, and the *Baimalun* in particular, have already been accepted by experts in the history of Chinese philosophy. One ancient China specialist told me that he would consequently change the standard misconception of *báimǎfēimǎ* as sophistry.

Moreover, much of the discussion of logical thinking in earlier books on the Mohist, Confucian and legalist philosophers is either incomprehensible or superficial. These books contain much prejudice and misunder-

---

[24] A term from Marxist dialetic logic: *yībān yǔ gèbié* 一般与个别

standing which must eventually be removed.

It is worth mentioning that some historians of science have been considering whether the history of logic should be included in their subject, since logic is quite clearly a tool for science. At the Chinese Academy of Sciences, the Laboratory for Mathematical Logic was originally located in the Mathematical Institute, then moved to the Computer Science Institute and is now based in the Computer Software Institute. In the late 1980s, two prominent historians of science came to talk to me. They hoped that we three would jointly organise a seminar on the *Mojing*. I supported this idea and we held three seminars at the University of Science and Technology of China in Anhui, and set up the *Mojing* Research Council. At each seminar, I was invited to introduce the historians of science to the wealth of logical thinking can be found in the *Mojing*. So we can see that research in the history of Chinese logic has already begun to attract the attention and be considered seriously by historians of science.

Related publications

(co-edited with Liu Peiyu) *Xiānqín luójishǐ* 《先秦逻辑史》(The Pre-Qin History of Logic), Beijng: Zhongguo Shehuikexue Chubanshe, 1984.

(co-edited with Li Kuangwu and Zhou Wenying) *Zhōngguó Luójishǐ* 《中国逻辑史》(The History of Chinese Logic), five volumes. Lanzhou: Gansu Renmin Chabanshe, 1989.

Xiānqín Míngbiàn Luóji Zhyào 《先秦名辩逻辑指要》(Companion to Pre-Qin Ming-Bian Logic), Chengdu: Sichuan Jiaoyu Chubanshe, 1993.

Mòjīng Jiàozhù.Jīnshì.Yánjiū—Mòjīng Luójíxué 《墨经校注.今释.研究—墨经逻辑学》(Notes, Translation and Study on Mohist Cannons: Logic of Mohist Cannons), Lanzhou: Gansu Renmin Chubanshe 1993.

Gōngsūnlóngzǐ Zhèngmíngxuéshuō Yánjiū-Jiàoquán.Jīnyì.Pōuxī.Zǒnglùn 《公孙龙子正名学说研究—校诠.今译.剖析.总论》(A Study of Gongsunlunzi's Theory of the Rectification of Names - Correction, Translation, Analysis and Evaluation), Beijing: Zhongguo Shehui Kexue Chubanshe, 1994.

Míngbiànxuélùn 《名辩学论》(On Names and Argumentation), Shenyang: Liaoning Jiaoyu Chubanshe, 1996.

Zhōu yúnzhī Wénjí 《周云之文集》(Zhou Yunzhi Collection), Beijing: Huaxia Hanlin Chubanshe, 2005.

Chapter 13

Chris Fraser 方克濤

The University of Hong Kong

1. Why did you begin working on the history of logic in China?

My initial interest wasn't in logic, but in philosophy of language, philosophy of mind, and epistemology. Since I had studied Classical Chinese as an undergraduate, I naturally got interested in understanding what traditional Chinese thinkers had said about language, mind, and knowledge. It turns out that in early Chinese texts, these subjects are consistently treated hand-in-hand with what contemporary academics might classify as logic, but what ancient Chinese thinkers called *biàn* 辯 (distinction-drawing). The reason the four fields intertwine is that, as these ancient writers saw things, the proper use of language—or, more specifically, *míng* 名 (name)— is explained by norms for drawing distinctions; the *xīn* 心 (heart/mind), for them, is the organ that draws distinctions; and knowledge depends on getting distinctions right. What we would call "judgment", they conceive of as the attitude of distinguishing something as similar to or different from things of some kind, and predication is an act of distinguishing something as being some kind of thing.

Logic is not equivalent to *biàn*, but the two overlap, as logical norms or laws are part of the grounds for *biàn*, which also includes semantic theory and rhetoric. Ancient Chinese *biànzhě* (distinction-drawers), did not really investigate logic in the specific sense of valid inference patterns. They did not develop formal logic and probably did not have a clear conception of logical consequence. Their conception of what *bì* 必 (necessarily) follows from something else encompasses logical consequence, but it also refers to semantic entailment, causal regularity, and even ethical norms. Mainly they were interested in analogical reasoning and informal persuasive rhetoric. The one recorded step they took toward investigating inferences based on formal structure is the Mohists' discussion in the *Xiaoqu* of *móu* 侔, a type of inference based on syntactic parallelism between phrases, not inferential relations between sentences or propositions. The Mohists concluded that inferences based on such parallelism are often unreliable.

I have always been fascinated by the distinctive conception of mind, action, and knowledge expressed in early Chinese texts, which I find both deeply insightful and very different from familiar western conceptions. This interest led me to study Mohism, both early and late, along with the logical-semantic parts of *Xunzi*, *Lüshichunqiu*, and other texts. Another of my chief interests has been Daoist ethics, and, as a graduate student, following the example of A. C. Graham and Chad Hansen,[1] I concluded that deep familiarity with Mohism was essential to understanding Daoism, especially the *Zhuangzi*.

2. What is the best way to define your area in terms of historical period, textual sources, methodology or other factors?

The work I've published so far is mainly on classical Chinese philosophy, the thought of the Warring States era, although I also draw quite a bit on Han dynasty material. My sources range across the corpus of early Chinese texts. It is important not only to examine sources that obviously deal with language, epistemology, and logic, such as the *Mohist Canons*, but to see how our interpretations cohere with the conceptual framework, background assumptions, and rhetorical practices of a range of texts, including even historical texts such as the *Zuozhuan* and mathematical texts such as the *Zhoubisuanjing*.

My methodological approach is two-pronged, as I am interested in two fundamental sorts of questions. One set of questions revolves around an attempt to understand what ancient texts are doing in their own terms. Here the methodological focus is on pursuing a coherent, reasonably comprehensive reconstruction of the background assumptions, conceptual framework, issues, and proposed solutions that drive early Chinese philosophical discourse. My focus is as much on the discourse as a whole as it is on the views expressed in particular texts within the discourse. For this interpretive work to succeed, it is crucial to try to avoid importing assumptions, concepts, or philosophical concerns alien to those of early

---

[1] A. C. Graham (Gé Ruìhàn 格瑞汉), 1919-1991, British sinologist and author of the seminal translation into English and analysis of the *Mojing*: *Later Mohist Logic Ethics and Science*, Chinese University Press, Hong Kong, 1978. Chad Hansen (Chén Hànshēng 陳漢生), 1942-, American philosopher and long-term resident of Hong Kong, well-known for his application of the techniques of analytic philosophy to the study of Chinese philosophy and logic, professor at the University of Hong Kong.

Chinese thinkers themselves. The other set of questions concerns the significance of ancient Chinese theories of language, mind, knowledge, and action for contemporary philosophy. Here we are free to decontextualise or recontextualise ideas and theories from Chinese discourse in the course of our own philosophical explorations.

3. What is your favourite example of logical acumen by an early Chinese thinker?

I have several favourites. One of them is Mohist canon B73, concerning whether the notion of the "limitless"—that is, infinity—makes all-inclusive moral care logically impossible. The text of the canon reads: "The limitless doesn't interfere with all-inclusiveness. Explained by: Filling or not."[2] The "explanation" to the canon poses the following objection to the Mohist ethical ideal of all-inclusive care for others:

《墨子·經說下》：南者有窮，則可盡。無窮則不可盡。有窮無窮未可智，則可盡不可盡(不可盡)未可智。人之盈之否未可智，(而必)人之可盡不可盡亦未可智，而必人之可盡愛也，誖。(B73)

> If the south has a limit, then it can be exhausted [that is, its end can be reached]. If it is limitless, then it cannot be exhausted. Whether it has a limit or not cannot yet be known, so whether it can be exhausted or not cannot yet be known. Whether or not people fill it not yet being known, [and so] whether or not people can be exhausted also not yet being known, it is perverse to insist that one can care about all people.

The point of the objection seems to be this. We don't know whether the mass of humanity is infinite or not, since we don't know whether the south —the direction of the top of an ancient Chinese map—has a limit, and we don't know whether the mass of humanity fills it, and is thus finite or infinite. So it is unacceptable to insist on the ethical standard that we must care all-inclusively about all of humanity, since humanity could turn out to be infinitely vast.

The Mohists reply as follows:

《墨子·經說下》：人若不盈先窮，則人有窮也，盡有窮無難。盈無窮，則無窮盡也，盡有窮無難。

> If people do not fill the limitless, then people have a limit. Exhausting what has a limit presents no difficulty. If people do fill the limitless, then the limitless can be exhausted. [So] exhausting the limitless presents no difficulty.[3]

The argument is that even if the world is limitless in size, inclusive care is possible, as shown by a dilemma: Either humanity fills the limitless or it doesn't. If it doesn't, then the mass of humanity is limited, and it can be "exhausted"—that is, its end can in principle be reached. If it does, then the

---

[2] 《墨子·經下》：無窮不害兼，說在盈否。(B73)
[3] This passage is also discussed by Thierry Lucas on 184

limitless can be "exhausted", and obviously so can the mass of humanity inside it. Either way, there is no logical problem involved in holding that one should care inclusively for all of humanity.

This one is a favourite for me because of the intriguing way the objection wields the concept of the limitless to pose a conceptual obstacle for the Mohist ethical ideal and then the crispness with which the writers deploy their understanding of the limitless and "exhausting" to dispose of the problem.

Other favourites include canons B71, B77, and B79, all of which employ arguments from pragmatic contradiction to refute anti-language or anti-learning positions associated with texts such as the *Daodejing*. For instance, canon B71 claims that "to treat all statements as perverse is perverse."[4] Here *bèi* 誖 (perverse) refers to what is "inadmissible",[5] because it violates logical, semantic, or other norms or is inconsistent or contradictory given the premises accepted in some rhetorical context. The Mohists are concerned to refute the claim that all explicit statements or teachings are inadmissible and the *dào* (way) is thus ineffable. The gist of their reasoning is this: "If this person's statement [that is, the person asserting 'all statements are perverse'] is admissible, then this is there being some statement that's admissible."[6] In other words, they notice that the statement "all statements are perverse" is self-referential, and thus deeming this statement itself admissible, or "non-perverse," commits the speaker to a pragmatic self-contradiction: if this statement is admissible, then it's not the case that all statements are inadmissible or perverse.

If we had space for an extensive sampling of amusing and intriguing bits of logical acumen, I'd recount numerous anecdotes from the *Lüshichunqiu*, *Shuoyuan*, *Zhuangzi* and *Gongsunlongzi*.

4. In your opinion what is the most difficult or problematic aspect of studying logical thought in China?

In the field of early Chinese thought, the most prominent difficulties are the extremely limited corpus of primary sources, the brevity and obscurity of these texts, and the severe textual problems they raise. Our most valuable set of sources is probably the *Dialetical Chapters of the Mozi*. These present a tremendous hermeneutical challenge, as they read like a series of compact notes for ancient readers either already familiar with their content or in a position to consult others familiar with it. Moreover, the texts are a philological minefield, full of lacunae, miscopied words, transpositions, and unknown, archaic graphs. Many parts can be interpreted only with a significant amount of educated conjecture. Some are so

---

[4] 《墨子·經下》：以言為盡誖，誖 。(B71)
Elsewhere in this volume *bèi* 誖 has been interpreted more narrowly as "self-contradictory". See, for example, Sun Zhongyuan page 48.

[5] *bùkě* 不可 (inadmissible), opposite of *kě* 可 (admissible).

[6] 《墨子·經說下》：(出)*{之} 人之言可，(是不誖)，則是有可也 。(B71)

corrupt or obscure as to be unintelligible. An unfortunate consequence of the sorry state of the texts is that some of the interpretive work published on them amounts more to an exercise in creative imagination than to disciplined scholarship.

Other important early sources, such as the rest of the *Mozi*, the *Xunzi*, and the *Lüshichunqiu*, are in much better shape textually, but still these provide only a limited amount of material to work with. And of course most of the texts that Han bibliographers attributed to the School of Names, which might have constituted an important part of early Chinese logical-semantic inquiry, vanished long ago.

Given the limited scope of the sources we have to work with, many of our interpretive conclusions about early Chinese philosophy of language and logic will always remain somewhat tentative.

Another problematic aspect of the study of language and logic in traditional Chinese thought is a widespread methodological tendency to read the texts on the assumption that the views expressed or concepts employed will inevitably converge with those of other traditions, principally Greek thought. As an example of how this sort of assumption leads interpreters astray, consider B66 of the *Mohist Canons*, which treats the issue of picking out features that genuinely distinguish one kind of thing from another. Although oxen and horses are different kinds of animals, the "explanation" to the canon points out, we can't distinguish them on the basis of oxen having molars and horses having tails, since the two kinds share these features. We need to find characteristics that one kind has and the other lacks. I've read discussions in the literature suggesting that here the Mohists must be alluding to a notion of "essence" similar to Plato's εἶδος or Aristotle's οὐσία, something shared by all objects of a kind that makes them the objects they are. But to the contrary, what's particularly interesting about the passage is precisely that it does *not* introduce any concept with a theoretical role comparable to "essence". The Mohists are simply looking for features that in practice allow us to reliably draw a distinction between the two kinds.

5. Which other areas of study could benefit from a better understanding of Chinese logic, or vice versa?

In my view, the concepts and procedures of *biàn* either influenced or intertwine with many areas of early Chinese thought, including epistemology, psychology, action theory, ethics, political philosophy, mathematics, and natural science. So a better understanding of the purpose and conceptual structure of *biàn* is likely to improve our understanding of all these areas. To give just a quick hint of the many interconnections between these fields, what classical writers say about *biàn* tells us not only how they understood the process of supporting a claim in a public persuasion or debate, but also how they understood cognition, reasoning, judgment, and knowledge. These points in turn help us to see how they understood the structure of action, which provides clues as well to their understanding of moral psychology and moral development and even to the structure of their ethical theories. Of course, I am biased—just a bit!—by my own philosophical interests. But I believe the various dimensions of what early texts call *"biàn"* form part of the conceptual core of classical Chinese philosophical discourse. Moreover, looking beyond the history of Chinese thought, the approach to language, reasoning, knowledge, and action that we find in Chinese texts may benefit our philosophical understanding of these topics today.

Related publications

The School of Names, *Stanford Encyclopedia of Philosophy*, 2005, revised 2009.

Mohist Canons, *Stanford Encyclopedia of Philosophy*, 2005, revised 2013.

Truth in Mohist Dialectics, *Journal of Chinese Philosophy* 39(3) : 351–368, 2012.

Distinctions, Judgment, and Reasoning in Classical Chinese Thought, *History and Philosophy of Logic* 34(1) : 1–24, 2013.

Language and Logic in the Xunzi, Forthcoming in Eric Hutton, ed., *the Dao Companion to Xunzi*, Dordrecht: Springer.

Chapter 14

Yiu-Ming Fung 馮耀明

Hong Kong University of Science and Technology

1. Why did you begin working on the history of logic in China?

My interest in working on logical thinking in ancient China began in the 1980s, the period of my PhD study. The topic of my thesis was the philosophy of language and logic in ancient China, which includes ideas from the *Mobian, Gongsunlongzi, Zhuangzi* and *Xunzi*.

At that time, very few scholars in the field of Chinese studies were interested in applying the methods of analytic philosophy. Thinking that this was a bit of a shame, I decided to focus on analysing philosophical problems about language and logic in ancient Chinese texts.

After my PhD work, my interest in the topic never faded. Even when I branched out into other areas such as Confucianism, Buddhism and comparative philosophy, I kept working on several projects on the Later Mohists, the School of Names and Buddhist logic, producing various articles in both Chinese and English. My main achievement is my book *Gongsun Longzi* (in Chinese), published in 2000, and my current research in this area is represented by an English book provisionally titled "Language and Logic in Early China", which will be submitted to review for publication very soon.

2. What is the best way to define your area in terms of historical period, textual sources, methodology or other factors?

The period of the Warring States was a golden time for philosophical thinking in the analytic spirit. Philosophical reflection on language and reality was one of the major concerns of Zhuang Zi, Xun Zi, Gongsun Long and the Later Mohists. The Later Mohists explicitly constructed a theory of logical reasoning and Gongsun Long used logic implicitly. Unfortunately, this analytic stream ran dry and was lost to the later tradition of Chinese philosophy.

Some scholars, including Marcel Granet, Joseph Needham and A. C. Graham consider the Chinese way of thinking to be essentially different from the western way, and take concepts and theories expressed in Chinese to be incommensurable with those expressed in western languages. They label the ancient Chinese way of thinking as "correlative" in contrast to the western "analytic" approach, and take the non-abstract and non-analytic character of Chinese thought to suggest that the main function of Chinese language is figurative or poetic. According to them, ancient Chinese thinkers could not even express the idea of causality, and lack the logical capacity to represent a rule of non-contradiction.

But this non-logical, illogical or trans-logical description of the ancient Chinese is not endorsed by all western scholars. Janusz Chmielewski, one of the few western pioneers of the study of Chinese logic has a quite different opinion:

> Such characteristic features of early Chinese as monosyllabism of lexical units, lack of inflections and lack of clearly delimited grammatical word-classes (especially the lack of a clear morphological distinction between nominal and verbal forms) could hardly have any negative bearing on Chinese implicit logic; in fact they are beneficial rather than detrimental to this logic, since they make the Chinese language more similar to the symbolic language of modern logic than any tongue of the Indo-European type can claim to be.[1]

I completely agree with Chmielewski on this matter.

Perhaps more fundamentally, the thesis of incommensurability cannot be sustained in any case because it is self-refuting. It seems to me that those who assert there is an essential difference between analytic and correlative thinking have never given any evidence for their view. But according to Donald Davidson's principle of charity, if there is any difference between "western analytic thinking" and "Chinese correlative thinking", we cannot explain the difference without having some common ground from which to compare them, and this defeats the claim that they are incommensurable. I have argued for this in more detail before and will not repeat the details here.

Thinking in terms of correlation or association is not thereby non-analytic; it is still within "rational space". To think "analytically" does not mean that one is always concerned to base one's claims on empirical evidence or to provide causal explanations; it means only to think in rational space and so to be bound by logic. Thinking in this way makes it impossible to assert a contradiction (although, as mentioned by Davidson, based on

---

[1] Janusz Chmielewski, Notes on Early Chinese Logic, Rocznik Orientaistyczny (Warsaw), part IV, vol: 26, no: 2 (1965), 103.

the idea of compartmentalisation of the mind, one could simultaneously make two assertions which are mutually contradictory).

Even in the case of metaphor, say, when we use some speech act to go beyond an assertion of literal meaning, we do not necessarily go outside rational space. And the same holds for correlation and association. In Chinese thinking, although the pair of *yīn* 陰 and *yáng* 陽 and the *wǔxíng*,[2] may not be fully grounded in the empirical evidence from the physical world, they should not be understood as illogical (or irrational) or non-logical (or non-rational). Thinking from a non-factual or non-physical perspective, such as a moral or aesthetic, metaphysical or religious perspective, or thinking in a way that is not fully based on factual evidence need not be seen as thinking in a way that is fundamentally non-analytic or somehow beyond rational space.

In my view, there is no significant gap between the ancient Chinese language and western languages, or between the Chinese way of thinking and the western way of thinking. We can use western mathematical logic to elaborate the reasoning of the *Baimalun*[3] and in the discussion of the validity of parallel arguments in the *Xiaoqu*.[4] Although the Later Mohists express their theory in the material mode of speech, their ideas can be understood in terms of western logic; and although they appeal to semantic sensibility instead of syntactic structure, we can still feel the analytic force of their discussion.

So the fact that these ancient Chinese arguments are delivered in a way that is different from what we find in western philosophy does not mean that they cannot be understood or explained in terms of western logic. And when we do this we can show that their thinking is analytic, and that "Chinese thinking", in this respect, is not essentially different from western thinking. To the extent that they differ, it is that western thinkers tend to express their analytic thoughts in a formal or syntactic way whereas the Later Mohists opt for a material or pragmatic way.

3. What is your favourite example of logical acumen by an early Chinese thinker?

Logical thought in ancient China can be divided into two kinds: an explicit theory of logic and the implicit use of logic in practice. The only clear example of an explicit theory is that of the Later Mohists; the most sophisticated use in practice is the *Baimalun* of *Gongsunlongzi*. These can both be taken as partial evidence to refute the thesis that thinking in ancient

---

[2] *wǔxíng* 五行 (five phases), basic aspects of change, also known as the five elements: *mù* 木 (wood), *huǒ* 火 (fire), *tǔ* 土 (earth), *jīn* 金 (metal) and *shuǐ* 水 (water).
[3] *Báimǎlùn* 《白馬論》 (White Horse Discourse), essay by Gongsun Long containing arguments for and against the claim *báimǎfēimǎ* 白馬非馬 (white horse not horse).
[4] *Xiǎoqǔ* 《小取》 Hsiao-ch'ü (Small Pick), chapter 45 of the *Mobian*, containing a general discussion of logical themes and many examples of reasoning patterns, also translated as "Minor Illustrations".

China is non-analytic and essentially different from analytical thinking in the western tradition.

My first example of ancient Chinese logical acumen is the view of reference, that is to say the relationship between *míng* 名 (name) and *shí* 實 (object), to be found in the *Gongsunlongzi*, especially in the *Baimalun*. This topic, which in Chinese is known as *zhèngmíng* 正名 (correcting names) is a vexed one, with no consensus in the field about the supposed logical function of the *míng*, the kind of *shí* involved, and the nature of the relationship between them. As far as I know, the many accounts proposed in the literature are variants of one of the following four:

A. Hu Shi's "description-theoretical interpretation", which seems to be an application of Bertrand Russell's theory of definite descriptions or, more accurately, it is an interpretation that is unconsciously based on Russell's theory.

B. Feng Youlan's "realistic interpretation", an application of the Platonic *idea* to the text in a quite consistent way.

C. Janusz Chmielewski's "set-theoretical interpretation", which assigns Gongsun Long the status of a logician and uses a peculiar notion of "set".

D. Chad Hansen's "nominalistic interpretation", which is based on a bold hypothesis about mass nouns and is considered by him to be a replacement of the above three as well as other kinds of "abstract interpretation".

My own opinion is that none of these four interpretations are acceptable, neither in addressing the textual evidence nor in terms of theoretical adequacy. None of them is sustainable, each having unsolvable difficulties in answering questions that arise either inside or outside the *Baimalun*. By contrast, my approach is to use first-order predicate logic to analyse the logical structures of both Gongsun Long and his opponent's arguments, and then borrow the direct theory of reference (from Saul Kripke and others). In this way, I can provide not only a comprehensive and coherent interpretation of the text, but also a solid base for the interpretation and explanation of the remaining chapters of *Gongsunlongzi*, a target that cannot be reached by the old interpretations.

My second example of logical acumen is the logical parrellism in the *Xiaoqu* chapter of the *Dialetical Chapters of the Mozi*, the simplest examples of which are the following:

《墨子·小取》：白馬，馬也；乘白馬，乘馬也 。驪馬，馬也；乘驪馬，乘馬也 。(NO 14)

> White horse is horse; riding white horse is riding horse. Black horse is horse; riding black horse is riding horse.

A. C. Graham was right to say that this is about deduction. Unfortunately, he lacks a consistent explanation of how the Later Mohists identified which deductions are valid and which are not. Instead, he thinks that the tendency to use parallelism is characteristic of correlative thinking.[5] By contrast, Chad Hansen thinks that these parallel sentences "are not plausibly treated as deductive forms since the Mohist is at pains to show that they can 'go wrong'."[6] Some further examples from the text:

《墨子·小取》：車，木也；乘車，非乘木也 。船，木也；(人)*{入}船，非(人)*{入}木也 。盜人，人也，多盜，非多人也，無盜非無人也 。(NO 15)

> Boat is wood; entering boat is not entering wood. Thief is person; many thieves is not many people; no thieves is not no people.

He regards the analysis before these examples, which concludes "So they cannot be left unexamined; they cannot always be used."[7] as a warning, claiming that the point of the Mohist analysis is not to prove that these techniques and forms of inference are correct, but to show their limits - to deny their universal validity.[8] Based on this destructive or deconstructive view and his mass-like interpretation of the terms in the parallel sentences, Hansen concludes,

> I read the tone of Hsiao Ch'u [Xiaoqu] as being defeatist. In spirit, the Mohists seem to have joined hands with Chuang-tzu [Zhuang Zi]. Language is capricious, arbitrary, and merely conventional.[9]

In general, I greatly appreciate Hansen's analytic and pragmatic approach, which can help us dig deep into the important problems of ancient Chinese philosophy. Nevertheless, I disagree with him on some textual matters and think that his peculiar, if not extreme, interpretation fails to support some of his other conclusions about Chinese language and thinking.

My view is that these parallel inferences can be given a logical analysis and justification. On the methodological level, Chinese thinkers, including the Later Mohists, lack a syntactic sensibility and are not interested in using what Rudolf Carnap called the "formal mode of speech". Instead, they tend to use the "material mode of speech", which employs and reinforces their semantic and pragmatic sensibilities.[10] This lack of formality, however, does not prevent their thinking from being analytical and logical.[11]

The third example of logical acumen is the consideration of "paradoxes" by the dialectician,[12] principally the lìwùshíshì and the biànzhě èrshíyīshì, which are listed in the Tianxia chapter of Zhuangzi. Here are a few examples of the latter:

---

[5] A. C. Graham, *Yinyang and the Nature of Correlative Thinking*, Singapore: The Institute of East Asian Philosophies, 1986, p.25.
[6] Chad Hansen, *Language and Logic in Ancient China*, Ann Arbor: University of Michigan Press, 1983, p.127.
[7] 《墨子·小取》：則不可不審也，不可常用也 。(NO 12)
[8] Ibid, p.129.
[9] Ibid, p.139.
[10] This is a distinction that assumed great importance to Carnap, particularly in his *Logical Syntax of Language* (1934).
[11] The parallel sentences discussed here are also considered by Yang Wujin, p. 69.
[12] biànzhě 辯者 (dialectician), those skilled in biàn 辯 (disputation), who were poorly regarded in the Chinese tradition because of a reputation for sophistry as represented by the biànzhě èrshíyīshì.

《庄子·天下》：飛鳥之景未嘗動也，鏃矢之疾而有不行不止之時，狗非犬，...一尺之捶，日取其半，萬世不竭。

> The shadow of a flying bird never moves. Swift the arrowhead, but at times it neither moves nor stops. A dog is not a hound. ...From a foot long stick take half every day and it will not be gone in ten thousand eons.

From the late Warring States period on, almost all traditional Chinese scholars objected to this sort of thing and to the dialectician, whose cognitive and logical approach they did not appreciate, accusing them of merely spreading confusion. In modern times, they have had a better reception from scholars who find their ideas philosophically interesting and somewhat similar to their western sophist counterparts. One view among sinologists and western scholars of Chinese philosophy, such as Needham, Graham and Hansen, is that many of these statements are paradoxes. The Chinese scholar Feng Youlan regards some of them as paradoxes and some of them, which he attributes to Gongsun Long as not. Chad Hansen and Christoph Harbsmeier go further and identify some of the self-referring sentences in the *Dialetical Chapters of the Mozi* also as semantic paradoxes.

Almost all these so-called "paradoxes" have the appearance of ridiculous, absurd, puzzling, surprising or counter-intuitive expressions. But, in what sense can they be called "paradoxes"? It seems to me that this question has not yet been addressed by the scholars mentioned above. W. V. O. Quine divides paradoxes into three kinds: (1) veridical or truth-telling paradoxes, (2) falsidical paradoxes, and (3) antinomies. He identifies the barber's paradox, some of the Zeno's paradoxes and the liar paradox as the respective examples of each of these three kinds.[13] If we look carefully at the text of the *biànzhě èrshíyīshì*, it is clear that they are not antinomies. So perhaps we can say that they are either veridical or falsidical paradoxes, if they are not understood as just surprising or puzzling statements.

4. In your opinion what is the most difficult or problematic aspect of studying logical thought in China?

The most difficult aspect of studying logical thinking in ancient China is related to the figurative use of classical Chinese in the *Zhuangzi*. Although it is obvious that Zhuang Zi did express his views in the text and argued for them, his reasons can be interpreted in different, even conflicting, ways, mainly because his use of language is figurative rather than descriptive. His butterfly dream, for example, has been interpreted very differently by different scholars. The elaboration of this kind of implicit reasoning is far from easy.

---

[13] W. V. O. Quine, *The Ways of Paradox and Other Essays*, New York: Random House, Inc., 1966, p.5.

The dialecticians' 21 theses which are regarded by some as "paradoxes", are also a source of great difficulty because all that remains of them are single statements, without any argument. In other words, what we have is the conclusion only; there are no premises found in the text. And, to make matters worse, the sentences used to express these theses use various ambiguous terms, ensuring that their meaning cannot be ascertained without doubt.

5. Which other areas of study could benefit from a better understanding of Chinese logic, or vice versa?

The areas of study with the closest connection to Chinese logic are the philosophy of language and the grammatical study of classical Chinese. I think each side can contribute to a better understanding of the other. For example, some scholars, including Chad Hansen, maintain that ancient Chinese philosophers lack the concepts of proposition, sentential belief and the one-many relation, and think instead in terms of non-sentential phrases, term beliefs and the mereological part-whole relation. Based on the fact that classical Chinese language is mass-like and non-inflected, some say that ancient Chinese thinkers cannot express their thoughts in a causal and logical way and that their mode of thinking is correlative rather than analytic.

I do not agree, preferring a constructive view of the linguistic data for classical Chinese, which include the logical and semantic characteristics of mass terms, causative terms, *jiānyǔ* 兼語 (a term used in an expression both as an object of a main sentence and a subject of a clause), classifiers and measure words, class words, assertive terms such as *rán* 然, *shì* 是 and *xìn* 信, sentence forms with *yǐwéi* 以為, parallel sentence forms, and different modes of compound terms. Without going into details, my view is that there is a functional equivalent to the propositional form of belief sentences and truth-based sentences in the western languages, a way of expressing the one-many relation, and so on. All these can be used to defeat the thesis of incommensurability.

For example, that-clause sentences can sometimes be expressed using a *jiānyǔ jù* 兼語句 (pivotal sentence) construction involving the pronoun *zhī* 之 (it) which can be used both as an object of the first verb and a subject of the second:[14]

<blockquote>
吾　　必　　謂　　之　　學　　矣
Wú　　bì　　wèi　　zhī　　xué　　yǐ
I　　must　　call　　[pivot]　　learn　　[final]
I must say of [it] is learning
I'd surely say that is (a case of) learning.
</blockquote>

---

[14]*Lunyu Xue'er*《論語·學而》

There is a similar construction in Old English and Middle English. Likewise, some compound sentences with anaphoric reference can be recognised as functionally equivalent to a that-clause in English:[15]

吾	聞	之	也	君子	不以其所以養人者害人。
Wú	wén	zhī	yě	Jūnzǐ	bù yǐ qí suǒyǐ yǎng rén zhě hài rén.
I	hear	it	,	gentleman	not injure people with what he nourishes people.

I hear that a gentleman does not injure (his) people with the very thing he uses to nourish them.

Related publications

Gōngsūnlóngzǐ《公孫龍子》(Gongsun Longzi: A Perspective of Analytic Philosophy), Taipei: Dongda Tushu Gongsi, 2000.

A Logical Perspective on "Discourse on White-Horse", *Journal of Chinese Philosophy* 34 (4): 515–536, 2007.

(with Chad Hansen, Bo Mou and Chung-Ying Cheng) Gongsun Long and Contemporary Philosophy, *Journal of Chinese Philosophy* 34 (4): 473-560, 2007.

School of Names. In Bo Mou ed., *Routledge History of Chinese Philosophy*, Routledge, 2008.

A Logical Perspective on the Parallelism in Later Moism, *Journal of Chinese Philosophy* 39 (3): 333-350, 2012.

---

[15] *Mengzi Lianghuiwangxia*《孟子·梁惠王下》

Chapter 15
Chad Hansen 陳漢生

The University of Hong Kong

1. Why did you begin working on the history of logic in China?

I was convinced that understanding classical views about fundamental things would be importantly helpful in understanding other aspects of their philosophy as well as help us identify and analyse philosophical thought within its context. It also seemed the key to being able to philosophise along with classical thinkers and probably the place where my combinations of interest and aptitude allowed me to make the greatest contribution both to philosophy and the western understanding of Chinese culture.

2. What is the best way to define your area in terms of historical period, textual sources, methodology or other factors?

My main historical period is the classical period with strong connected interest in the period of Buddhist importation and the Confucian Renaissance. My main textual resources are the philosophically most dense texts: the *Mozi* and *Mobian*, the scattered theorists about language and names, *Zhuangzi* and *Xunzi*. My methodology is essentially radical translation combined with the principle of humanity which I consider to rest on a use theory of language with a norms-of-inference conception of meaning or conceptual content. I'm also interested is using the causal-historical theory of reference which helps me reconstruct a dominant form of use theory I find in classical China.

3. What is your favourite example of logical acumen by an early Chinese thinker?

I suppose it is the Later Mohists' "'all statements are self-contradictory' is self-contradictory."[1]

4. In your opinion what is the most difficult or problematic aspect of studying logical thought in China?

The weight of western assumptions about meaning and of Chinese Confucian-oriented tradition.

5. Which other areas of study could benefit from a better understanding of Chinese logic, or vice versa?

Pretty much all of it, but the one I find most interesting now is broadly normative and ethical theory.

Related publications

Mass Nouns and "A White Horse Is Not a Horse", *Philosophy East and West* 26 (2):189-209.

Language and Logic in Ancient China, University of Michigan Press, 1983.

A Daoist Theory of Chinese Thought: A Philosophical Interpretation, Oxford University Press, 1992.

The Relatively Happy Fish, *Asian Philosophy* 13 (2 and 3): 145–164, 2003.

Prolegomena to Future Solutions to "White-Horse Not Horse", *Journal of Chinese Philosophy* 34 (4): 473–491, 2007.

---

[1]《墨子・經下》：以言為盡誖，誖。(B71)
See also the discussion of this passage by Sun Zhongyuan, p. 48, and Chris Fraser, p. 118.

Chapter 16

Dan Robins 羅丹

The University of Hong Kong

---

1. Why did you begin working on the history of logic in China?

I wouldn't say that I work on the history of logic in China, but I do work on the Later Mohists, so I'll talk about how I got to doing that. It's a bit indirect.

When I started university, I was a bit under the spell of the idea that the languages you speak affect how you think, and I decided to study a language very different from English. I settled on Mandarin. I can't remember what other options McGill offered at the time (I briefly considered Russian), but a couple of my close friends were Chinese-Canadians, and that probably influenced my choice.

I took my second year of Mandarin the next summer at Xiamen University. The trip was led by Ken Dean, and one of the results of the trip was that I wanted to take one of his courses when I got back to Montreal. At his suggestion, I signed up for a course in which we read early Chinese texts dealing with ritual alongside Foucault's *History of Sexuality*. That was my first proper exposure to Chinese philosophy, and I ended up with a lasting love for the *Zhuangzi*. (My term paper was a crazy thing that threw the *Zhuangzi* together with punk music and the Situationist International —Greil Marcus's *Lipstick Traces* loomed large in it.)

Somewhere in there I read Chad Hansen's "A Tao of Tao in Chuang-tzu."[1] That was probably my first encounter with the idea that to under-

---

[1] In Victor H. Mair, ed., *Experimental Essays on Chuang-Tzu*, Honolulu: University of Hawaii Press, 1983, pp. 24-55.

stand the *Qiwulun*[2] you had to know the Later Mohists. That led to me devouring Hansen's *Language and Logic in Ancient China* and A. C. Graham's *Later Mohist Logic, Ethics and Science*. (In effect *Later Mohist Logic* served as my intermediate text in classical Chinese.)

Anyway, I ended up going to the University of Hong Kong to study with Chad, and the next term Chris Fraser ended up there too. Chris and I would meet regularly to read and discuss texts—mostly the *Zhuangzi* and the *Mojing*. So I maintained those interests even though neither one played much of a role in my dissertation project.

It wasn't until 2010 that I first published on the Later Mohists, but appropriately enough it was a paper called "The Later Mohists and Logic"—it was a study of the *Xiaoqu*. The idea for the paper had been simmering away for about ten years. I read the *Xiaoqu* as arguing that we can't trust linguistic parallelism to guide inference, and wondered whether it made sense to think of the argument as an argument against formal logic. Unfortunately I concluded that it doesn't especially make sense to think of the argument that way; but it's still a pretty good paper.

2. What is the best way to define your area in terms of historical period, textual sources, methodology or other factors?

I work on the philosophy of the Warring States period. Recently I've mostly worked on the *Mozi*, including the *Mojing*, though I've also done substantial work on the *Mengzi* and the *Xunzi*. I've only published one thing on the *Zhuangzi*—for the most part I don't seem to have figured out a way to write about that wonderful text. (Though the one thing I did publish was tremendous fun to write.)

As for methodology, I suppose the most general thing I can say is that I think of the texts as products of human activity, and what I want to understand is why the people who produced them did so, what they were trying to accomplish, and how they understood their own activity. Unsurprisingly I tend to be most interested in texts where the activity seems to be in some sense philosophical, though of course there are lots of things that could mean. For me anyway it implies a particular interest in texts that present explicit reasoning and texts that develop concepts and put them to work.

Some of my work focuses on very (maybe excruciatingly) close readings of particular texts. Maybe that's just my temperament. I do think there's a lot going on in these texts that you can miss if you aren't sensitive to detail and specificity.

---

[2] *Qíwùlùn*《齊物論》 (On Equalising Things), chapter of the *Zhuangzi* containing the most explicitly analytical passages.

3. What is your favourite example of logical acumen by an early Chinese thinker?

I'm going to mention three examples, I'm afraid. They're all examples of early Chinese philosophers being very precise in their attempts to construct and work with concepts.

The first is Xun Zi in *Xing 'e*. The care with which Xun Zi constructs his concept of *wěi* is really astonishing:

《荀子·性惡》：不可學，不可事，而在人者，謂之性；可學而能，可事而成之在人者，謂之偽 。

> What is in people but can neither be learned nor enacted, we call *xìng* (nature); what is in people but can be learned proficiently and enacted completely, we call *wěi* (artifice).

This is just the beginning of the analysis. I'm especially impressed by the bit where he follows things to their logical conclusion and concludes in effect that it is impossible for a human being to follow her *xìng*. Of course this means that *xìng* can't be bad, and that bad actions are as artificial as good ones—that contradicts quite a bit of what's in *Xing 'e*, but fits pretty well with relevant texts from the rest of the *Xunzi*.

Then of course there are the Later Mohists. They made a serious attempt to regiment their vocabulary and their syntax. This is actually part of what makes the *Mojing* so hard to read. They invented characters so that they could mark distinctions not marked in the ordinary Chinese of the time, and so that they could distinguish their technical terms from the everyday terms from which they derived. But later scribes couldn't have recognised these strange characters, and often tried to correct them. The first example you meet is in the sixth canon:

《墨子·經上》：恕，明也 。
《墨子·經說上》：恕也者，以其知論物而其知之也著 。若明 。(A6)

> Wisdom (?) is illumination.
> Wisdom (?): by means of one's intelligence, in discourse about the thing one's knowledge of it is apparent. Like clearness of sight.

Here the Later Mohists introduce their invented character "恕"—it's right in the canon, but "corrected" to "恕" in the explanation. What remains of their technical vocabulary is still very impressive.

My third example is also from the Later Mohists. They introduce the technical term *jiānbái* 堅白 (hard-white) for entities such as hardness and whiteness that can "fill" each other.[3] Then they apply this term in two canons on space and time. They say "space and time are not *jiānbái*"[4], because "space moves through time"[5]—which is to say that space does not fill the past or the future. But "space *is jiānbái* with the present moment."[6] (So, we can say with surprising confidence that in today's terms the Later

---

[3] 《墨子·經上》：堅白，不相外也 。(A66)
[4] 《墨子·經下》：宇久不堅白 (B14)
[5] 《墨子·經說下》：宇徙久 。(B14)
[6] 《墨子·經下》：無久與宇堅白 (B15)

Mohists were three-dimensionalists but not presentists.) And I love the precision with which they're able to state these ideas.

4. In your opinion what is the most difficult or problematic aspect of studying logical thought in China?

I guess the main tricky thing is knowing what the subject matter is supposed to be. I take it that the point of saying "logical thought" rather than "logic" is so that we can include more things; but then I'm not sure what purpose the broader category is supposed to serve or how broad it's actually supposed to be. (Does it include everything that's not flat-out irrational?) Anyway I've never thought of myself as working on something called logical thought.

I do do a fair bit of work on the Later Mohists, though, so I'll say something about that. With them of course you always run into trouble because of the state of the texts. We are very lucky that some of their difficulties can be addressed systematically—for example, with Liang Qichao's insight that each explanation comes with a head character, Luan Tiaofu's discoveries concerning the physical history of the *Mojing*, or Graham's work on the Later Mohists' use of stock examples and technical terminology.[7] But there are still many difficulties, and probably a frustrating number of things we will never be able to read with any confidence.

I suppose the most common sort of objection I have to work that's presented as being about logic in China is that it takes the idea of logic too much for granted. It's as if logic is a sort of given, so that, first, you kind of expect a philosophical tradition to give rise to the study of logic (and there's something wrong with one that doesn't), and, second, we know from western logic or Buddhist logic what sorts of ideas and concepts we can expect to find in, say, the Later Mohists. So you get really hasty identification if Later Mohist concepts with concepts drawn from other traditions as if we should just expect convergence on these things. I'll give a pair of examples, which sometimes seem ubiquitous—very often Later Mohist references to *míng* 名 (name) and *cí* 辭 (phrase) get interpreted as if the Later Mohists were talking about concepts or propositions. As far as I can tell the only reason anyone would think this is that those are supposedly the sorts of things that you expect logicians to talk about; in fact *míng* and *cí* are both certainly linguistic items. Just to draw a contast: I think A. C. Graham was wrong to conclude that *cí* for the Later Mohists were sentences, but at least he recognised that he had to supply an argument based on things the Later Mohists actually wrote, and that

---

[7]Liáng Qǐchāo 梁啟超, 1873–1929, prominent scholar and reformist who had significant philological insights into the structure of the *Mojing*, whose connection to western logic he was one of the first to recognise; one of the four principal scholars of the Tsinghua academy of *guóxué*. Luán Tiàofǔ 欒調甫, 1889–1972, scholar who debated with the Liang Qichao about his *Mojing Jiaoshi*.

it wouldn't do just to take it for granted that the concept of a sentence is self-evident or essential to logic or whatever.

One last thing that's been especially brought home to me by the History of Logical Thought in China project is how little effective communication there has been scholars working primarily in Chinese and the rest of us. A symptom of this is how little known Shen Youding's work is in western scholarship, and how little known A. C. Graham's work is within mainland China.[8]

5. Which other areas of study could benefit from a better understanding of Chinese logic, or vice versa?

The early Chinese texts that you might consider logical come to us with very little context, so anything that could add to our knowledge of their context would help. For example, we rarely know with any precision who they were responding to or who might have been responding to them, and we rarely know with what philosophical motivations and goals they were written. What got the Later Mohists interested in the relation between space and time? How are the texts in the *Qiwulun* responding to or taking up the religious and cosmogonic ideas they present? Anything that would help us with questions like these would be extremely valuable. (Maybe there's a tomb waiting to be discovered of a prince who was also a logic geek.)

There are lots of particular cases where we could benefit a great deal from knowing just a little bit more—about the precise sense of an idiom, about the significance of a metaphor or an example, or about the use or construction of a tool, for example. Anything that casts light on the language of these texts or on the culture in which they were written— including the material culture—could be helpful.

There are also plenty of early Chinese texts that aren't about logic but which do important work with terms and ideas we also find in the logical texts. Maybe some of these were influenced by the logical texts, and maybe the logical texts were making explicit assumptions shared by the authors of these other texts. And you could say the same thing about the kinds of reasoning employed in nonlogical texts, if and when they correspond to kinds of reasoning treated in the logical texts (that's assuming there are logical texts that treat kinds of reasoning, of course).

The logical texts are also important test cases for general claims about how human beings think about language and thought. Maybe you're inter-

---

[8] Shěn Yǒudǐng 沈有鼎, 1908-1989, philosopher, logician and author of *Mojing de Luojixue*, who studied at Harvard in the 1920s under Sheffer and Whitehead, in Germany under Jaspers and Heidegger, and later visited Oxford; he was professor at Tsinghua University, Peking University and a fellow of the Chinese Academy of Social Sciences. A. C. Graham (Gé Ruìhàn 格瑞汉), 1919-1991, British sinologist and author of the seminal translation into English and analysis of the *Mojing*: *Later Mohist Logic Ethics and Science*, Chinese University Press, Hong Kong, 1978.

ested in the question of whether human beings inevitably think of these things in terms of truth or representation. Then the question of whether, say, the *Xiaoqu* discusses things in those terms should be important to you.

Alternatively, maybe you think we have independent reason to suppose that human beings think about language and thought in certain ways. Then that will presumably inform how you read early Chinese logical texts. (But approaches of that sort have a pretty lousy track record, in my view.)

Related publications

The Later Mohists and Logic, *History and Philosophy of Logic* 31 (3): 247-285, 2011.

Names, Cranes, and the Later Moists, *Journal of Chinese Philosophy* 39 (3): 369-385, 2012.

Chapter 17

Hsien-Chung Lee 李賢中

National Taiwan University, Taipei

1. Why did you begin working on the history of logic in China?

Most people believe that Chinese traditional thought neither emphasises logical thinking, nor expresses thought using rigorous deduction and proof. Nonetheless, the ancient Chinese made many significant scientific discoveries, developed intricate industrial techniques, and pondered philosophically on both ethical virtues and the nature of the universe. So how were their thoughts formed? What methods of reasoning were involved? If they had such methods, what rules governed them? And were they similar to the methods of other cultures or quite unique? Questions such as these made me interested in the reasoning of the ancient Chinese and gave me the motivation to study further.

In *Mojing de Luojixue*, Shen Youding[1] observed: "The character of language conditions the patterns and forms of the way of thinking that is common to all of humanity. So the means of expression in Chinese has inevitably affected the development of logic in China, giving it certain ethnic features"[2] In other words, logic is common to all, but its method of expression has ethnic and regional differences according to language. But we can take this further. Linguistic expression arises from cognition,

---

[1] Shěn Yǒudǐng 沈有鼎, 1908-1989, philosopher, logician and author of *Mojing de Luojixue*, who studied at Harvard in the 1920s under Sheffer and Whitehead, in Germany under Jaspers and Heidegger, and later visited Oxford; he was professor at Tsinghua University, Peking University and a fellow of the Chinese Academy of Social Sciences.

[2] 《墨经的逻辑学》：语言的特性制约著人类共同具有的思惟规律和形式，在中国语言中所取得的表现方式的特质，这又不可避免地影响到逻辑学在中国的发展，使其在表达方面具有一定的民族形式。

and cognition is dependant on cognitive methods, as well as the worldview and metaphysical categories of the person concerned. So the particular way logic is expressed depends on culture: the thought, language, and cognition of the people. And in this way, exploration of the logic of the Chinese promises a glimpse into the grandness of Chinese philosophy. This was the second point of attraction for me.

Finally, people often feel that Chinese philosophy is grandiose but unstructured and difficult to grasp; I felt the same way when studying it at university. So I hoped that by exploring the reasoning methods of ancient Chinese philosophers, I could find some regularity in their thoughts, methods, and developmental contexts, so as to help me both to grasp the meaning of Chinese classics and to express Chinese philosophy in clearer terms.

And that's how I began studying the history of Chinese logic.

2. What is the best way to define your area in terms of historical period, textual sources, methodology or other factors?

The categorising of textual sources into historical stages and the referencing of western logical theoretical frameworks is how the history of Chinese logic is currently being studied. Selection of literature is basically based on occurrences of key terms such as *míng* 名 (name/concept), *cí* 辭 (phrasing/statement), *shuō* 說 (discourse/reasoning), *biàn* 辯 (debate/argumentation), and reasoning principles found in the texts. Historical materials are interpreted by the researcher to find parts relevant to logic and the temporal sequence of the texts are used to construct a "history of Chinese logic". This sort of definition of the field accords with the sequential character of "history" and has the systematic character of "research", but it lacks what is particular to Chinese logic and its context in the history of logic as a whole. Much of the Chinese literature on the history of logic appeals to various "reasoning methods" but does explain them. Simply put, the conception of "logic" being used is neither clear nor distinct.

I believe that the delineation of the subject "history of Chinese logic" can be improved by referring to a fixed systematic framework, composed of connections and reasoning relationships between different "units of thought". This is necessary if we are to elucidate both the distinctiveness of Chinese logic and the context of its historical development. What I call a "unit of thought" is not necessarily a term or phrase but rather a meaningful context for thought; it may be expressed by a whole paragraph and includes not only the text but various factors particular to the author's subjective perspective. The contextual blending between one unit of thought and another is also an important factor in the reasoning process.

Our conception of the history of Chinese logic should define the scope within which each thinker in each era or school can be seen as a part, so that their thoughts are somehow connected to those of others, and have position and value, effecting and being influenced by the whole. And to do this we must realise that Chinese logic is not a mechanic logical system and that the history of Chinese logic is an organic dialectical development, in the process of continual modification through reasoning in specific contexts by actual thinkers. It includes a changing system of non-inevitable but necessary rules: "non-inevitable" because as rules of reasoning they may not be valid, and "necessary" because they make up the world of thought of the thinkers themselves and so cannot be avoided.

A further concept that is useful here is "relative prevalence". Rules of reasoning in Chinese logic, such as the method of analogy common in pre-Qin period, may be applicable in only a contextually given range of cases. Difference in application result from differences or changes in the cognitive contexts of the people involved. The sense in which rules of reasoning are valid has to be sensitive to such issues, and so although some rules considered as part of Chinese logic may not be valid, strictly speaking, they should not be ignored if we are to understand the historical process of logical development in China.

My methodology is first to find the units of thought; second, to find relationships among them; third, to determine which of them involve reasoning and which do not; fourth, to distill rules of reasoning from those that do; and, fifth, to compare the rules extracted from textual sources of different historical periods. In the process of comparison, one should also consider how the same rule operates in different units of thought and how different rules operate in the same unit. By these means, we may discover contextual relationships in the development of Chinese logic, and in this way construct its history.

3. What is your favourite example of logical acumen by an early Chinese thinker?

Hui Shi's discussion of similarities, Yinwen's[3] categorisation of *míng* 名 (name) and discovery that "general classification follows specific form"[4] and Gongsun Long's reasoning about *báimǎfēimǎ* 白馬非馬 (white horse not horse). All these are examples of sharp logical insights by early Chinese thinkers.

Hui Shi grasped the difference between large and small categories, compared concepts with different extensions, and then named the things being compared:

---

[3] Huì Shī 惠施, 380–305 B.C.E., logician, proto-scientist and intellectual sparring partner of Zhuang Zi, whose work is mostly lost. Yǐnwén 尹文, 360-280 B.C.E., thinker whose ideas are believed to range over many topics; the book *Yinwenzi* purports to be a record of his views.
[4] 《尹文子·大道上》：通稱隨定形 。

《庄子·天下》：大同而與小同異，此之謂小同異。

major similarity (major categories) is different from small similarity (small categories), this is a small similarity and difference

The *Yinwenzi Dadaoshang* divides *míng* into three types:

《尹文子·大道上》：一曰命物之名，方圓白黑是也；二曰毀譽之名，善惡貴賤是也；三曰況謂之名，愚賢愛憎是也。

One is *mìngwùzhīmíng* 命物之名 (name for things), such as "square", "round", "black", and "white"; the second is *huǐyùzhīmíng* 毀譽之名 (appraisal name), such as "good", "bad", "noble", and "base"; the third type is *kuàngwèizhīmíng* 況謂之名 (contextual name), such as "worthy", "stupid", "loveable", and "despicable".

Here, *mìngwùzhīmíng* are names based on external features of objects, which can only be grasped through senses such as sight or touch. *Míng* fixed in this way refer to concrete tangible objects identified by such features as shape and colour. Then *huǐyùzhīmíng* are names based on subjective evaluation, as to whether something is good or bad, etc. *Míng* fixed in this way may refer to abstract and intangible things identified by the subjective evaluation standards of the person who names them. And *kuàngwèizhīmíng* are names concerning a subject's evaluative reaction to an object, such as love and disgust.

Yinwen's classification includes concrete, abstract, and relative concepts. He also points out the relationship between concrete concepts and abstract concepts: "'Good' is a general classification of things, and 'cow' is the specific form of a thing; general classification follows specific form, but cannot be exhausted."[5]. When "good" is used in naming, it can be attached to many other *míng*, such as "good cow", "good horse", "good person", "good book", etc. And so, he says, "it cannot be exhausted." Interest in this issue continued with Gongsun Long, who proposed the notorious *báimǎfēimǎ*. His first argument for this surprising statement is

馬者，所以命形也；白者，所以命色也。命色者非命形也。

"Horse" is how the shape is named; "white" is how the colour is named. That which names colour does not name shape.

Later, Gongsun Long also uses the method of *reductio ad absurdum*:

《白馬論》：
曰：以「有白馬為有馬」，謂有白馬為有黃馬，可乎？
曰：未可。
曰：以有馬為異有黃馬，是異黃馬於馬也；異黃馬於馬，是以黃馬為非馬。以黃馬為非馬，而以白馬為有馬，此飛者入池而棺槨異處，此天下之悖言亂辭也。

---

[5] 《尹文子·大道上》：好，則物之通稱，牛，則物之定形；以通稱隨定形，不可窮極者也。

(Gongsun Long) says: If "there is a white horse" is equal to "there is a horse", then is saying "there is a white horse" the same as "there is a yellow horse"?
(The opponent) says: No.
(Gongsun Long) says: If you take the situation of there being a horse to be different from there being a yellow horse, then you differentiate the yellow horse from the horse; to differentiate the yellow horse from the horse is to take the yellow horse to be a non-horse. Taking the yellow horse to be a non-horse, but taking the white horse to be a horse - this is like flying creatures entering a pond, or the inner and outer coffin put at different places. It is "confusing language".[6]

While the Yinwenzi states that "general classification follows specific form", Gongsun Long emphasised that each *míng* refers to a different *shí* 實 (object). So "white" and "horse" cannot be seen as equal, and the combination of "white" and "horse" to form "white horse" cannot be equated to "horse". By carefully examining the relationship between the thoughts of Hui Shi, Yinwen and Gongsun Long, we can observe a small piece of the history of Chinese logic.

4. In your opinion what is the most difficult or problematic aspect of studying logical thought in China?

Reasoning is typically done without any awareness of method, and so it is hard to determine what method was used, solely from examining the text. There are significant problems interpreting the text and even in selecting appropriate materials.

When interpreting a text, we are pulled by two forces: the desire to find the objective unit of thought it expresses and the constraints enforced by the need to maintain scholarly standards and to be reasonable when attributing this unit of thought to an ancient thinker. We are also influenced by our theoretical framework and general premises. Conducting research with an expectant attitude, hoping to find the imagined "Chinese logic", we are bound to be influenced in the way we interpret the texts.

In selecting material to study, we are also influenced by our logical training. It is easy to use what we already know about the rules of logic and our own reasoning methods to guide what we look for in the texts, thereby filtering them for "logical" material, and sometimes even adding or deleting words to suit our purpose. This can result in our overlooking or corrupting valuable material.

We should aim to investigate how the ancients actually thought and reasoned, and how their thinking developed, rather than subject their ideas to our logical standards. Our goal would then be to clarify the principles governing their thinking, first by investigating the particular

---

[6] *bèi* 誖 (self-contradictory/perverse), contrary to accepted practice; in logical contexts it can have the more specific meaning of self-contradictory, also written as 悖 outside the *Mojing*; see also the discussions of *bèi* on p.48 and p.118.

thoughts and methods of the various ancient philosophers. By summarising them, we hope to discover what they have in common and to explain the general direction of thought about logic among the various schools and across time periods.

In addition, we should find out *why* their thoughts about logic exhibit the forms they do. This requires relating their thinking to the historical culture in which they lived. But here too there are dangers. For example, some scholars believe that Chinese logic is biased toward practicality, but reasoning is of course used in many texts dealing with abstract ontological or metaphysical matters, such as *xuánxué* 玄學 (neo-Daoism) in the Wei and Jin periods and Buddhism in the Sui and Tang. Therefore we must be very careful not to use limited cases to make general claims about Chinese logic.

By comparing the forms of reasoning and logical thought of different schools and different periods, we may also find correlations and indications of development, thereby locating the history of logic within the history of Chinese philosophy. The problems here are that the development of logical thought may not be continuous, different reasoning types may be used for different topics, and there may be other jumps in intellectual history that are relevant to the development of logic. All these may disrupt our attempts to form a holistic view of the history of Chinese logic.

Yet, finally, a holistic view is needed if we are to discover the principles of "Chinese logic". It may be that a comparison with western logic can serve as a useful reference but if the reasoning forms of Chinese and western logic are very different, how should we compare them? With even broader scope, we should aim to investigate the meaning and value of this logic in the rational development of all people; and there are difficulties and challenges here too.

5. Which other areas of study could benefit from a better understanding of Chinese logic, or vice versa?

Research on Chinese philosophy and the methodology of Chinese philosophy can all benefit from the research on the history of Chinese logic.

Characteristics of the history of Chinese philosophy include systematicity and connection. By "systematicity" I mean the internal principles and theoretical framework of particular schools of philosophical thought, or in particular texts or along particular developmental paths. By "connection" I mean the lines of heritage between different schools or developmental branches, who criticised whom about which issues, and similarities and difference in the content of different philosophical systems.

The history of Chinese logic is fundamentally relevant to these two characteristics. We may hope that our progress can help to clarify the developmental paths of Chinese philosophical thought, and provide standards relevant to evaluating both their systematic character and the nature of the connections between them. Moreover, a grasp of the relevant rules of reasoning can help with the discovery and development of Chinese philosophical methodology.

Of course, logic is closely related to language, which serves as the vehicle for our thoughts and a tool of expression. So understanding the form and character of the Chinese language from the perspective of philology and linguistics is sure to help our research.

Related publications

Xiānqín Míngjiā "Míngshí" Sīxiǎng Tànxī 《先秦名家 "名實" 思想探析》 (Analyzing the Ideas of the School of Names Concerning 'míngshí '), Taipei: Wenshizhe Chubanshe, 1992.

Gōngsūnlóngzǐ 公孫龍子 (Gongsun Longzi), *Zhexue yu Wenhua* 哲學與文化 256: 855-857, 1995.

Míngjiā Zhéxué Yánjiū 《名家哲學研究》(Research in the Philosophy of the School of Names), Xinbeishi: Huamulan Wenhua Chubanshe, 2012.

Zhànguó Zònghéngjiāshū zhī Sūqín Sīwéifāngfǎ Tànxī 《戰國縱橫家書》之蘇秦思維方法探析 (Study of Suqin's Way of Thinking in *Letters in the Warring States period*), *Fuda Zhexuelunji* 輔大哲學論集 46: 1-18, 2013.

Mòzǐ - Dǎodú jí Yìzhù 《墨子一導讀及譯注》(Mozi–Introduction and Interpretation), Hong Kong: Zhonghua Shuju, 2014.

Chapter 18
Jer-Shiarn Lee 李哲賢

Yunlin University of Science and Technology, Taiwan

---

1. Why did you begin working on the history of logic in China?

I think it's maybe better for me to talk about "when", before talking about "why". It was in 2004 when I started working on the history of Chinese logic, or specifically, on Xun Zi's *míngxué* 名學 (study of names), which most Chinese scholars consider identical to western logic. As for Xun Zi, he was a great scholar in early Confucianism, a major school of thought in ancient China. His dates are not definitely known, but probably lay between the years 298 and 238 B.C.E.

In pre-Qin times, Confucius, Mencius, and Xun Zi were the most original and creative contributors to their tradition, proposing all the main Confucian ideals of life and culture and a view of the universe centring on the ideal of human life as a life of sagehood, with every man able to become a sage by cultivating his own moral potential. This idea remained a fundamental strand of the Confucian tradition.

From that early period, Xun Zi was the last great figure to appear in the Confucian School, and is best known for his doctrine that "human nature is bad". Through the Han dynasty, his influence on Confucian thought and classical scholarship was significant and extensive, although subsequently he was mostly neglected, right up until the 19th century. During these years, Xun Zi never enjoyed high favour, and even today, outside of China, even those who are familiar with Mencius may be quite uncertain as to who Xun Zi was, despite his important role in Chinese intellectual history.

During the pre-Qin period, except for the School of Names and the Mohists, the most important figure in *míngxué* was Xun Zi. Xun Zi's major contribution was to criticise but also develop the School of Names and Mohist versions of *míngxué*. He also inherited and significantly developed Confucius' doctrine of "correcting names".

I have been closely engaged in the study of Xun Zi's thought since 1982, especially his ideas about mind, human nature, heaven/nature, and ritual. But it wasn't until 2004, when I was planning a book for promotion to professor, that I started to explore his *míngxué*. My reasons for picking the study of names was that I needed teaching materials for a course in general education entitled "An Introduction to Methods of Thinking", the core of which is western logic. So I looked for examples of logic in ancient Chinese texts, hoping that these materials would be easily accessible to my students. And since I had been studying Xun Zi for more than 20 years, I felt that it was right for me to start with him, also hoping that an understanding of his *míngxué* would improve my understanding of his thought in general.

2. What is the best way to define your area in terms of historical period, textual sources, methodology or other factors?

Xun Zi is one of the most eminent and brilliant Confucian scholars in ancient China, and except for the School of Names and the Mohists, he is the most important pre-Qin thinker to write about *míngxué*. His theory, which is mostly contained in the *Zhèngmíng*《正名》chapter, concerns the relationship between *míng* 名 (name) and *shí* 實 (object). The term *zhèngmíng* 正名 (correcting names) originated with Confucius, who said: "Let the ruler be ruler, the subject be subject; let the father be father and the son be son."[1] Since Confucius' orientation was ethical and political, his application of *zhèngmíng* was restricted mainly to ethics and politics. Xun Zi inherited the doctrine and extended it, also in a logical direction. When Xun Zi talks about the origin and use of names, he says that "the wise make distinctions and establish *míng* so as to point out *shí*, firstly to shed light on what is noble and base, and secondly to *biàn* 辯 (distinguish) similarities and differences."[2]

Xun Zi's *míngxué* has been neglected by Chinese and foreign scholars alike, both in the past and until very recently, and even now, lack good insights into the essence of his theory. In summary, their opinions range as follows:

A. An American scholar contends that ancient China had semantic theory but no logic. It was because western historians, who confused logic and theory of language, used the term "logicians" to refer to those philosophers of the School of Names. Another American scholar, in a

---

[1]《論語·顏淵》：君君 、臣臣 、父父 、子子 。
[2]《荀子·正名》：知者為之分別制名以指實，上以明貴賤，下以辨同異 。

chapter entitled "Logical Theory" of his book on Xun Zi states that in Chinese the term for logic is "*míngxué*", and logical problems are taken to be problems about names rather than about judgments.

B. Most scholars from mainland China maintain that Xun Zi's *míngxué* is identical to western logic. There are only few scholars who disagree.

C. Almost all Japanese scholars also describe Xun Zi's *míngxué* as "western logic", taking for granted that it is concerned with logic. Just one of them raises a question as to whether there is logic in ancient China, and his answer is negative, saying that if "logic" means traditional logic or Aristotelian logic, then there is no logic in ancient China.

D. In Taiwan, a scholar who studies Later Mohist philosophy, points out if "logic" refers to deductive logic, then he thinks it's proper to say that there is no logic in ancient China.

For the moment, I am the only scholar in this field who has published a book on Xun Zi's *míngxué*, which has an objective assessment of its essential features and explores both its significance within the tradition of *míngxué* and its contribution to the intellectual history of the pre-Qin period.

The divergence of opinion as to whether Xun Zi's *míngxué* is identical to western logic, can only be settled by making a proper comparison with traditional western or Aristotelian logic.

3. What is your favourite example of logical acumen by an early Chinese thinker?

Xun Zi had a logical mind as well as profound scholarship, and his thought is systematic and rigorous. His *míngxué* has not only ethical interest but also a logical orientation, and it is full of examples of logic acumen. Below are a few:

A. *Giving definitions.* The term "*zhèngmíng*" which is used as the title of Xun Zi's chapter on *míngxué* highlights the importance of the correct use of names. So it is no surprise that he pays much attention to the function of definitions, and is particularly careful in giving definitions himself. Words such as *suǒwèi* 所謂, *kěwèi* 可謂, *zhīwèi* 之謂 and *wèizhī* 謂之 are all used to introduce definitions. For example, a whole paragraph in the chapter on "self-cultivation" consists of nothing but a series of 22 definitions, such as

> 《荀子·修身》: 是是非非謂之知, 非是是非謂之愚。...多聞曰博, 少聞曰淺。多見曰閑, 少見曰陋。

> To endorse what is right and condemn what is wrong is called "wisdom". To endorse what is wrong and condemn what is right is called "stupidity"....To have heard many things is called "broadness". To have heard few things is called "shallowness". To have seen many things is called "erudition". To have seen few things is called "boorishness".[3]

Obviously, Xun Zi is good at defining his terms.

B. *The use of arguments.* In the *Xunzi* we find a remarkable preoccupation with arguments, and this is evident in the chapter *Xìng 'e*[4] named with his most famous doctrine that "human nature is bad", which means that following our nature, which is to satisfy the desires we are born with, will result in strife and disorder. In support, Xun Zi sustains a series of arguments, carefully leading us to his conclusion. But if human nature is bad, how can someone become good? To answer this question, Xun Zi presents another argument. He thinks that people cannot live without a social organisation. And to have social organisation, people need *lǐ*,[5] whose purpose is to set limits on the satisfaction of desires. By constraining human nature, we create a framework within which people can become good. In fact, all of Xun Zi's ideas, about human nature, the role of *lǐ*, etc. are strongly connected by logical argument.[6]

C. *Systematic classification.* In arguing for specific definitions, Xun Zi shows his desire to systematise. He has a view of the world as divided into kinds according to their properties, even ranking them in a hierarchy:

> 《荀子‧王制》: 水火有氣而無生，草木有生而無知，禽獸有知而無義，人有氣、有生、有知，亦且有義，故最為天下貴也。

> Water and fire have *qì* (matter/energy) but not life; grass and wood have life but not understanding; birds and beasts have understanding but not a sense of right and wrong; humans have *qì*, life, understanding and a sense of right and wrong, so in all the world, they are the noblest.

In fact, discriminating kinds based on distinguishing properties, of which this is an example, is taken by Xun Zi to be *the* distinguishing property of humans when applied to social matters, namely the recognition of distinctions within human society and behaviour:

> 《荀子‧非相》: 人之所以為人者，何已也？曰：以其有辨也。...非特以二足而無毛也...今夫狌狌形相亦二足而無毛也，然而，君子啜其羹，食其胾。故人之所以為人者，非特以其二足而無毛也，以其有辨也。

---
[3] This and the other translations of *Xunzi* are based on *Xunzi: the Complete Text* by Eric Hutton, Princeton University Press, 2014.
[4] *Xìng 'e* 《性惡》 (Human Nature is Vile), chapter of the *Xunzi*.
[5] *lǐ* 禮 (ritual propriety), central concept of Confucian philosophy including social etiquette, ritual performance and role-specific norms such as those of being a father or ruler, son or minister.
[6] See also Luo Dan's discussion of Xun Zi's argumentation in the *Xìng 'e* on p. 133.

> What is it that makes humans human? I say it's their having *biàn* (distinctions)....not the characteristic of having two legs and no feathers... Now the ape also has two feet and no feathers but the gentleman drinks ape soup and eats ape flesh. So, what makes a human human is not the characteristic of having two feet and no feathers, but rather having *biàn*.

4. In your opinion what is the most difficult or problematic aspect of studying logical thought in China?

The development of *míngxué*, subsequent to its inception in ancient China, is tied up with the introduction of western logic after which "*míngxué*" became equivalent to "Chinese logic". Scholars from mainland China have been engaged in the study of the *míngxué* for more than one hundred years, generally relying on western logic for interpretation and comparison. Once they found some elements of *míngxué* to be similar to elements of western logic, they assumed that they were identical, despite observing that the dominant type of reasoning in *míngxué* is analogical, in contrast to that of Aristotelian logic which is deductive or syllogistic. But if we don't explore the essential characteristics of *míngxué* properly before making a comparison, we should not rely on such a simple identification. I think this is the most problematic aspect of contemporary research on *míngxué*.

5. Which other areas of study could benefit from a better understanding of Chinese logic, or vice versa?

As far as I know, the study of western logic and intellectual history could both benefit from a better understanding of Chinese logic. For example, as I have been saying, we should first come to understand Xun Zi's *míngxué* thoroughly and profoundly, and only then compare it to western logic. This would result in an objective comparison, enabling us to discover similarities and differences between these two traditions, and that will be of interest to both.

Also, in studying Xun Zi's *míngxué* we should explore its significance in the development of *míngxué* across Chinese history, and this would be a contribution to intellectual history more generally. One aspect of this would be further investigation of the transition from Confucius' doctrine of *zhèngmíng* to Xun Zi's *míngxué*, elucidating just how Xun Zi was influenced by and in turn developed Confucius' ideas. Another is to properly assess the relationship between Xun Zi and the Later Mohists, whose ideas he both criticised and developed.

Related publications

Xúnzǐ zhī Míngxué Xīlùn《荀子之名學析論》(On Xun Zi's Mingxue), Taipei: Wenjin Chubanshe, 2005.

Lùn Xúnzǐ Míngxué zhī Běnzhì jí Dìngwèi 論荀子名學之本質及定位 (On Xun Zi's Mingxue: Essence and Assessment), *Hanxue Yanjiu Jikan* 漢學研究集刊, No.4, pp.1-16, 2007.

Lùn Mòjiā Míngxué zhī Běnzhì jíqí Fǎnsī 論墨家名學之本質及其反思 (On Later Mohist Mingxue: Essence and Reflection), *Zhida Xuebao* 職大學報, No.6, pp.11-17, 2011.

Chapter 19
Chung-Ying Cheng 成中英

University of Hawaii, Manoa

1. Why did you begin working on the history of logic in China?

Even as a high school student I was worried by the doubt whether the Chinese have a tradition of logic as the West or the Greeks have. The three laws of logic seem to me to be obvious, and I thought that the Chinese mind, as a human mind, must embody them in its way of thinking. But I also observed that in concrete situations, things may not conform to logic but rather to the laws of change, as disclosed in the *Yijing*.[1] The contrast intrigued me and set me to find out how Chinese logic started and how the Chinese mind has moved in the direction of existential change. I found to my surprise that the Chinese noticed the laws of change before the laws of logic and established the *Yijing* system through the practice of divination, finding it practically useful and cosmologically meaningful. I came to see that by the 4th century B.C.E., the Neo-Mohists[2] started to argue according to implicit laws of formal logic and eventually worked out a formal logic, based on our understanding of categories of things such as identity and difference and forms of debates, for proving objective points of truth. This means that the human mind, whether Chinese or Greek, needs logic for objective knowledge and for validity of reasoning and the formal discourse of argument or debate.

Historically, I came to see that the Chinese mind developed logic as a result of rational criticism and perceived it as necessary and required for

---
[1] *Yijīng*《易經》I-ching (Book of Changes), the *Zhouyi* divination text together with the *Yizhuan* commentaries.
[2] "Neo-Mohists" is another name for the Later Mohists.

establishing objective truth. In fact, I came to see that in the actual use of discourses and languages, formal logic was always assumed even in other schools of classical philosophy such as *rúxué*[3] and *dàoxué*.[4] The content of Confucianism and Daoism may contain many dialectical truths to do with cosmic genesis and human existence, but in linguistic discourse the formal logic of reasoning has been always followed. We have many good examples of *modus ponens* or *modus tollens* in the classical texts of Confucianism and Daoism which were used for the purpose of communication, persuasion or for identifying a coherent feature of a concept or a statement of truth. In this sense formal logic is preserved in the form of communication and linguistic discourse whereas dialectics remains a matter of cosmological understanding, not to do with linguistic presentation.

In the year of 1965, when I started as an Assistant Professor of Philosophy at University of Hawaii at Manoa, I began to think how to explicate Neo-Mohist logic. I tried to show that it has the same basic laws as Greek logic and more than Greek or Stoic logic in its rich exploration of semantic contexts for unmediated logical reasoning. I also noticed how analogy and metaphor often guided reasoning that seeks validity and consistency or coherence, and have explored ontological reasons for reasoning like Gongsun Long's "white horse not horse".[5] I came to the conclusion that Chinese reasoning could be about ontological and cosmological matters even if its expression in discourse conforms to formal logic, drawing a distinction between *logica utens* and *logica docens*, following the american philosopher C. S. Peirce, whom I studied as part of my PhD dissertation at Harvard. My preliminary inquiries into Chinese logic are well known. I continued this inquiry from time to time but did not engage in producing a comprehensive systematisation as I had originally planned. Instead, I was beset with many other urgent issues in Chinese philosophy and comparative philosophy, all demanding my attention. Even at present I consider my inquiries into Chinese logic to be a substantial part of my whole philosophy of knowledge and language, and to be well-represented in my work from the 60's.

From studying Chinese logic, I came to realise that although no philosophy is separable from logic, logic itself is not separable from philosophy, especially not from ontology. My understanding of Chinese logic also affects my understanding of Quine, who was one of my teachers of modern logic at Harvard. (The other one was Arthur Smullyan at the University of Washington, where I studied philosophy for my MA in 1959.) For as I see it, not only is the ontogenesis of logic a matter of the ontogenesis of language, as logic must be rooted in language, but also, as I came to see, language is rooted in life or experience of the world and in the human mind. It is from

---

[3] *rúxué* 儒學 (Confucianism), the study of Confucian texts and ideas.
[4] *dàoxué* 道學 (*Taoism*, Daoism), the study of *dào* and Daoist texts, not to be confused with *dàojiào* 道教 (Daoist religion).
[5] Gōngsūn Lóng 公孫龍, c. 325–250 B.C.E., dialectician famous for his discussion of "white horse not horse", associated with the School of Names and the *Gongsunlongzi*.

this perspective that I came to my work on "onto-hermeneutics" or "onto-generative" hermeneutics or, in other words, a theory of interpretation as founded on reference and meaning and their unity.

This suggests an answer to my earlier question of how logic relates to dialectics: dialectics has to take logic as its form and logic has to consider dialectics as its application to concrete events. I see this as a matter of existential and cosmological development, which I later identify with dialectics. I see how formal logic has to become dialectics in the ontogenesis of things, by which negation is not absolute but a matter of degree, namely in not being a platonic idea.

It is clear that I never considered the study of Chinese logic simply as a historical matter, but rather a matter of how logic can transform itself into dialectics and yet remain as the form of dialectics. It is by considering this relationship between logic and dialectics that I came to appreciate some insights from Hegel's dialectics.

2. What is the best way to define your area in terms of historical period, textual sources, methodology or other factors?

I have basically confined myself to the logic of discourse in the classical or pre-Qin period of Chinese philosophy. I have dealt with the logical approaches of all schools of the classical period and with their logical concerns, such as zhèngmíng[6] and reasoning to acceptable or desirable (not necessarily true) conclusions. Over a period of four decades, I have considered the following issues, as can be seen in my publications, including those in the *Journal of Chinese Philosophy* and *Philosophy East and West*:

A. Origins and beginnings of Chinese logic in Chinese language: I have dealt with the subject structure of classical Chinese and logical particles such as zé 則 and gù 故 and jí 即 and ér 而.

B. Questions of names, zhèngmíng: from Confucius to Mencius to Xun Zi and Han Fei in their positive rectificational projects, from Lao Zi to Zhuang Zi and other Daoists in their negational approach, and finally, from Mo Zi to the Later Mohists and even Gongsun Long in their formal reasoning approach with different considerations of language uses.[7]

C. Ontological and cosmological issues: as shown in my study of the *Yijing* onto-cosmology and its onto-hermeneutic concerns.

D. Comparative studies of dialectics and logic involving western philosophy.

---

[6]zhèngmíng 正名 (correcting names), doctrine concerning the relationship between míng 名 (name) and shí 實 (object), discussed mostly by Confucians.
[7]These names are all of well-known pre-Qin philosophers; consult the glossary for further information.

3. What is your favourite example of logical acumen by an early Chinese thinker?

Three good examples are:

A. *Zhongyong*: "*dào* cannot be separated from life and thus what is separable is not *dào*"[8]

B. *Zhuangzi*: " if you asked me, Zhuang Zi, how I knew that the fish are happy in the stream, you, Hui Shi, must assume that I already knew this and you just wanted to know how."[9] For Zhuang Zi, we do not have to be fish in order to know whether the fish are happy.[10]

C. A third example might be drawn from the *Hanfeizi*: it is to do with the famous story of selling an invincible shield and an all-piercing lance.[11]

4. In your opinion what is the most difficult or problematic aspect of studying logical thought in China?

In my view the most difficult aspect of studying logical thinking is to correctly separate the form from the content of a thought or a system of thought. As we can see, this separation is not a simple matter, but involves consideration of levels. As I suggested, we should see logic as a formal abstraction from language and see language (reference and meaning and intention) as a form of abstraction from our experience of life and world. Hence we have to see how logic as form relates to the levels of thinking, not just to its sequential order. I do not think that we can identify the past as isolated from the present, as we have to interpret the past in light of the present and our understanding of what is the case. This is a meta-logical methodology of onto-hermeneutics for the study of Chinese logic or any other historically evolved form of logic in other cultures.

5. Which other areas of study could benefit from a better understanding of Chinese logic, or vice versa?

I have answered this already, but in summary, primarily one has to know Chinese dialectics which is based on Chinese onto-cosmology and philosophy of change. To know the process of human development is also

---

[8]《中庸》：道也者，不可須臾離也，可離非道也 。
[9]《庄子·秋水》：請循其本 。子曰 "汝安知魚樂" 云者，既已知吾知之而問我 。
[10] See also the discussion of this passage by Zhou Shan, p. 97.
[11] This story is discussed by Liu Peiyu on p. 30.

essential to understanding the creative and logical (often metaphorical-logical) use of Chinese language for the practical purposes of transformation and communication.

Related publications

Inquiries into Classical Chinese Logic, *Philosophy East and West* 15 (3/4):195-216, 1965.

(with Richard H. Swain) Logic and Ontology in the Chih Wu Lun of Kung-sun Lung Tzu, *Philosophy East and West* 20 (2):137-154, 1970.

Aspects of Classical Chinese Logic, *International Philosophical Quarterly* 11 (2): 213-235, 1971.

On Implication (tse) and Inference (ku) in Chinese Grammar and Chinese Logic, *Journal of Chinese Philosophy* 2 (3):225-244, 1975.

Remarks on Ontological and Trans-ontological Foundations of Language, *Journal of Chinese Philosophy* 5 (3):335-340, 1978.

Chapter 20

Jane Geaney 葛立珍

University of Richmond, Virginia

---

1. Why did you begin working on the history of logic in China?

I began studying the *Mobian*[1] as a graduate student at the University of Chicago in the early 1990s as a result of my interest in conceptions of language in Early China (5th to the first century B.C.E.). The only translation and study of the *Mobian* in English at the time was that of A. C. Graham. But while Graham's reconstruction of the text made it accessible, his own interpretive biases added to the complexity of the project of understanding it. I tried to piece together Graham's agenda and sort out its effects on his reconstruction of the text.

While some scholars describe the *Mobian* as "logic", I agree with those who note that the text does not develop propositional reasoning, so categorising it as "logic" seems misleading. As others have observed, there is nothing in the text to justify interpreting *cí* 辭 as being used to mean "sentence" or "proposition", even in A. C. Graham's reconstructed "Name and Objects" section.[2] In both the *Mobian* and the *Zhengming* chapter of the *Xunzi*, the word *cí* is used to mean "phrase". Since the *Mobian* does not identify a sentence structure, I do not think it should be read as even a preliminary attempt to evaluate structural inference patterns between propositions.

---

[1] *Mòbiàn* 《墨辯》 (Dialetical Chapters of the *Mozi*), the six chapters of the *Mozi* that concern the most abstract theoretic thought of the Mohist: the four chapters of the *Mojing* together with the *Daqu* and *Xiaoqu*.
[2] Chad Hansen, *A Daoist Theory of Chinese Thought*, Oxford: Oxford University Press, 1992, p. 241.

Instead, it makes sense to situate the *Mobian* in relation to other genres of writing in Early China. Chapters 40 and 41 (*Jingshang* and *Jingxia*) resemble the *Erya*[3] (also of the 3rd cent B.C.E.) more than any text in the traditional western canon of logic. Scholars have observed that the treatment of names in those chapters is not quite as "definitions".[4] Rather than attempting to identify the thing that makes something what it is, they make associations, which in some cases might inadvertently look like providing a definition. Like the entries in the *Erya*, the *Mobian*'s glosses provide guidance for the use of terms for a particular purpose. Both texts instruct their readers about the use of terms in response to concerns that are specific to their time. Moreover, the two texts are similarly organised in the sense that they are arranged according to what appear to be deliberate divisions on a breadth of topics. The *Mobian* is obviously not as encyclopaedic in its subject matter, but the topics in the *Mobian* are also surprisingly broad. This comparison to the *Erya* is not likely to shed much light on the specific nature of the *Mobian*, but it at least gestures toward a more suitable frame for locating the text.

2. What is the best way to define your area in terms of historical period, textual sources, methodology or other factors?

In general, I am interested in conceptions of bodies, language, and thought, and especially the interrelations between these things. I focus my research on texts from Early China. Unlike most scholars of Early Chinese philosophy, I come to these texts with a background in literary criticism and theory, while teaching in a Religious Studies department. My approach to texts is poststructuralist. I sift through all sorts of genres of texts that are more or less contemporaneous in search of references to language, thought, and bodies. I take note of patterns of word use, parallel structures, and terms that are frequently paired and I interpret these references in light of one another. Insofar as dates for the texts and their layers can be known, I aim to detect changes in their cultural constructions of conceptions of language, thought, and body.

My research is not restricted to a particular type of text. The topics that interest me (language, body, thought) occur implicitly in all sorts of genres, including, for instance, medical, ritual, and mathematical texts. As a result, I tend to produce interpretations that highlight the way the use of terms in philosophical texts is informed by usages in other sorts of texts. Except when philosophical texts explicitly signal an intentionally unusual use of a term, I do not assume that their usage is unrelated to more pedestrian ones. Instead, I presume that any pattern of usage shared by

---

[3] *Ěryǎ* 《爾雅》 (Approaching Eloquence), 3rd century B.C.E., oldest known Chinese book of word glosses.
[4] Chris Fraser, Mohist Canons, *Stanford Encyclopedia of Philosophy*, 2005, revised 2013.

other texts is as applicable to its occurrence in a philosophical text as any other.

Intertextuality is my starting point. It is an undeniable feature of Early Chinese texts, evident in the frequency with which they repeat parts of other texts. But foregrounding intertextuality means that, to some extent, my method departs from the way texts from Early China are traditionally read. In light of the implications of intertextuality, I pay scant attention to "schools of thought" to which texts might be said to belong. Moreover I do not tend to rehearse the overall goals of a text. This is deliberate because my own goal is to observe something new, not the explicit subjects of the texts' discussions. When I work with a passage, I supply it with a new context—that of similar patterns from other texts of the period that affect the possibilities for interpretation. The result is new ways of looking at Early Chinese philosophical texts.

3. What is your favourite example of logical acumen by an early Chinese thinker?

This question emphasises logical acumen, as distinct from something like intellectual acumen, so with that in mind, the *Mobian*'s analysis of compound names comes closest to the mark. But, as an outsider to the field of logic, I do not tend to call the *Mobian*'s analysis "logic".

The prerogative of defining "logic" belongs to that academic discipline, and on the basis of the content of U.S. higher education logic curricula, it seems that what counts as logic developed and flourished exclusively in "the West". We should be skeptical about universality of a discipline that just so happens to have developed almost exclusively in "the West", but in any case, it looks like aspirations for the *Mobian* to be included in the discipline of logic in the western academy are not likely to be met. While the scope of the discipline of logic could potentially change in the future, so far, the field of logic has been more recalcitrant than most about reassessing its own disciplinary assumptions in light of traditions of thinking that have emerged from non-western cultures.

From my perspective, this exclusion from the field of logic need not be disappointing. Logic no longer has the status of the "queen of the disciplines". Few people still see logic as the key to scientific or technological progress. Moreover, like the humanities in general, logic seems to be suffering from not being an obvious source of the kind of "returns" that are expected from an educational "investment". But in any case, the *Mobian*'s significance does not lie in its potential to infiltrate the more insular disciplines of higher education. Scholars are free to pursue work on the *Mobian* in a more interdisciplinary spirit that might actually contribute to chipping away at the disciplinary walls that consistently marginalise non-traditional areas of study like the texts of Early China.

4. In your opinion what is the most difficult or problematic aspect of studying logical thought in China?

As a sinologist located in "the West", the hardest thing about researching Early Chinese thought in general is settling on an approach that can make a topic that is distant in space and time seem important to the current academic establishment. There are pitfalls to every alternative. If we present Early Chinese texts as having only historical value, we reduce the value of our research to the relevance of one spatially and temporally remote historical moment. But making convincing connections to anything beyond that is tricky. Studies that compare Early Chinese texts with those of Ancient Greece seem too eager to legitimise Early Chinese texts by comparison to "the Classics". But the application of ideas from Early Chinese texts to anything in contemporary debate is anachronistic and therefore only more transparent in its eagerness to borrow relevance. Thus, if we focus on the potential for Early Chinese texts to denaturalise certain kinds of thinking in the dominant western philosophical tradition, as I tend to do, we risk being accused of creating an Orientalist caricature of "China" to solve problems of western philosophy. Or we appear to be selectively choosing evidence from the pool of Chinese texts, picking only what can be marshalled to contrast with something in the western philosophical tradition. Yet if we emphasise instead how Early Chinese ideas might fit into categories already present somewhere in the western philosophical tradition, we also expose ourselves to being labeled an Orientalist for letting "the West" set the terms for the discussion.

But the biggest challenge to studying the *Mobian* in particular is the condition of the text itself. The corruption of the text is the interpretive equivalent of quicksand. Moreover, the text frequently gives the impression of invoking examples that would be familiar to its intended audience but are entirely lost on us. These difficulties pose strong temptations to emend graphs and rearrange them to suit what seems most plausible to us. In order to guard against that impulse, it is necessary to establish a strict list of criteria for determining when to emend or rearrange graphs. And yet even those protective measures leave open possibilities for projection. Furthermore, a large percentage of the text offers tentative readings at best, hence any claim to have discovered the rationale for the overarching structure of the text is likely to lead the interpreter astray, rather than provide a foundation for moving forward. Moreover, interpreting one particular "Canon" or "Explanation"—or even one occurrence of a graph —often depends upon prior decisions about how other Canons and Explanations should be interpreted. Persuading other scholars to accept a particular reading of one passage often requires first convincing them to accept interpretations of other passages. The circularity of the process is exhausting.

5. Which other areas of study could benefit from a better understanding of Chinese logic, or vice versa?

The *Mobian* expands our knowledge of the range of possibilities for how humans have thought about what language is. Despite its corrupt state, when read in light of other texts from Early China, it reveals quite a bit about preconceptions regarding the nature of "language" in early Chinese texts. Language in other texts of the period is best understood as engaged social communication–voices, dialogue, and motivated speech–not formal structure.[5] This is true of the *Mobian* as well, but the interesting feature of the *Mobian* is that it seems to strive toward decontextualising more so than the other texts of the period. It does not analyse sentences or propositions, but we should not view that as a sign of logical backwardness. It contributes to our understanding of different ways of thinking about language through the specific form of its relatively detached approach to social communication, as compared with other texts from Early China.

Interpreting the *Mobian* requires willingness to dispense with certain familiar conceptions of language. As Chad Hansen has argued, it would not make sense for the Mohists to speculate about propositions or mental ideas. But this is only the beginning. When the *Mobian* discusses terms like *míng* 名 (name), *yán* 言 (speech), *cí* 辭 (phrase), *tōng* 通 (commune), and *yì* 意 (intent), it generally does so with the same emphasis on linguistic social interaction as other texts of the period. For brevity, I will focus on *míng* here and discuss the *Mobian*'s use of this term in a general way to avoid being mired in the thickets of textual interpretation.

Allowing leeway for emendations and interpretive debates, there are approximately three dozen occurrences in the *Mobian* of the terms *míng* 名 and *mìng* 命 used as "to name". The vast majority of these concern naming things, calling things by name, knowing what something is called, using names to pick out things, using names to show or inform people about things, and/or having the sound of a name spread as fame. The uses associate *míng* with things, as well as with mouths, sounds, and voices.

The *Daqǔ*[6] also contains a passage that resembles a pattern common in other early Chinese texts of matching *míng* to visible things. It begins by saying something about *míng* and *shí* (action/thing) that is obscure (one term might require emendation and the beginning of the passage is uncertain), but it is followed by a more intelligible discussion of stones being white and large. The latter part of the passage reads

《墨子·大取》：苟是石也白，敗是石也，盡與白同。是石也唯大，不與大同。是有便謂焉也。以形貌命者，必智是之某也，焉智某也。不可以形貌命者，唯不智是之某也，智某可也。諸以居運命者，苟（人）*{入}

---

[5] I emphasise voice here because *míng* 名 is the term used for fame or renown, that is, having one's name heard broadly. Graphs, being visible, are something other than *míng*. Although they are used to write *míng*, writing has its own privileged derivation independent of *míng*. Early Chinese texts take this for granted and do not explain the relation of graphs to *míng*. I discuss this more in my article "Grounding 'Language' in the Senses".

[6] *Dàqǔ* 《大取》 (Great Pick), chapter 44 of the *Mozi* and part of the *Mobian*, also translated as "Major Illustrations".

於其中者，皆是也，去之，因非也 。諸以居運命者，若鄉里齊荊者，皆是 。諸以形貌命者，若山丘室廟者，皆是也 。(NO 1,2)

> If this stone is white, and the stone is broken up, all of it will be exhaustively the same white. Although this stone is big, it is not the same as big. This has a convenience of calling in it. When naming by shape and visible features, we necessarily know this thing is X, and only then do we know X. If we cannot name by shape and visible features, although we do not know the thing is X, it is possible to know X. Of the things that are named by residence and movement, if there is entering into the inside, they all are this. If they have exited it, consequently, they are not. Of the things that are named by residence and movement, like districts, villages, Qi and Jing, all are this. Of all the things named by shape and visual features, like mountains, hills, houses, temples, they all are this.

We might assume at first that "stone", "white", and "large" are functioning as words that the passage examines, but when considered in light of audible/visible patterns in early Chinese texts, it appears instead that the passage describes applying names to those visible things. The discussion that follows affirms this because the things in question are visual traits (the shape and visible features of mountains, hills, etc.) or, in their absence, movements of entering and leaving something (also visible) and location in space (as in districts and villages). Thus, most of the *Mobian*'s uses of *míng* entail using names for purposes, and this one in particular highlights a pattern similar to other texts of audible naming of visible items. In sum, the majority of occurrences of *míng* in the *Mobian* are like those in other texts of the period. They are not examinations of the term independent of the things named or the production of names in sound.

There are, however, four out of (approximately) three dozen cases of *míng* in the *Mobian* that at least partially treat *míng* in abstraction from speakers or the things they name. When the *Mobian* treats *míng* in a way that is somewhat detached from the context of voices naming things, it addresses questions of categories or types of sameness. One example describes types of *míng*: "generally, by extension, and private."[7] Another concerns types of sameness: "two *míng* and one *shí* (action/thing) is duplicate sameness."[8] The other two both involve questions about having the same name: "same *míng*: Two and fight..."[9] and "same-name sameness"[10] This pattern indicates that insofar as the text considers *míng* in terms of something like form, it focuses on categorising names and/or kinds of sameness.

Thus, this philosophy of language that emerges from a conception of language rooted in speech situations begins with puzzles about different kinds of sameness in naming. As an account of linguistic communication, what the *Mobian* offers is not necessarily better or worse than a narrative

---

[7] 《墨子·經上》：名，達、類、私 。(A78)
[8] 《墨子·經說上》：二名一實，重同也 。(A86)
[9] 《墨子·經下》：同名：二與鬪…(B3)
[10] 《墨子·大取》：重同，具同，連同，同類之同，同名之同 。(NO 6)

that involves "words", "concepts", and "sentences". It is, however, different, and as such, has the potential to unsettle the obviousness of certain presumed ways of thinking about language.

Related publications

The Emergence of Word-Meaning in Early China: A Chinese Grammatology, SUNY Press Series in Chinese Philosophy and Culture, forthcoming.

Language as Bodily Practice in Early China: A Chinese Grammatology, SUNY Press Series in Chinese Philosophy and Culture, forthcoming.

What is *Ming* 名? In Yiu-ming Fung, ed., *Dao: A Companion to Chinese Philosophy of Logic*, New York: Springer (forthcoming).

The Sounds of *Zhèngmíng* (正名): Setting Names Straight in Early Chinese Texts, in Chris Fraser, Dan Robins, and Timothy O'Leary, eds., *Ethics in Early China: An Anthology*, pp. 107–118, Hong Kong University Press, 2011.

Grounding "Language" in the Senses: What the Eyes and Ears Reveal about *Ming* 名 (Names) in Early Chinese Texts, *Philosophy East & West* 60: 251–293, 2010.

Critique of A. C. Graham's Reconstruction of the Neo-Mohist Canons, *Journal of the American Oriental Society* 119: 1–11, 1999.

Chapter 21

Rens Bod 任博德

University of Amsterdam, Netherlands

---

1. Why did you begin working on the history of logic in China?

I got into the field via my work on the history of the humanities. By the humanities I mean the "humanistic disciplines" such as philology, musicology, linguistics, art theory, literary theory, rhetoric and historiography, or as the German philosopher Wilhelm Dilthey famously put it: the humanities are the disciplines that study the expressions of the human mind.[1] While the history of Chinese science, technology and medicine has received considerable attention thanks to Joseph Needham[2] and others, the history of the Chinese humanities (and actually of the humanities in general) is still largely an untrodden field, with the possible exception of linguistics and logic (e.g. volume 7 in Needham's series). This conspicuous gap in Chinese intellectual history is surprising because the humanistic disciplines were flourishing as much as the scientific disciplines were. For instance, in ancient China we find eminent historians like Sima Qian and Ban Gu, we find influential art theorists like Xie He, great philologists like Shu Xi, renowned music theorists like Liu An, and arguably China's greatest literary theorist, Liu Xie.[3] This impressive humanistic tradition continuous into later periods.

---

[1] Wilhelm Dilthey, *Einleitung in die Geisteswissenschaften. Versuch einer Grundlegung für das Studium der Gesellschaft und der Geschichte*, Teubner, 1959 [1883], pp. 14ff.

[2] Joseph Needham, *Science and Civilisation in China*, 27 volumes, Cambridge University Press, 1954-2008.

[3] Sīmǎ Qiān 司馬遷, c. 145 or 135 - 86 B.C.E., historian and renowned author of the *Shiji*, the completion of which required him to choose castration over death when he supported the wrong friends at court. Bān Gù 班固, 32-92, noted historian and author of the *Hànshū* 《漢書》 (Book of the Han Dynasty) Hetucakra-ḍamaru. Xiè Hè 謝赫, 5th century artist, writer

So when I was writing *A New History of the Humanities*, I naturally included China. And it was then when I decided to include logic as part of the humanistic disciplines. This may sound somewhat controversial, since logic is often viewed as part of the formal sciences rather than the humanities. But the study of logic is closely related to the study of language and rhetoric as well. In the West, for many centuries, logic together with grammar and rhetoric, formed the so-called *trivium* in the liberal arts curriculum (*artes liberales*). In the end I decided to be inclusive rather than exclusive, and I added the history of logic to my historiography of the humanities.

My first contact with the Chinese humanities was not through logic, however, but through historiography, in particular through the works by Sima Qian and Liu Zhiji.[4] I was searching for the methodological principles used by these historians which I wanted to compare with the principles used by other historians from other regions and periods, as well as with the principles used in other disciplines, including logic.

2. What is the best way to define your area in terms of historical period, textual sources, methodology or other factors?

I don't limit myself to any historical period, and I work both with translations and "original" sources (the latter mainly when I collaborate with sinologists). My methodology is to figure out the working principles employed by humanistic researchers, and next to flesh out the patterns or "laws" that these researchers have extracted from their material by means of the principles. I use a number of additional concepts to further categorise principles and patterns, such as procedural rule system, declarative rule system and analogy-based rule system. Let me give an example from Chinese literary theory. In his master piece, *Wenxin Diaolong*, Liu Xie starts by giving a descriptive overview of the writing styles known in his time. He discusses myths and sagas, the classics and their imitations, the different styles of poetry and poetic prose, hymns and eulogies, prayers and vows, laments, historical works (including an extensive stylistic description of Sima Qian's writings), philosophical works, offerings to heaven and earth, exam papers, reports and memoranda, and even declarations of war. In the second part of his work Liu Xie tries to come up with rules that aim at capturing the writing process itself, such as rules for composing a text in terms of its structural elements, i.e. words, sentences and paragraphs.

---

and art historian, known for his *Huìhuà Liùfǎ* 繪畫六法 (Six principles of Chinese painting)
. Shù Xī 束晳, c. 260-300, philologist and poet instrumental in reconstructing the *Zhúshū Jìnián* 竹書紀年 (Bamboo Annals) from excavated bamboo strips. Liú Ān 劉安, c. 179-122 B.C.E., editor of the *Huainanzi* and *Chuci*. Liú Xié 刘勰, 5th century literary critic and author of *Wenxin Diaolong*.

[4] Liú Zhījī 劉知幾, 661-721, historian and author of the *Shǐtōng*《史通》, China's first work on historiography.

He distinguishes between a first rough draft of a text, the revision of text and the adaptation of a text to a certain situation. The methodological question I asked myself was: what kind of rule system is actually proposed by Liu Xie? Is it a fully explicit procedure of rules, or does Liu Xie give only heuristic rules, or does he perhaps give the requisites (constraints) by means of what we might call declarative rules? And what new insights does Liu Xie find with his rules? I figured out that Liu Xie uses a declarative rule system that states the requisites for a literary text or rhetorical piece.

In the same vein I analysed other humanistic texts, such as Xie He's art theoretical *Guhuapin Lu*[5]. In this work Xie He proposes a number of principles for painting, such as the division and planning of the composition, the placing and arrangement of objects, and the treatment of light and colour. Similar to Liu Xie, Xie He seems to devise a system of declarative rules, a set of requisites that painters seem to follow. But Xie He uses his principles not only in a descriptive but also in a *prescriptive* manner: according to him the best painters are those who are able to integrate all principles. Thus while Xie He's principles may initially be seen as descriptive generalisations of Chinese art, they were also used as a normative system for criticising artists. Xie He's system was so influential that it defined Chinese art criticism for many centuries.

Besides elucidating the principles that Chinese researchers have come up with, I also want to figure out what kind of patterns or "laws" were discovered by these researchers. One of the most famous patterns is undoubtedly Sima Qian's *recurrent cycle of rise, glory and decline* of dynasties. Sima Qian believed that this recurrent cycle was not only valid for past Chinese dynasties but also for any future dynasties to come. Another historian, Ban Gu, believed instead that dynasties do not necessarily decline before they are overthrown – and he had indeed some convincing cases. So here we have two contrasting generalisations of history, of which only one can be true. It appears that Ban Gu was closer to the truth, even though Sima Qian's pattern was more influential, perhaps because it seemed in perfect agreement with Daoist philosophy.

The quest for principles and patterns is also found in Chinese logic, especially in the *Mohist Canons*. It has often been observed that the Mohists formulated basic principles for *biàn*,[6] though the link to "logic" is somewhat controversial. One of these principles says that of two contradictory statements one must be false: they cannot be true at the same time.[7] Another principle says that two contradictory statements cannot be both false, one of them must be true.[8] These principles loosely correspond to Aristotle's Law of Non-contradiction and Law of the Excluded Middle. But the Mohists were the first to discover these two basic principles, although

---

[5] *Gǔhuàpǐn Lù* 《古畫品錄》(Analyzing Old Paintings)
[6] *biàn* 辯 (disputation), also interpreted as "distinction-drawing", one of the Mohist *míngcíshuōbiàn*.
[7] 《墨子·經上》：(攸)*{反} 不可兩不可也 。(A73)
[8] 《墨子·經說上》：是爭(彼)*{反} 也 。是不俱當 。(A74)

for a different area, *biàn*.⁹ It remains surprisingly difficult to interpret or recognise principles proposed by the Mohists, especially because their *pìmóuyuántuī*¹⁰ are analogical rather than deductive. But it is crystal clear that the Mohists did actually derive general principles, just as others did in other humanistic disciplines. While the nature of the principles differ across disciplines, they can mostly be categorised into procedural, declarative and analogy-based.

Thus with my approach I place Chinese logic in a broader context and compare its methods with those in art theory, literary theory, music theory, historiography and other fields (including the sciences). While it should be kept in mind that the quest for principles does not always constitute the main focus amongst Chinese "humanists", their common use across humanistic disciplines has been underestimated – if not to say entirely neglected – in previous studies.

3. What is your favourite example of logical acumen by an early Chinese thinker?

My favourite example is constituted by the two basic principles that bring so beautifully together Chinese argumentation and Greek logic, and that have been somewhat controversially referred to as the Law of Non-contradiction and Law of the Excluded Middle. How is it possible, one could ask, that these principles were discovered both by the Mohists and Aristotle, who were unaware of each other's existence? Moreover, this surprising parallel between China and Greece is far from the only one. The great historian Sima Qian, who was well aware of the Mohists' patterns (see book 130 of *Shiji*), discovered also a pattern himself: the pattern of rise, glory and fall of dynasties. This same pattern was also claimed by Herodotus in Greece, and later by Ibn Khaldun in the Arabic world. And there is more: from common principles in the art theory of Pliny and Xie He, to the principles of musical scales by Pythagoras and Liu An.

4. In your opinion what is the most difficult or problematic aspect of studying logical thought in China?

It is not just logical thinking that is difficult to study and interpret, it is all texts from the past that are hard to interpret. I found Liu Xie's literary theory no easier reading than the *Mohist Canons*. Some believe that what is especially difficult about logic is the complexity (as well as the

---

⁹ See for example Jialong Zhang and Fenrong Liu, "Some Thoughts on Mohist Logic", in Johan van Benthem, Shier Ju and Frank Veltman, eds., *A Meeting of the Minds: Proceedings of the Workshop on Logic, Rationality and Interaction*, College Publications, 2007, pp. 85-102.

¹⁰ *pìmóuyuántuī* 辟侔援推 (four modes of reasoning), discussed at the beginning of *Mozi Xiaoqu*.

sheer pleasure) that one can observe in ancient riddles and arguments. But in the poetics of Liu Xie or in the rhetoric of Chen Kui[11] one finds a very similar complexity, which is equally difficult to interpret. Not to speak of the complex philological works by Gu Yanwu,[12] the founder of *xùngǔxué*,[13] who uses inference methods for deriving the archetypical text from extant copies. Thus to some extent one could say that logic is found in all humanities and sciences. This makes it even harder to determine what is a logical text and what is not. But perhaps there is no need to do this either. Logical thinking is found everywhere, not only in "logical" texts.

5. Which other areas of study could benefit from a better understanding of Chinese logic, or vice versa?

It probably won't come as a surprise when I say that I believe that all humanistic and scientific areas will benefit from a better understanding of Chinese logic – and vice versa. The quest for underlying principles and patterns is found in all disciplines and in all periods. The analysis of these principles in terms of systems of rules and laws has only just begun. Of course, Mohist logic disappeared from the scene with the Qin dynasty. But the *use* of logic, and the search for principles and laws, continued in all disciplines, from music theory to philology. In this respect the history of the humanities in China very much resembles developments in other regions, from India to pre-Columbian America. It suggests that, at a methodological level, there is no unique Chinese practice.

Related publications

"A Comparative Framework for Studying the Histories of the Humanities and Science", *Isis*, Vol. 106, No. 2, 2015, pp. 367-377.

(with Julia Kursell) "The History of the Humanities and the History of Science", *Isis*, Vol. 106, No. 2, 2015, pp. 337-340.

(co-edited with Jaap Maat and Thijs Weststeijn) *The Making of the Humanities*, Vol. I, II and III, Amsterdam University Press, 2010, 2012, 2014.

A New History of the Humanities: The Search for Principles and Patterns from Antiquity to the Present, Oxford University Press, 2013. (Originally published in Dutch as *De Vergeten Wetenschappen: Een Geschiedenis van de Humaniora*, Prometheus, 2010; Chinese translation to appear with Peking University Press.)

---

[11] Chén Kuí 陳騤, 1128-1203, author of the book Wénzé 《文則》(The Rules of Writing).
[12] Gù Yánwǔ 顧炎武, 1613–1682, philologist and Confucian scholar known for detailed study of the language of ancient texts including phonology based on rhyming pairs.
[13] *xùngǔxué* 訓詁學 (critical interpretation of antiquity), late Ming early Qing dynasty movement concerned with establishing objective knowledge about ancient texts.

Chapter 22

Christoph Harbsmeier
何莫邪

University of Oslo

---

1. Why did you begin working on the history of logic in China?

My interest was general and philosophical. At the age of 16, I started to study seriously formal logic and in particular ancient Greek logic with Professor G. Patzig of Göttingen University. My special interest at the time was in the philosophical logic of Aristotle, in particular his *Categories* and *De Interpretatione*.

My thought at the time was that it would be nice to get an angle on the Greek achievement by asking to what extent ancient Greek philosophical logic was shaped by the fact that it was articulated in the ancient Greek language and never considered languages of a different type. As the only non-Indo-European language with an indigenous tradition of logical reflection. I felt that classical Chinese logic was the natural subject to study.

2. What is the best way to define your area in terms of historical period, textual sources, methodology or other factors?

My main interest has been in three stages:
    1. pre-Buddhist logical theory and logical practice

2. *Yinming* Buddhist logical theory
3. the introduction of western logic in the 17th century.

3. What is your favourite example of logical acumen by an early Chinese thinker?

Hui Shi: "The ten thousand things are all similar and are all different."[1]

4. In your opinion what is the most difficult or problematic aspect of studying logical thought in China?

Lack of sustained training in philosophical logic and its history. An exaggerated interest in the technicalities of modern formal logic and a corresponding lack of interest in fundamental problems of philosophical logic and its history in ancient Greece, Rome, early medieval times, late medieval times and particularly in modern analytic philosophy of language.

5. Which other areas of study could benefit from a better understanding of Chinese logic, or vice versa?

Intellectual history in general, general history of moral argumentation, scientific method, Chinese intellectual history, comparative linguistics.

The potential of the study of the specificities of Chinese logical theories and Chinese logical forms of argumentation for analytic philosophy of language in general has hardly begun to have any significant well-defined effect on the interested scholarly community at large.

In particular, the study of Chinese logic has not so far had any significant impact on the study of the parochial specificities of western and Indian developments in this area.

The study of Chinese logic is far from having made the kinds of contributions to comparative philosophy of language and indeed comparative philosophy more generally that one would think it should be capable of.

Useful work will require a difficult combination of advanced training in formal and philosophical logic on the one hand, and very sophisticated training in traditional Chinese philology and classical western philology on the other. Separately each of these fields is difficult to master well. Each of these required skills is extremely hard (and time-consuming) to achieve. But all of them together are needed for the kind of work that will put Chinese logic on the global intellectual map in an intellectually substantial, well-argued and precise way.

---

[1] 《庄子·天下》：萬物畢同畢異 。

Related publications

Aspects of Classical Chinese Syntax, London: Curzon Press, 1981.

The Mass Noun Hypothesis and the Part-whole Analysis of the White Horse Dialogue, in H. Rosemont, Jr. La Salle eds., *Chinese Texts and Philosophical Contexts*, Illinois: Open Court, 1991, pp.49-66.

Conceptions of Knowledge in Ancient China, in Hans Lenk and Gregor Paul eds., *Epistemological Issues in Classical Chinese Philosophy*, Albany: SUNY Press, 1993, pp.11-33.

Language and Logic in Traditional China (Science and Civilisation in China, Vol. 7.3), Cambridge University Press, 1998.

Some Philosophical Notes On the Guodian Manuscript Yucong 1, *Studies in Logic*, Vol. 4, No. 3, pp.3-56, 2011.

Chapter 23

Michiel Leezenberg 李仁伯

University of Amsterdam

1. Why did you begin working on the history of logic in China?

First, there was of course the challenge and the excitement of studying a tradition in logic and philosophy of language that is entirely unrelated to the ones I am familiar with. More specifically, what looked particularly promising was the radically different framing of questions of correct language use from the ones we have grown accustomed to in modern analytical philosophy. Originally, when I had just finished my dissertation (which, among others, traced the history of the concept of metaphor and the historical and cultural variability of the literal-figurative divide), I was curious to see how the classical Chinese view of literal and figurative language was articulated. Quickly, however, I became intrigued by the problematic of *zhèngmíng*[1] as discussed by Confucius and later thinkers, which drew my attention to questions of the role of social authority and power in determining correct and literal (and, by extension, figurative) language use. A related question that continues to fascinate me is the disciplinary embedding of logical matters in ancient Chinese thought. In some cases, questions concerning, say, the validity of a particular kind of argument are to be found next to statements and discussions that are barely recognisable as logic in the modern sense of the word. The easy way out would be to argue that ancient Chinese thought did not know any "real" logic; but a more interesting line of exploration than such yes-no questions would focus on the definition and delimitation of disciplines, and

---

[1] *zhèngmíng* 正名 (correcting names), doctrine concerning the relationship between *míng* 名 (name) and *shí* 實 (object), discussed mostly by Confucians.

chart how and why particular kinds of questions concerning logic and language came to be raised, and in what disciplinary and other context. From my own earlier study of the division of the sciences in the mediæval Islamic tradition, I have learned that one can get a much deeper understanding of possibly radically different ways in which knowledge is conceived of by studying how the different disciplines are classified and ordered.

2. What is the best way to define your area in terms of historical period, textual sources, methodology or other factors?

Unfortunately, given my other activities and obligations, I have not been able to devote as much time to these topics as I would have liked; but the work I have published has focused on the earliest phase of Chinese thought, in particular Confucius and the Mohists. Perhaps more than anyone else, and certainly more than anyone else writing in English, it was Angus Graham who called attention to the fact that the most ancient forms of Chinese thought had a much more rigorous and systematic character than had hitherto been believed. Especially in the pre-Han period, one can see a variety of explicit and implicit argumentation and debate between the different currents among the "Hundred Schools", which becomes less intensive and less visible with the consolidation and institutionalisation of more "official" schools of thought, or religions, in particular Confucianism, Daoism, and Buddhism during and after the Han dynasty. It seems that this later period knew a less intensive and innovative intellectual activity concerning questions of logic, language, and argumentation; but it may well be that we simply haven't studied the later periods intensively enough with an eye on such matters.

My own methodological approach to Chinese thought has primarily been one of contrastive linguistics; thus, I have confronted Confucian doctrines on language use, and in particular correct naming, with modern western conceptions of pragmatics, like J.L. Austin's Speech Act Theory, H.P. Grice's theory of conversational implicature, and Pierre Bourdieu's theory of language and symbolic power. In particular, I have used such contrastive studies with the aim of explicating the different linguistic ideologies, or tacit and perhaps not entirely systematic beliefs about words and their place, role and effects in the world, that are implicit in these very different authors. In recent decades, such linguistic ideologies have become a prime topic of investigation in linguistic anthropology, as they carry the promise of helping to provide an empirically more adequate and conceptually more sophisticated account of linguistic practice.

More recently, I have also been developing an interest in early modern and modern developments, in particular the rise of the spoken vernacular as the basis both for a novelistic literature and for learning and written communication more generally, as argued for by modern literary and other authors like, most famously, Lu Xun. This modern process of vernacularisation appears to be an almost worldwide phenomenon that starts, roughly, in the eighteenth century. The Chinese path towards vernacularisation, however, appears to have distinct features both chronologically and conceptually. I would very much like to further explore these changing practices and ideologies of language in early modern and modern China.

3. What is your favourite example of logical acumen by an early Chinese thinker?

I think the paradox of the white horse is a beautiful example of the excitement of discovering the power of argumentation and logical reasoning, and of formulating an apparently valid argument that leads to an intuitively obviously absurd conclusion. One sees different authors attempting to come to come to terms with this apparently impossible result in different ways, some (like Xun Zi) appealing to common sense and visual perception, others (like Zhuang Zi) happily embracing the apparent paradoxes as part of a more general rejection of strictly rationally regimented forms of language use.

4. In your opinion what is the most difficult or problematic aspect of studying logical thought in China?

For most non-Chinese scholars, the primary problem is of course the language barrier. Relatively few texts are available in English, and much of the frontline research in this area depends on a thorough acquaintance with *wényán* 文言 (classical Chinese), and more specifically with the technical vocabulary that was developed in it, and which has come to be recognised as such only in relatively recent times. At the same time, however, these difficulties constitute precisely what is most fascinating about comparative and historical studies of intellectual traditions: they provide a vista on entirely different worlds of thought.

Another difficulty is the above-mentioned problem that sometimes we hardly even recognise ancient Chinese thought as "real" philosophy or "real" logic at all. This perception could be correct, but it could also be an indication that we may simply be looking for the wrong answers, for the wrong questions, or perhaps even in the wrong places. Ancient Chinese logic, and ancient Chinese thought more generally, should be studied on their own terms, and one should avoid imposing modern or western preconceptions and norms on them.

5. Which other areas of study could benefit from a better understanding of Chinese logic, or vice versa?

Apart from its obvious inherent interest, the study of history of Chinese logic and philosophy of language would seem to be of interest primarily for comparative and/or intercultural philosophy. Comparing or contrasting history of Chinese logic, not only with, most obviously, the premodern (especially ancient Greek and mediæval) and modern western logical tradition, but also logical traditions like those in the Islamic world or the Indian subcontinent, may bring new rigour to comparative approaches to philosophy that generally tend to focus more on other philosophical subfields. These comparative or contrastive insights, in turn, may help us explore linguistic ideologies and other ethnocentric preconceptions in the field of logic and philosophy of language, which— tacitly or explicitly—think of themselves as providing universally applicable concepts and universally valid norms or values of thought, rationality and communication. In short, they may help in developing more self-critical and culturally more self-aware forms of knowledge.

Another field for which the study of history of Chinese logic is of particular relevance is intellectual history, or what used to be called the history of ideas. In particular, for intellectual historians of a neo-Kantian orientation, the study of beliefs about how language relates to the world and the ways in which arguments are defined as valid may provide new insights into the very architecture of more ancient and more modern stages of Chinese thought. I am convinced that the further study of Chinese ideas on logic and language in both the ancient and modern period will yield many unexpected and indeed surprising insights. To conclude on a somewhat moralising note: a more systematic exploration of the Chinese study of logic, language and argumentation may help in countering, and eventually perhaps even putting to rest, the still-widespread misconception that China only has a tradition of conceptually uninteresting moralising and no tradition of "real" philosophy, i.e., of systematic, rigorous, and/or speculative thought. This myth should have been dispelled long ago, but unfortunately, not only is it still widely believed by many a western philosopher; it is also institutionally entrenched, witness the near-total lack of attention to Chinese philosophy in most philosophy departments in Europe and America.

Related publications

Gricean and Confucian Pragmatics: A Contrastive Analysis, *Journal of Foreign Languages*, pp: 2-21, 2006, reprinted in D.F. Shu and K.P. Turner (eds.) *Contrasting Meaning in Languages of the East and West*, Berlin: Peter Lang, 2010, pp. 3-32.

(with H. van Rappard) (eds.) *World Philosophy: Philosophical Thought in Different Cultures* (Wereldfilosofie: Wijsgerig denken in verschillende culturen), Amsterdam: Bert Bakker 2010.

Chapter 24
Thierry Lucas 卢卡斯

Catholic University of Louvain (Louvain-la-Neuve)

---

1. Why did you begin working on the history of logic in China?

Let me answer with an image which is traditional and quite naive but is still working very well: it is a seed which happened to fall on good ground. By good ground, I do not mean that I would be particularly gifted for that, but that I received a training; I got an experience which prepared me for that and I met the people who drew my attention to the field. I began my work in logic first with algebraic logic, then concentrated on the foundations given by categorical logic; by nature, I feel inclined to look at the foundations, always feeling dissatisfied if some concept is not clear enough and my impression is that formal logic is especially "honest" in that respect; when you have a formal system, you clearly announce things which are basic and are not to be explained: the basic vocabulary, the terms and formulas, the axioms, the rules; but the rest becomes fully clarified simply by being reduced or "virtually concentrated" in those notions. I must also complete the picture of my basic training by saying that I also received a complementary formation in philosophy, which happened to give me still more motivation for the search for foundations and for the clarification of notions. That is it for the formal training. For a less formal training, let me say that I have always been interested by the study of foreign languages and of language in general. Here again, the problem is not very far from some aspects of logic: real logic is always expressed in a language, a human language; what is the influence of the language on logic? Some twenty years ago, I became particularly interested in the Chinese language, because it is so far from the structure of our Indo-European languages. Contrary to a popular view (among Chinese as well as non-Chinese people), it is far from being devoid of structure, but linguists have well shown that it has a quite definite structure and that that structure is built along lines which are very different from those of Indo-European languages. Enough for the ground on which the seed fell. Now for the seed: twenty years ago, I also had the chance of meeting Chinese colleagues who drew my attention to the famous *báimǎfēimǎ* 白馬非馬, a provocative thesis defended in the 3rd century B.C.E. by the famous Chinese sophist Gongsun Long. As a logician, I couldn't but be intrigued and wanted to propose my solution — I should be modest and say the nth solution — to a problem which nonetheless or precisely for that reason remains very interesting. I realised later that Mo Zi was still much more documented and showed the characteristics of the "true logician": systematic comparisons of similar sentences, logical arguments to support ethical theses, use of quantifiers and variables, etc. On the other hand, the *Mohist Canons* show characteristics which are very far from the traditional Aristotelian syllogistic: this is what makes them interesting, which is a quite different view from that of the first Chinese thinkers (e.g. Hu Shi[1]) who wanted to bring together western "science" with Chinese tradition. Being now retired as a professor, I can spend more time on the study of texts, bringing together my three (professional!) loves: formal logic, philosophical logic and languages.

2. What is the best way to define your area in terms of historical period, textual sources, methodology or other factors?

At this moment, I am particularly interested in the *Mohist Canons*, but I hope that later I can expand my considerations to all Mohist texts and to other pre-Qin texts, such as *Xunzi*, *Mengzi* or the *Analects*. It is much more akin to what we call "argumentation"; typical examples are the very frequent arguments by analogy, or by appeal to the authority of the "sage-kings", or by chains of implications. But that it is argumentation is not a good reason for logicians to give up; let me explain this by a memory dating back to the beginning of the sixties. When I began my career, I had some contacts with Chaïm Perelman who had just renewed interest in argumentation with his "Treatise on Argumentation".[2] He wanted to explain to me that argumentation was very different from logic, taking the example of a lawn on which it is written "forbidden to walk on the grass"; a logician comes by, stands outside the lawn and damages the grass

---

[1] Hú Shì 胡適, 1891-1962, influential scholar, writer, philosopher, and literary reformist, who studied at Columbia University under John Dewey; his dissertation *Xianqin Mingxueshi* was the first book on the history of Chinese logic in English.

[2] Chaïm Perelman and L. Olbrechts-Tyteca, *The New Rhetoric: A Treatise on Argumentation*, Notre Dame: Notre Dame Press, 1991.

by savagely pulling it up but telling everybody that he respects the letter of the interdiction; you guess the sequel of the story: if the case goes to court, the logician will obviously be condemned typically on the basis of the "a fortiori argument". Pace Perelman, I can now say that I was not convinced by his example: I never worked out the details, but already at that moment it seemed obvious to me that we could introduce an order relation between sentences which would not be logical consequence but would explain much of what we expect of an "a fortiori relation". I give that example to explain my methodology: logical techniques are now so diverse and so well defined that we have scores of techniques at our disposal to explain the coherence of unusual types of reasonings, of deviant or apparently absurd systems and my plan is to use those techniques or, more exactly, to use their spirit or adapt them to explain texts of the pre-Qin period. I already said above why I was interested in that period, but I should also say that I do realise the difficulties of the task; I will mention two: finding the true text and determining its meaning, or rather what its meaning was at the time. For the "true text", I obviously have to rely on experts of pre-Qin Chinese, but I try to follow their discussions and to remain critical when applying their results; for the "true meaning", I also have to rely on the methods of philologists and I would not dare propose completely new interpretations, but I am convinced that the formal methods of logic introduce some independence from that "true meaning". To take otherwise well-known examples, you can work out and explain in a quite satisfactory way paraconsistent reasonings, i.e. admitting contradictions without admitting the *e falso* rule; there remains room for a critique of those systems, for what their good points and defects are and for a nuanced view of their applicability, but your decisions will be enlightened by your discussions. And of course, you have to remind yourself of one of the first things you learn when beginning philosophy: there is no absolute, no purely independent point of view.

3. What is your favourite example of logical acumen by an early Chinese thinker?

I would like to mention many examples. Gongsun Long's *báimǎfēimǎ* is provocative but its underlying argumentation is too crude. Mo Zi's " a robber is a man, but killing a robber is not killing a man"[3] is almost equally provocative; its underlying argumentation is already very formal in spirit, involving a systematic comparison of sentences obeying similar laws and variations on the theme "X is Y / ZX is (is not) ZY". I should also mention the use of variables, the interdefinability of quantifiers in the *Mojing*, the presence of paradoxes, and its already great sensitivity to definitions. But the example I like best, for many reasons, is the argument

---

[3] 《墨子·小取》：雖盜人人也，…，殺盜人非殺人也 。(NO 15)
 This and similarly parallel statements are also discussed by Yiu-ming Fung, p. 124, and Yang Wujin, p. 69.

in Canon B73 in favour of *jiānài* 兼愛 (impartial care[4]). It is based on concepts which at first sight are not in the least related to ethics: limitless/ limited, exhaustible/ inexhaustible, knowable/ unknowable, necessary/ unnecessary. The logical words it uses are all defined in the text. And it presents both an objection and an answer, each using a quite elaborate disjunction of cases. So this, for me, is a very nice example of the logical sensibility of the author, and I do not resist repeating it in A. C. Graham's translation:

《墨子·經下》: 無窮不害兼，說在盈否。

Canon: Their being limitless is not inconsistent with doing something to everyone. Explained by: whether it is filled or not.

《墨子·經說下》:「南者有窮，則可盡。無窮則不可盡。有窮無窮未可智，則可盡不可盡(不可盡)未可智。人之盈之否未可智，(而必)人之可盡不可盡亦未可智，而必人之可盡愛也，誖。」人若不盈(先)*{無} 窮，則人有窮也。盡有窮無難。盈無窮則無窮盡也。盡(其)*{無} 窮無難。

Explanation:
(Objection). The south if limited is exhaustible, if limitless is inexhaustible. If whether it is limited or limitless is unknowable a priori, then whether it is exhaustible or not, whether men fill it or not, and whether men are exhaustible or not, are likewise unknowable a priori, and it is fallacious to treat it as necessary that men can be exhaustively loved.
(Answer). If men do not fill the limitless, men are limited, and there is no difficulty about exhausting the limited. If they do fill the limitless, the limitless has been exhausted, and there is no difficulty about exhausting the limitless. (B73)[5]

4. In your opinion what is the most difficult or problematic aspect of studying logical thought in China?

Well, having a reliable text and understanding the context of the epoch is certainly a difficulty. Corruption of pre-Qin Chinese texts is especially important and Chinese is particularly misleading because the written characters are the same as now but syntax and meanings have changed significantly. Those two difficulties should, however, not be exaggerated. It all depends on what you want to do with the history of logic, be it western or Chinese or Indian or whatever. You can try to reconstitute as faithfully as possible the way of thinking, of arguing, of people of the past and their own views on that activity. It is a very nice endeavour, and in that sense it is not different from other historical endeavours, but it is, I guess, subject to similar difficulties: unless you limit history to a list of statistics, history always involves a good deal of interpretation; it is always made from our contemporary point of view and it has to be rewritten by

---

[4] This translation of *jiānài* is now preferred to "universal love".
[5] This passage is also discussed by Chris Fraser on page 117.

every generation. There is a very good example of that attitude in the 20th century interpretations of "Chinese logic": most writers, especially Chinese, starting with Hu Shi, wanted at any price to find syllogisms in early Chinese thought; that is a view which is now completely abandoned. We should not fall into the same error now and think that we have the definitive interpretation which will not suffer any further amendment. Personally, I think that the history of logic as well as the history of mathematics and of science has a specificity which is not as clearly marked as the history of politics or of society or of civilisations: we can hope that studying the history of logic will give us inspiration for new concepts or give new arguments or new applications for contemporary concepts. For example, I like to think that Mo Zi's notion of *lèi* 類 is very close to our contemporary conception of category in the mathematical sense of the term and that that "identification" explains many formal features of the text; for me, it is also a good argument in favour of the formal approach and a good "propaganda" for our modern concepts. The real difficulty or problematic aspect is that that kind of formalism is not written in black and white in the text and that other people come and say: I have a better interpretation using, say, default logic or non-monotonic reasoning, which explains this or that feature which your approach fails to explain; or quite a number of Chinese writers will come by and question the applicability of "western" formal methods (which I have taken for granted): they stress less formal methods or think that there is a very specific Chinese way of doing logic. That difficulty is in fact a richness: we cannot hope to explain a not yet mature logic by a single theory and it is only later that we will be able to give a balanced view of Chinese pre-Qin logic. We can however already say that we have nice challenging problems of interpretation and nice sources of inspiration.

5. Which other areas of study could benefit from a better understanding of Chinese logic, or vice versa?

Here are a few examples of what the study of ancient Chinese Logic could bring to logic and argumentation: bring again to the fore the problem of generalisation (not in the sense of induction, but in the sense of passing from a "typical element" to "all elements"); reasoning by analogy is another example of a problem which merits attention; disputation is another one; definitions of the *Mojing*, being unconventional, set again the problem of what a definition is, etc. I think that the history of Chinese thought can also benefit from the study of Chinese logic: writers such as Hu Shi, and have already considerably changed the previously oversimplified views of the history of Chinese thought.[6] Pre-Qin sources and the study of their logic will certainly help us to complete and correct such insights.

---

[6] (Féng Yǒulán 馮友蘭), 1895–1990, philosopher and professor at Tsinghua University and Peking University who studied in the U.S.A. and whose *A Short History of Chinese Philosophy*,

But for me the greatest benefit would be that it could bring new ideas on the relation between logic and other fields of philosophy such as ethics or philosophy of science and perhaps bring a less western centred view on philosophy in general. I have no precise idea on how that could be done, but I am particularly confident that the study of early Chinese thought could help us to enrich our views on ethics: ethics has always been a dominant motive in Chinese thought; Confucianism, Mohism, Daoism, Legalism, study of names are all different approaches within which language and logic play a non-negligible role; let us look at them with all means at our disposal!

Related publications

Hui Shih and Kung Sun Lung an Approach from Contemporary Logic, *Journal of Chinese Philosophy* 20 (2): 211-255, 1993.

Later Mohist Logic, Lei, Classes, and Sorts, *Journal of Chinese Philosophy* 32 (3): 349–365, 2005.

Definitions in the Upper Part of the Moist Canons, *Journal of Chinese Philosophy* 39 (3): 386-403, 2012.

Why White Horses are not Horses and other Chinese Puzzles, *Logique Et Analyse* 56: 185-203, 2012.

Parallelism in the Early Moist Texts, *Frontiers of Philosophy in China* 8 (2): 289-308, 2013.

1948, made the study of Chinese philosophy accessible to the English-speaking world. (Chén Róngjié 陈荣捷), 1901-1994, Chinese-born philosopher who attended Harvard in the 1920s and later became a leading exponent of Chinese philosophy in the United States.

Chapter 25

Gregor Paul 葛保罗

Karlsruhe Institute of Technology

1. Why did you begin working on the history of logic in China?

The main reason I began working on the history of logic in China was that I regard as unacceptable the exoticism, esotericism, obscurantism, and cultural relativism so influential in intercultural studies. Many scholars and politicians even maintain that there are no universally valid laws of logic, or, more precisely, logical form, and that logical laws depend on the cultures of their origin, i.e., differ according to their cultural origin. One German scholar even wrote in an influential German newspaper that the members of different cultures cannot but have different ideas of human rights for, in their thinking, they follow different logics. In my opinion such views amount to denying the unity of mankind and the basic identity of all members of the species homo sapiens sapiens. As a consequence, intercultural understanding would be impossible in principle. For if there actually existed classes of fundamental logical laws that are incompatible with each other, humans who, in their reasoning, follow a class A, and others who follow a class B, would usually arrive at different conclusions even from identical premises. Believing in, and even propagating such nonsense, is not only epistemologically and empirically untenable, but also ethically, politically and socially dangerous. Authoritarian and despotic politicians could use logical relativism to justify their inhumane politics as a unique and valuable cultural tradition that people from "foreign" cultures cannot understand and that is therefore no legitimate aim of "foreign" criticism. Actually, everybody who believes in logical relativism could easily refuse critical discussion with "foreigners". Driven to its logical extreme (in which a culture is erroneously conceived of as a very specific closed system), Nazis could maintain that only Nazis can understand and judge them. Thus, to refute the often voiced idea that there exists a "Chinese logic", incompatible with "western logic" (also a misnomer), was, and remains, one of my main motives to deal with the "theory and practice" of logic in Chinese (but also in Indian and Arabic) history. Thereby, studying history of logic in China can also be regarded as an application of the principle of charity, and it can preclude falling into the trap of linguistic relativism, i.e. of confusing rules of logic with rules of (a specific) language which in turn may result in fatally misunderstanding Chinese texts.

2. What is the best way to define your area in terms of historical period, textual sources, methodology or other factors?

As far as theory of logic is concerned, I focus on texts from the Mohist and School of Names texts, which date back to the 5th and 4th centuries B.C.E., and Tang Buddhist (yīnmíng) texts from the 7th century C.E. But I also analyse the ways logical rules are applied in Chinese texts. In principle, all Chinese texts are of interest, though I restrict myself mainly to the earlier philosophical texts. Among the main problems I deal with are the following questions: (i) Do Chinese texts include phrases that can adequately be interpreted as formulations of such laws as, e.g., the principles of identity, non-contradiction, excluded middle, and transitivity? (ii) Do Chinese texts expressly demand logical consistency? (iii) Do they include examples of reductio ad absurdum? (iv) How do they handle paradoxes? (v) How do Chinese texts express negations? Etc. Pursuing such problems and questions I argue extensively and in detail (a) that there are universally valid laws of logical form and formal logical deduction, (b) that these laws should not be confused with specific principles put forward in specific theories and that (c) they should be distinguished from principles of consistent language use that reflect the particularities of different languages as for instance different usages of quantifiers or different expressions of the copula.

As to points (i), (ii) and (iii), Chinese texts include numerous respective examples. As to (iv), (v) and (c), a few illustrations (to which others could easily be added) may facilitate understanding of what I want to say.

(iv) In Mohist texts criticising Daoist contempt of speech we find such ironical arguments as for instance the remark that who maintains that we cannot communicate thereby implies that he himself does not communicate, i.e., that his statement is self-refuting.

(v) There are several forms of negation used again and again to intentionally express contradictories and, on this basis, to formulate formally arguments that cover the whole realm of discourse, thus presupposing and applying the laws of non-contradiction and excluded middle. The most prominent pairs are *shì* 是 (this/is this) and *fēi* 非 (not/is not); *rán* 然 (is so) and *bùrán* 不然 (is not so); *yǒu* 有 (has) and *wú* 無 (lacks), etc.

(c1) In most (if not all?) European languages, "some x" can also mean/include "all x", whereas in Mohist texts "some" means "at least one, but not all". As a matter of consequence, the rules of the so-called Aristotelian square (according to which we can deduce "some" from "all") do not apply to Mohist arguments.

(c2) Also, in English the so-called copula is usually (though not necessarily) explicitly expressed by words such as "is" or "are", e.g. "A is B". However, there are languages in which such explicit expressions are not (regularly) used, though every native speaker immediately understands that, in respective phrases, (a logical relation of) identity and/or diversity between A and B is expressed. In both cases (c1 and c2), language rules differ, though the logical rules remain the same.

3. What is your favourite example of logical acumen by an early Chinese thinker?

Sunzi Bingfa (5th century B.C.E.), the Later Mohist works, *Xunzi* (4th-3rd centuries B.C.E.), and *Hanfeizi* (3rd century B.C.E.). If "early" also refers to Tang thinkers, I would include some Buddhist scholars, especially Xuan Zang.[1] The *Sunzi Bingfa*, better known as the famous *Sunzi's Art of War*, intentionally employs contradictories to cover the whole (respective) realm of discourse. The *Mohist Canons* refutes opponents, such as the Daoists, by pointing out the paradoxical and self-refuting character of Daoist arguments. The *Xunzi* points out that language use ought to be logically consistent. For instance, if you name something "round", things similar in this respect should also be called "round" – actually a rule of naming already put forward in Mohist texts and implicit in the *Analects*. However, the *Xunzi* also makes it clear that in logically distinguishing concepts one must not go too far, for this would confuse the important and the unimportant and would mislead those who are not so well versed in over-sophisticated argument. The *Hanfeizi* is a text in which the means to ensure or even further a ruler's power and welfare are developed in almost ruthless logical consequence. Xuan Zang, who translated two Sanskrit treatises on *hetuvidyā*, a discipline that deals, among other things, with problems of (non-)contradiction and valid logical inference, again and again emphasised that arguments ought to be consistent to be acceptable.

---

[1] Xuán Zàng 玄奘, 602-664, monk, scholar, traveller and teacher, who studied in India and translated many Buddhist texts, including the logical texts *Zhenglimenlun* and *Ruzhenglilun*.

4. In your opinion what is the most difficult or problematic aspect of studying logical thought in China?

Actually, I fail to see any difficulties that significantly differ from the difficulties one encounters by studying pre-modern "western" history of logical thinking. Studying logic can be a hard job. Comparable to mathematics, logic poses difficult intellectual problems. Moreover, studying logic may be a dry, if not boring and superfluous undertaking – for human beings can, and usually try to, think logically without having studied logic and/or without any need of studying logic.

One should, however, not misunderstand my interest in studying history of Chinese logic. As indicated above, in my opinion, knowledge of this history does not only provide means to argue against logical and cultural relativism (etc.), but also facilitates understanding of Chinese texts and Chinese culture in general. Such study precludes that you all too easily attribute strange and awkward, if not nonsensical, views to Chinese writers, or that you all too easily give up the task of understanding their "foreign thinking". In particular, to learn how to distinguish between logical rules and Chinese language rules and use is important.

Actually, if we want to understand a foreign culture, we must presuppose that its members are able to think logically, and that they usually try to do this. *This is an indispensable methodological and methodical principle for every kind of understanding.* When interpreting a text we must presuppose that the text is – in one way or other, intentionally or unintentionally, consciously or unconsciously, on the level of object-language or meta-language – a function of fundamental logical principles. The same applies if we want to translate a text, for a translation is but a special kind of interpretation. By making such a presupposition, we do not read any logic into the respective text. We do not fall victim to a vicious circle, for our procedure permits for the conclusion that the respective text cannot be understood at all. This, then, could indeed imply that the text not only violates "our" logical principles, but is a function, a result, or reflexion of "something" completely different from them. Mere violations are irrelevant, for we also violate, e.g., mathematical laws. In the second case, however, we would not be able to identify the "something". I do not know of any interpretation of a text which arrived at the conclusion that the text reflected, or was determined by, such a mysterious "something", not to mention interpretations of a whole culture. Some Daoists and Zen Buddhists have attacked logical principles. However, certain western philosophers did the same. One need only remember the so-called Greek sophists. But whoever thereby tried to convince his opponents, had himself to employ logical laws and rules.

There are other rather general arguments for the hypothesis that there are universally valid logical principles. There are of course also further counter-arguments besides the argument that logical principles depend on, and differ according to, the specific features of the specific languages in which they are put forward, among them the often religiously motivated contention that existentially relevant knowledge can only be gained by violating or transcending logical laws. All these arguments and counter arguments influenced the way I approached the study of history of logic in China, and the way in which I analyse the particular expression they found in Chinese texts.

5. Which other areas of study could benefit from a better understanding of Chinese logic, or vice versa?

Every area of study could benefit from a rational approach, i.e., from not falling to the temptations of exoticism, esotericism, obscurantism, or cultural relativism. Of course, acknowledging the universal validity of basic logical principles is only one presupposition for avoiding such traps. Critical common sense, i.e., empiricism and belief in the validity of every day causal laws (e.g., if you are standing naked in the rain, you are getting wet), are equally important.

Related publications

Reflections on the Usage of the Terms "logic" and "logical", *Journal of Chinese Philosophy* 18 (1): 73-87, 1991.

Equivalent Axioms of Aristotelian, or Traditional European, and Later Mohist Logic: An Argument in Favor of the Universality of Logic and Rationality, in Hans Lenk and Gregor Paul, eds., *Epistemological Issues in Classical Chinese Philosophy*, State University of New York Press, 1993.

Logic and Culture, in Shoun Hino and Toshihiro Wada, eds., *Three Mountains and Seven Rivers*, Delhi: Motilal Banarsidass, 2004, pp. 463-485.

Logic in Buddhist Texts, with Particular Reference to the Zhonglun, in *Horin* 11, München: iudicium, 2005, pp. 39-56.

(with Hans Lenk) Logic and Culture [...], in Hans Lenk, ed., *Comparative and Intercultural Philosophy: Proceedings of the IIP Conference Seoul 2008*, Berlin: LIT, 2009, pp. 183-210.

Ed., *Logic in Buddhist Scholasticism*, Nepal: Lumbini International Research Institute, 2015.

Glossary of People

Ordered by pinyin spelling

Ài Yuēsè 艾約瑟 Joseph Edkins, 1823-1905, British protestant missionary who lived in China for over 50 years, a philologist, author and translator of many books, including *Bianxue Qimeng*.

Bān Gù 班固 Pan Ku, 32-92, noted historian and author of the *Hànshū*《漢書》(Book of the Han Dynasty) *Hetucakra-ḍamaru*.

Bǎo Sēng 宝僧, 1969-, scholar in Tibetan Buddhist logic.

Chén Chéngzé 陈承泽, 1885-1922, linguist who studied in Japan, editor and translator for Shangwu Yinshuguan.

Chén Hànshēng 陳漢生 Chad Hansen, 1942-, American philosopher and long-term resident of Hong Kong, well-known for his application of the techniques of analytic philosophy to the study of Chinese philosophy and logic, professor at the University of Hong Kong.

Chén Nà 陳那 Dignāga, c.480 – c.540, Indian scholar and Buddhist logician, pioneer of *hetuvidyā*.

Chén Róngjié 陈荣捷 Wing-Tsit Chan, 1901-1994, Chinese-born philosopher who attended Harvard in the 1920s and later became a leading exponent of Chinese philosophy in the United States.

Chén Yínquè 陳寅恪, 1890-1969, historian, linguist and polymath, who studied in Europe in the 1920s; one of the four principal scholars of the Tsinghua academy of *guóxué*, also pronounced Chén Yínkè .

Chéng Zháoxiá 程朝侠, 1979-, scholar of Japanese Buddhism and *hetuvidyā* in Japan.

Chéng Zhōngyīng 成中英 Chung-Ying Cheng , 1935-, Chinese American philosopher and professor at the University of Hawaii.

Cuī Qīngtián 崔清田, 1936-, scholar of the history of Chinese logic and professor at Nankai University.

Dà Xī Zhù 大西祝 Ōnishi Hajime, 1864-1900, Japanese philosopher who studied in Germany; a leading exponent of western philosophy in modern

Japan.

Dèng Xī 鄧析 Têng Hsi, d.501 B.C.E., lawyer and philosopher associated with the School of Names, notorious for his ability to argue for both sides of an argument *liǎngkězhīshuō*《列子·力命》: 鄧析操兩可之說.

Dǒng Zhìtiě 董志铁, 1945-, scholar of the history of Chinese logic and professor of Beijing Normal University.

Fǎ Chēng 法稱 Dharmakīrti, fl. c. 7th century, Buddhist scholar and logician who significantly revised Dignāga's system of *hetuvidyā*, teacher at the Nālandā School and famous for his skill at debate.

Fāng Kèlì 方克立, 1938-, scholar of Chinese philosophy and professor at Nankai University and the Chinese Academy of Social Sciences.

Fāng Kètāo 方克濤 Chris Fraser, 1942-, Canadian scholar of early Chinese philosophy and professor of the University of Hong Kong.

Féng Yàomíng 馮耀明 Yiu-Ming Fung, professor at Hong Kong University of Science and Technology.

Féng Yǒulán 馮友蘭 Fung Yu-lan, 1895–1990, philosopher and professor at Tsinghua University and Peking University who studied in the U.S.A. and whose *A Short History of Chinese Philosophy*, 1948, made the study of Chinese philosophy accessible to the English-speaking world.

Fù Fànjì 傅汎際 Francisco Furtado, 1587–1653, Portuguese Jesuit, trained at the University of Coimbra, who with Li Zhizao translated western works of logic into Chinese, specifically the *Mínglǐtàn*《名理探》(Exploration of Names and Principles).

Fùchā Yēnà 富差耶那 Vātsyāyana, fl. c. 3rd century, Indian scholar believed to be the author of the *Kāmasūtra* and a commentary on the *Nyāyasūtra*.

Gě Bǎoluó 葛保罗 Gregor Paul, 1947-, German philosopher and professor at Karlsruhe Institute of Technology.

Gě Lìzhēn 葛立珍 Jane Geaney, American scholar of philosophy and literature in early China at the University of Richmond, Virginia.

Gé Ruìhàn 格瑞汉 A. C. Graham, 1919-1991, British sinologist and author of the seminal translation into English and analysis of the *Mojing: Later Mohist Logic Ethics and Science*, Chinese University Press, Hong Kong, 1978.

Gōngshū Pān 公输盤, 507–440 B.C.E., carpenter, engineer, and inventor, a contemporary of Mo Zi, and the patron saint of Chinese builders and contractors, also known as Lǔ Bān 魯班.

Gōngsūn Lóng 公孫龍 Kung-sun Lung, c. 325–250 B.C.E., dialectician famous for his discussion of "white horse not horse", associated with the School of Names and the *Gongsunlongzi*.

Gù Yánwǔ 顧炎武, 1613–1682, philologist and Confucian scholar known for detailed study of the language of ancient texts including phonology based on rhyming pairs.

Guō Zhànbō 郭湛波, 1905-?, historian of ideas, known for his *Xiānqín Biànxuéshǐ*《先秦辩学史》(History of pre-Qin Dialectics), Zhonghua Shuju, 1932.

Hán Fēi 韩非, 280–233, student of Xun Zi who synthesised the work of various legalist thinkers as the *Hanfeizi*.

Hé Mòyé 何莫邪 Christoph Harbsmeier, linguist and professor of Chinese at the University of Oslo, noted for his *Language and Logic*, volume 7(1) of *Science and Civilisation in China* and the *Thesaurus Linguae Sericae*.

Hú Màorú 胡茂如, translator of the book *Lunlixue* by Japanese scholar Ōnishi Hajime.

Hú Shì 胡適 Hu Shih, 1891-1962, influential scholar, writer, philosopher, and literary reformist, who studied at Columbia University under John Dewey; his dissertation *Xianqin Mingxueshi* was the first book on the history of Chinese logic in English.

Huáng Shàojī 黄紹箕, 1854-1908, a prominent Qing dynasty scholar who commented and corrected Sun Yirang's *Mozixiangu*.

Huì Shī 惠施, 380–305 B.C.E., logician, proto-scientist and intellectual sparring partner of Zhuang Zi, whose work is mostly lost.

Jiǎ Nǔzī 贾努兹 Janusz Chmielewski, 1916-1998, Polish sinologist and philosopher whose "Notes on Early Chinese Logic I to VIII" *Rocznik Orientalistyczny*, 1962-1969, was the first systematic western study of logical thought in China.

Jiǎng Wéiqiáo 蔣維喬, 1873-1958, Buddhist scholar, educator and philosopher, who taught logic and psychology.

Jiè Xián 戒賢 Śīlabhadra, 529–645, Buddhist monk and abbot of the Nālandā monastery, where he taught Xuán Zàng 玄奘.

Jīn Yuèlín 金岳霖, 1895-1984, philosopher and logician, studied in Columbia University, whose *Luoji* is one of the earliest books on modern logic in Chinese; founder of the philosophy department at Tsinghua University.

Jìngyǎn 淨眼, a student of Xuan Zang.

Jù Zōnglín 剧宗林, 1938-, scholar of Tibetan Buddhist logic and professor at Minzu University of China.

Kǒng Zī 孔子 Confucius, 551-479 B.C.E., founding figure of Chinese philosophy and iconic teacher whose main concerns were social and ethical, but whose doctrine of *zhèngmíng* is taken as the starting point for discussions of the relationship between language and reality.

Kuījī 窺基, 632–682, student of Xuan Zang and author of *Yinmingdashu*.

Lǎo Zǐ 老子 Lao Tzu, literally "old master", this is the name associated with the *Daodejing*, the founding text of Daoist.

Lǐ Rénbó 李仁伯 Michiel Leezenberg, Dutch philosopher and professor at the University of Amsterdam.

Lǐ Xiánzhōng 李賢中 Hsien-Chung Lee, 1957-, philosopher and professor at National Taiwan University.

Lǐ Yuēsè 李约瑟 Joseph Needham, 1900-1995, British biochemist and sinologist noted for his work on the history of science in China in particular as the main editor of *Science and Civilisation in China*, 27 volumes, Cambridge University Press, 1954-2008.

Lǐ Zhéxián 李哲賢 Jer-Shiarn Lee, 1953-, philosopher and professor at National Yunlin University of Science and Technology (Taiwan) .

Lǐ Zhīzǎo 李之藻, 1564-1630, translator of the *Minglitan* with Francisco Furtado.

Liáng Qǐchāo 梁啟超, 1873–1929, prominent scholar and reformist who had significant philological insights into the structure of the *Mojing*, whose connection to western logic he was one of the first to recognise; one of the four principal scholars of the Tsinghua academy of *guóxué*.

Liú Ān 劉安, c. 179–122 B.C.E., editor of the *Huainanzi* and *Chuci*.

Liú Fènróng 刘奋荣, 1975-, logician and professor at Tsinghua University.

Liú Péiyù 刘培育, 1940-, scholar of the history of Chinese logic and fellow of the Chinese Academy of Social Sciences.

Lóngshù 龍樹 Nāgārjuna, influential 2nd century Buddhist philosopher.

Lú Kǎsī 卢卡斯 Thierry Lucas, Belgian logician and professor at the Catholic University of Louvain (Louvain-la-Neuve).

Lǚ Shèng 魯勝, scholar of Jin period, known for his *Mobianzhuxu* in the *Jinshu*; he tried but failed to revive an interest in Mohist logic.

Luán Tiàofǔ 欒調甫, 1889-1972, scholar who debated with the Liang Qichao about his *Mojing Jiaoshi*.

Luō Dān 羅丹 Dan Robins, Canadian philosopher at the University of Hong Kong.

Lǚ Búwéi 呂不韋, 291–235 B.C.E., prime minister of the Qin state and sponsor of the *Lüshichunqiu*.

Lǚ Chéng 呂澂, 1896-1989, scholar of Buddhist philosophy and logic, and fellow of the Chinese Academy of Social Sciences.

Lǚ Shūxiāng 呂叔湘, 1904-1998, prominent linguist and fellow of the Chinese Academy of Social Sciences, studied at Oxford.

Mèng Zǐ 孟子 Mencius, 372 – 289 B.C.E., Confucian philosopher whose ideas are recorded in the *Mengzi*; he used the Mohists methods of reasoning to oppose them.

Mò Zǐ 墨子 Mo Tzu, c. 470 - c. 391 B.C.E., philosopher who defended his political and ethical ideas with reason and argument (uncharacteristic of the period), which lead to the development of "Mohist logic" by his followers.

Qínshǐhuáng 秦始皇, king of Qin and subsequently first emperor of China after his victories over all rival states, which thereby effectively ended both the Warring States period and the Hundred Schools, killing many philosophers and destroying almost all philosophical texts.

Rèn Bódé 任博德 Rens Bod, Dutch computational linguist and professor at the University of Amsterdam with an interest in the history of the humanities.

Shěn Jiànyīng 沈劍英, 1932-, scholar of Indian logic and professor at Huadong Normal University.

Shěn Yǒudǐng 沈有鼎, 1908-1989, philosopher, logician and author of *Mojing de Luojixue*, who studied at Harvard in the 1920s under Sheffer and Whitehead, in Germany under Jaspers and Heidegger, and later visited Oxford; he was professor at Tsinghua University, Peking University and a fellow of the Chinese Academy of Social Sciences.

Sīmǎ Qiān 司馬遷 Ssu-ma Chien, c. 145 or 135 - 86 B.C.E., historian and renowned author of the *Shiji*, the completion of which required him to choose castration over death when he supported the wrong friends at court.

Sòng Sàihuā 宋賽花, scholar of the history of Chinese logic and professor at the China Women's University.

Sūn Yíràng 孫詒讓, 1848-1908, influential editor and commentator on the *Mojing*, author of *Mozixiangu*.

Sūn Zhōngyuán 孙中原, 1938-, scholar of the history of Chinese logic and professor at Renmin University of China.

Tán Jièfǔ 譚戒甫, 1887-1974, professor at Wuhan university and scholar of pre-Qin philosophy, especially the *Mobian* and *Gongsunlongzi*, author of *Mòbiàn Fāwēi*《墨辯发微》, Beijing: Kexue Chubanshe, 1958.

Tāng Míngjūn 汤铭钧, 1982-, scholar of Buddhist logic and fellow of the Shanghai Academy of Social Sciences.

Wāng Diànjī 汪奠基, 1900-1979, logician and philosopher who compared western and Chinese history of logic; he studied in Paris in the 1920s and was fellow of the Chinese Academy of Social Sciences.

Wáng Guówéi 王國維, 1877-1927, philosopher and literary scholar who studied in Japan; he translated *Bianxue* and was one of the four principal scholars of the Tsinghua academy of *guóxué*.

Wáng Kèxǐ 王克喜, scholar of the history of Chinese logic and *yǔyánluóji*, and professor at Nanjing University.

Wáng Lì 王力, 1900-1986, prominent linguist who studied in Paris in the 1930s and was later professor at many Chinese universities.

Wáng Xiànjūn 王宪钧, 1910-1993, logician and professor at Tsinghua University and Peking University who studied with Gödel in Austria in the 1930s.

Wáng Zànyuán 王讚源, 1940-2011, author of *Mojing Zhengdu* and professor at Taiwan Normal University.

Wēn Gōngyí 温公颐, 1904-1996, philosopher and professor at Nankai University who wrote extensively on the history of Chinese logic.

Wén Guǐ 文軌, 615-c.675, monk in the Zhuāngyán 莊嚴 temple, student of Xuan Zang and author of the *Ruzhenglilun Wenguishu*.

Wǔ Fēibǎi 伍非百, 1890-1965, philosopher and author of *Mojing Jiegu*.

Wú Jiāguó 吴家国, 1936-, philosopher and professor at Beijing Normal University; one of the authors of *Putong Luoji*.

Wú Wénjùn 吴文俊, 1919-, prominent mathematician and fellow of the Chinese Academy of Sciences who studied in Strasbourg in the 1940s; also active in the history of Chinese mathematics.

Xiè Lìmín 谢立民 Jeremy Seligman, 1964-, British logician and philosopher, long-term resident of New Zealand.

Xú Zōngzé 徐宗澤, 1886-1947, historian of religion who wrote a preface to the 2nd edition of the *Minglitan*.

Xuán Zàng 玄奘, 602-664, monk, scholar, traveller and teacher, who studied in India and translated many Buddhist texts, including the logical texts *Zhenglimenlun* and *Ruzhenglilun*.

Xún Zi 荀子 Hsün Tzu, ca. 312–230 B.C.E., Confucian philosopher and head of the *Jìxià* 稷下 Academy, who used some of the concepts and methods of reasoning of the Mohists and whose essay on *zhèngmíng* is an important contribution to *míngxué*.

Yán Fù 嚴複, 1854-1921, scholar and translator of western books, include *Mule Mingxue* and *Mingxue Qianshuo*.

Yán Shīgǔ 顔師古, 581-645, Confucian scholar, philologist and historian.

Yáng Wǔjīn 杨武金, 1964-, scholar of the history of Chinese logic and professor at Renmin University of China.

Yǐnwén 尹文, 360-280 B.C.E., thinker whose ideas are believed to range over many topics; the book *Yinwenzi* purports to be a record of his views.

Zhái Jǐnchéng 翟锦程, 1964-, scholar of the history of Chinese logic and professor at Nankai University.

Zhāng Dōngsūn 張東蓀, 1886-1975, philosopher and government official who studied in Japan in the 1900s, known for the view that different cultures have different logics.

Zhāng Jiālóng 张家龙, 1938-, logician, philosopher and fellow of the Chinese Academy of Social Sciences.

Zhāng Shìzhāo 章士钊, 1881-1973, philosopher, government official and author of *Luojizhiyao*, who studied in Japan and the U.K. (Aberdeen) where he learned logic.

Zhāng Tàiyán 章太炎, 1868-1936, philologist, philosopher, journalist and revolutionary; author of *Guogulunheng*.

Zhāng Yán 张颜 Ian Johnston, Australian professor of neurosurgery, scholar of Chinese, and translator of poetry, medical texts and philosophy, in particular a complete bilingual annotated translation of *Mozi*, Hong Kong: The Chinese University Press, 2010.

Zhào Yuánrèn 赵元任, 1892-1982, linguist, poet, musician and polyglot who studied mathematics at Cornell and philosophy at Harvard; he was a professor at many leading universities in the U.S.A. and one of the four principal scholars of the Tsinghua academy of *guóxué*; he was the translator for Bertrand Russell during his visit to China.

Zhēn Dì 真谛 Paramārtha, 499-569, Indian monk, translator into Chinese of the works of Vasubandhu including the *Rushilun*.

Zhèng Wěihóng 郑伟宏, 1948-, scholar of Buddhist logic and professor at Fudan University.

Zhōu Lǐquán 周礼全, 1921-2008, philosopher and fellow of the Chinese Academy of Social Sciences; pioneer of *yǔyánluóji*.

Zhōu Shān 周山, scholar of history of Chinese logic and fellow of the Shanghai Academy of Social Sciences.

Zhōu Wényīng 周文英, 1928-2001, scholar in the history of Chinese logic and professor at Jiangxi College of Education.

Zhōu Yúnzhī 周云之, 1934-, scholar of the history of Chinese logic and fellow of the Chinese Academy of Social Sciences.

Zhū Zhìkǎi 朱志凯, philosopher and professor at Fudan University.

Zhuāng Zǐ 莊子 Chuang Tzu, 4th century B.C.E. thinker whose reflections on life language and the human condition are recorded in the *Zhuangzi*; with Lao Zi he is regarded as one of the founders of Daoism.

Glossary of People

Ordered by "other" name

Rens Bod 任博德 (Rèn Bódé), Dutch computational linguist and professor at the University of Amsterdam with an interest in the history of the humanities.

Chung-Ying Cheng 成中英 (Chéng Zhōngyīng), 1935-, Chinese American philosopher and professor at the University of Hawaii.

Janusz Chmielewski 贾努兹 (Jiǎ Nǔzī), 1916-1998, Polish sinologist and philosopher whose "Notes on Early Chinese Logic I to VIII" *Rocznik Orientalistyczny*, 1962-1969, was the first systematic western study of logical thought in China.

Dharmakīrti 法稱 (Fǎ Chēng), fl. c. 7th century, Buddhist scholar and logician who significantly revised Dignāga's system of *hetuvidyā*, teacher at the Nālandā School and famous for his skill at debate.

Dignāga 陳那 (Chén Nà), c. 480 – c. 540, Indian scholar and Buddhist logician, pioneer of *hetuvidyā*.

Joseph Edkins 艾約瑟 (Ài Yuēsè), 1823-1905, British protestant missionary who lived in China for over 50 years, a philologist, author and translator of many books, including *Bianxue Qimeng*.

Chris Fraser 方克濤 (Fāng Kètāo), 1942-, Canadian scholar of early Chinese philosophy and professor of the University of Hong Kong.

Yiu-Ming Fung 馮耀明 (Féng Yàomíng), professor at Hong Kong University of Science and Technology.

Francisco Furtado 傅汎際 (Fù Fànjì), 1587–1653, Portuguese Jesuit, trained at the University of Coimbra, who with Li Zhizao translated western works of logic into Chinese, specifically the *Mínglǐtàn*《名理探》(Exploration of Names and Principles).

Jane Geaney 葛立珍 (Gě Lìzhēn), American scholar of philosophy and literature in early China at the University of Richmond, Virginia.

A. C. Graham 格瑞汉 (Gé Ruìhàn), 1919-1991, British sinologist and author of the seminal translation into English and analysis of the *Mojing*: *Later Mohist Logic Ethics and Science*, Chinese University Press, Hong Kong, 1978.

Chad Hansen 陳漢生 (Chén Hànshēng), 1942-, American philosopher and long-term resident of Hong Kong, well-known for his application of the techniques of analytic philosophy to the study of Chinese philosophy and logic, professor at the University of Hong Kong.

Christoph Harbsmeier 何莫邪 (Hé Mòyé), linguist and professor of Chinese at the University of Oslo, noted for his *Language and Logic*, volume 7(1) of *Science and Civilisation in China* and the *Thesaurus Linguae Sericae*.

Ian Johnston 张颜 (Zhāng Yán), Australian professor of neurosurgery, scholar of Chinese, and translator of poetry, medical texts and philosophy, in particular a complete bilingual annotated translation of *Mozi*, Hong Kong: The Chinese University Press, 2010.

Hsien-Chung Lee 李賢中 (Lǐ Xiánzhōng), 1957-, philosopher and professor at National Taiwan University.

Jer-Shiarn Lee 李哲賢 (Lǐ Zhéxián), 1953-, philosopher and professor at National Yunlin University of Science and Technology (Taiwan).

Michiel Leezenberg 李仁伯 (Lǐ Rénbó), Dutch philosopher and professor at the University of Amsterdam.

Thierry Lucas 卢卡斯 (Lú Kǎsī), Belgian logician and professor at the Catholic University of Louvain (Louvain-la-Neuve).

Nāgārjuna 龍樹 (Lóngshù), influential 2nd century Buddhist philosopher.

Joseph Needham 李约瑟 (Lǐ Yuēsè), 1900-1995, British biochemist and sinologist noted for his work on the history of science in China in particular as the main editor of *Science and Civilisation in China*, 27 volumes, Cambridge University Press, 1954-2008.

Ōnishi Hajime 大西祝 (Dà Xī Zhù), 1864-1900, Japanese philosopher who studied in Germany; a leading exponent of western philosophy in modern Japan.

Paramārtha 真諦 (Zhēn Dì), 499-569, Indian monk, translator into Chinese of the works of Vasubandhu including the *Rushilun*.

Gregor Paul 葛保罗 (Gě Bǎoluó), 1947-, German philosopher and professor at Karlsruhe Institute of Technology.

Dan Robins 羅丹 (Luō Dān), Canadian philosopher at the University of Hong Kong.

Jeremy Seligman 谢立民 (Xiè Lìmín), 1964-, British logician and philosopher, long-term resident of New Zealand.

Śīlabhadra 戒賢 (Jiè Xián), 529–645, Buddhist monk and abbot of the Nālandā monastery, where he taught Xuán Zàng 玄奘.

Vātsyāyana 富差耶那 (Fùchā Yēnà), fl. c. 3rd century, Indian scholar believed to be the author of the *Kāmasūtra* and a commentary on the *Nyāyasūtra*.

Glossary of Texts

Báimǎlùn《白馬論》(White Horse Discourse), essay by Gongsun Long containing arguments for and against the claim *báimǎfēimǎ* 白馬非馬 (white horse not horse).

Biànjīng《辯經》(Classic of Disputation), alternative name for *Mojing* or *Mobian*, used by Lu Sheng.

Biànxué《辯學》(Study of Disputation), translation by Wang Guowei of the textbook *Elementary Lessons on Logic* by W. S. Jevons, published in China in 1908.

Biànxué Qǐméng《辯學啟蒙》(Primer in the Study of Disputation), translation by Joseph Edkins of the volume *Logic* by W. S. Jevons in the series *Science Primers*, published in China in 1886, later re-translated by Yan Fu as *Mingxue Qianshuo*.

Chǔcí《楚辭》(Ch'u-tz'u, Songs of Chu), collection of poems from the Warring States and Han dynasty, compiled by Liu An.

Dàodéjīng《道德經》(Tao-te-ching, Classic of Way and Power/ Virtue), mid-to-late Warring States philosophical text traditionally attributed to Lao Zi, the text most closely associated with Daoism and the Daoist religion.

Dàozàng《道藏》(Tao-tsang, Daoist Canon), Collection of 1476 texts, assembled by daoist monks c. 400, and containing the oldest known version of the *Mobian*.

Dàqǔ《大取》(Great Pick), chapter 44 of the *Mozi* and part of the *Mobian*, also translated as "Major Illustrations".

Dèngxīzǐ《鄧析子》(Works of Deng Xi), text of doubtful authenticity.

Ěryǎ《爾雅》(Approaching Eloquence), 3rd century B.C.E., oldest known Chinese book of word glosses.

Fāngbiànxīnlùn《方便心論》(Upāyakauśalyahṛdaya śāstra, On the Heart of Skilful Means), 5th century translation of an Indian text controversially attributed to Nāgārjuna.

Fēigōng《非攻》(Against War), chapters of the *Mozi* containing arguments against the use of military power by a stronger state against a weaker one.

Gōngsūnlóngzǐ《公孫龍子》(Works of Gongsun Long), text containing five essays attributed to Gongsun Long (*Baimalun, Zhiwulun, Tongbianlun, Jianbailun* and *Mingshilun*) and a more general chapter *Jifu* about his life and opinions; according to A. C. Graham only the *Baimalun* and *Zhiwulun* are authentic.

Guógùlùnhéng《國故論衡》(Discussion of the Chinese Classics), by Zhang Taiyan published in 1910; a study of philology, style, literary history and philosophy in the classics.

Hánfēizǐ《韓非子》(Works of Han Fei), treatise in political philosophy combining the views of early legalist thinkers with advice for rulers and ministers alike; it contains many examples of argumentation and coins the term "*máodùn* 矛盾" (contradiction); it also contains the first commentary on the *Daodejing*.

Huáinánzǐ《淮南子》(Works of the Masters of Huainan), 2nd century B.C.E. compendium of Chinese philosophy, compiled by Liu An.

Huángdìnèijīng《黃帝內經》(Internal Classic of the Yellow Emperor), late Warring States or early Han dynasty text by unknown authors using an analogical approach to medical reasoning via, for example, the concepts of *yīnyáng* and *wǔxíng*.

Jiānbáilùn《堅白論》(On Hard and White), chapter of the *Gongsunlongzi* concerning the concept of *jiānbái* but of doubtful authenticity.

Jíliàng《集量》(Pramāṇasamuccaya, Compendium on Means of Valid Cognition), central text on logic and epistemology by Dignāga.

Jīngshàng《經上》(Canons A), chapter 40 of the *Mozi* and part of the *Mojing*, notable for its precise and concise definition-like statements.

Jīngshuōshàng《經說上》(Explanations of the Canons A), chapter 42 of the *Mozi* and part of the *Mojing*, consisting of explanations of the *Jingshang*.

Jīngshuōxià《經說下》(Explanations of the Canons B), chapter 43 of the *Mozi* and part of the *Mojing*, consisting of explanations of the *Jingxia*.

Jīngxià《經下》(Canons B), chapter 41 of the *Mozi* and part of the *Mojing*, notable for its clear formulation of technical concepts and claims.

Jìnshū《晉書》(Book of Jin), official record of the Jin dynasty compiled in 648, containing the *Mobianzhuxu*.

Lùnlǐxué《論理學》(Study of Rational Discourse), translation by Hu Maoru of the logic book by Ōnishi Hajime, published in 1906.

Lùnlǐxué Jiǎngyì《論理學講義》(Lecture Notes on the Study of Rational Discourse), by Jiang Weiqiao, Shangwu Yinshuguan, 1924.

Lúnyǔ《論語》(Analects), record of sayings attributed to Confucius and his students, one of the Four Books that became the core of literary education throughout Chinese imperial history.

Luóji《邏輯》(Logic), by Jin Yuelin, Shangwu Yinshuguan, 1936; one of the earliest books on modern symbolic logic in Chinese.

Luójizhǐyào《邏輯指要》(Outline of Logic), first written in 1917 by Zhang Shizhao, officially published at the Chongqing Zhongxin Yinshuguan in 1943; a new edition was published by Sanlian Shudian in 1959.

Lǔshìchūnqiū《呂氏春秋》(Spring and Autumn Annals of Mr. Lü), late Warring States compilation of philosophical texts, collected by Lü Buwei.

Mǎshìwéntōng《馬氏文通》(Grammar of Mr. Ma), the first systematic work on Chinese grammar, edited by Ma Jianzhong and published by Shangwu Yinshuguan in 1898.

Mèngzǐ《孟子》(Works of Mencius), record of the teaching and dialogues of Mencius and one of the Four Books.

Mínglǐtàn《名理探》(Exploration of Names and Principles), translation by Li Zhizao and Francisco Furtado of *In universam dialecticam*, the Coimbra commentary on Aristotle, published in Hangzhou in the 1630s.

Míngshílùn《名實論》(On Names and Objects), chapter of the *Gongsunlongzi*.

Míngxué Qiǎnshuō《名學淺說》(Introduction to the Study of Names), translation by Yan Fu of the logic textbook by W. S. Jevons, previously translated as *Bianxue Qimeng*.

Mòbiàn《墨辯》(Dialetical Chapters of the *Mozi*), the six chapters of the *Mozi* that concern the most abstract theoretic thought of the Mohist: the four chapters of the *Mojing* together with the *Daqu* and *Xiaoqu*.

Mòbiànzhùxù《墨辯注序》(Preface to the Mohist Dialectical Chapters), short preface in the *Jinshu* by Lu Sheng.

Mòjīng《墨經》(Mohist Canons), the four chapters of the *Mozi* containing a definition-like systematisation of Mohist thought: *Jingshang*, *Jingxia*, *Jingshuoshang*, and *Jingshuoxia*; Chinese scholars also include in this list the remaining two chapters of the *Mobian*.

Mòjīng de Luójíxué《墨经的逻辑学》(Logic of the *Mojing*), by Shen Youding, published as a series of articles in *Guangming Ribao* from 1954-55 and later as a book, published by Zhongguo Shehuikexue Chubanshe in 1980.

Mòjīng Jiàoshì《墨經校釋》(Corrections and Interpretation of the Mohist Canons), by Liang Qichao, Shangwu Yinshuguan, 1922.

Mòjīng Jiěgù《墨經解故》(Interpretation of the Mohist Canons), by Wu Feibai, Zhongguo Daxue Chenguangshe, 1922.

Mòzǐ《墨子》(Works of Mo Zi), collection of the Mohist school, now in 53 chapters, including a record of the thoughts of Mo Zi himself and the Later Mohist *Mobian*.

Mòzǐxuéàn《墨子學案》(Critical Survey of the *Mozi*), by Liang Qichao, published by Shangwu Yinshuguan in 1921.

Mòzǐxiángǔ 《墨子閒詁》 (Critical Edition of the *Mozi*), by Sun Yirang, published by Shangwu Yinshuguan in 1935.

Mùlè Míngxué 《穆勒名學》 (A System of Logic), translation by Yan Fu of *A System of Logic* by John Stuart Mill, published by Shangwu Yinshuguan in 1905.

Nányī 《難一》 (Criticisms 1), chapter of the *Hanfeizi* containing advice to ministers on how to argue and survive politically.

Pǔtōng Luójí 《普通逻辑》 (Common Logic), widely used logic textbook, in many editions, first published in 1982, taken to be a definitive representation of western traditional logic.

Qiūshuǐ 《秋水》 (Autumn Floods), chapter of the *Zhuangzi* containing the Happy Fish story of debate between Zhuang Zi and Hui Shi.

Qíwùlùn 《齊物論》 (On Equalising Things), chapter of the *Zhuangzi* containing the most explicitly analytical passages.

Rúshílùn 《如實論》 (Tarkaśāstra, On Reasoning), translation by Zhen Di of a text about argumentation by Vasubandhu.

Rùzhènglǐlùn 《入正理論》 (Nyāyapraveśa, Primer on Logic), translation by Xuan Zang of the text by Śaṅkarasvāmin on Dignāga's *hetuvidyā*.

Rùzhènglǐlùn Hòushū 《入正理論後疏》 (Commentary on the Final Part of the Nyāyapraveśa), by Jingyan.

Rùzhènglǐlùn Luèchāo 《入正理論略抄》 (Commentary on the Nyāyapraveśa), by Jingyan.

Rùzhènglǐlùn Wénguǐshū 《入正理論文軌疏》 (Wen Gui's Commentary on the Nyāyapraveśa), also known as the *Zhuāngyánshū* 莊嚴疏, named after Wen Gui's temple.

Shǐjì 《史記》 (Shih-chi, Records of the Grand Historian), first substantial history of China from legendary beginnings to Emperor Wu of Han and the main textual source about the lives of the Hundred Schools philosophers, completed in 91 B.C.E. by Sima Qian about 30 years after it was started by his father.

Shījīng 《詩經》 (Shih-ching, Book of Odes), oldest existing collection of Chinese poetry comprising 305 works dating from the early Zhou (11th to 7th centuries B.C.E.) and part of the literary canon for all Chinese scholars even in pre-Qin times.

Shíyì 《十翼》 (Ten Wings), another name for *Yizhuan*.

Tiānxià 《天下》 (In the World), chapter of the *Zhuangzi* comprising the first history of philosophy in China and including important material on Hui Shi and others.

Tōngbiànlùn《通變論》(On Understanding Change), chapter of the *Gongsunlongzi* concerning the logic of kinds but of doubtful authenticity.

Xiānqín Biànxuéshǐ《先秦辯學史》(History of Pre-Qin Argumentation), by Guo Zhanbo published by Zhonghua Shuju in 1932.

Xiānqín Míngxuéshǐ《先秦名學史》(The Development of the Logical Method in Ancient China), by Hu Shi, originally a dissertation from 1917, published in English in 1922 by Shanghai Yadong Tushuguan, and finally in Chinese in 1983 by Shanghai Xuelin Chubanshe.

Xiǎoqǔ《小取》(Hsiao-ch'ü, Small Pick), chapter 45 of the *Mobian*, containing a general discussion of logical themes and many examples of reasoning patterns, also translated as "Minor Illustrations".

Xúnzi《荀子》(Hsün-tzu, Works of Xun Zi), Confucian text compiled in approx. 250 B.C.E.and attributed to the scholar Xun Zi, who developed the theory of *zhèngmíng*.

Yìjīng《易經》(I-ching, Book of Changes), the *Zhouyi* divination text together with the *Yizhuan* commentaries.

Yīnlúnlùn《因輪論》(Hetucakra-ḍamaru, On the Wheel of Reason), text on the classification of logically correct and incorrect reasons, by Dignāga, lost but preserved in Tibetan and finally translated into Chinese by Lü Cheng in the 20th century.

Yīnmíngdàshū《因明大疏》(Great Exegesis of *Yinming*), by Kuiji, an influential commentary on the *Ruzhenglilun*.

Yīnmíngdàshū Shānzhù《因明大疏刪注》(Great Exegesis of *Yinming*: Abridged with Commentary), by Xiong Shili, first published at Shangwu Yinshuguan in 1929, later published at Shanghai Shudian Chubanshe in 2008.

Yǐnwénzǐ《尹文子》(Works of Yinwen), purported to be the work of Yinwen but of doubtful authenticity.

Yìzhuàn《易傳》(Narratives of the Changes), the ten lengthy texts that accompany the divination text *Zhouyi* in the *Yijing*, traditionally attributed to Confucius; also known as *Shiyi*.

Yújiā Shīdìlùn《瑜伽師地論》(Yogācārabhūmi-śāstra, Discourse on the Stages of Yogic Practice), 7th century translation by Xuan Zang of the Yogacara Buddhist text, composed in between 300 and 350.

Zhànguócè《戰國策》(Chan-kuots'e, Legends of the Warring States), history of the Warring States focussing on strategy and political intrigue.

Zhènglǐménlùn《正理門論》(Nyāyamukha, Gateway to Logic), translation by Xuan Zang in 649 of Dignāga's primary text on *hetuvidyā*.

Zhèngmíng《正名》(Rectification of Names), chapter of the *Xunzi*, and the main Confucian text on logical topics.

Zhǐwùlùn《指物論》(On Pointing at Things), chapter of the *Gongsunlongzi* concerning the relationship between names and things but of doubtful authenticity.

Zhōubì Suànjīng《周髀算經》(Arithmetical Classic of the Zhou Gnomon), one of the oldest and most famous Chinese mathematical texts, ostensibly from the early Zhou dynasty but compiled in the 1st century B.C.E..

Zhōuyì《周易》(Chou-i, Zhou Book of Changes), early Zhou divinatory text in which lines of — and -- are combined in combinations of 6 to produce 64 symbols, and brief lines of interpretation; later combined with a series of commentaries in the *Yijing*.

Zhuāngzǐ《莊子》(Chuang-tzu, Works of Zhuang Zi), late Warring States text attributed to Zhuang Zi, together with the *Daodejing* one the founding text of Daoism, but also containing logically significant material, especially in the *Qiwulun*, *Qiushui* and *Tianxia* chapters.

Zǐmòzǐ Xuéshuō《子墨子學說》(Doctrines of Mo Zi), by Liang Qichao, published in the biweekly periodical Xinmin Congbao in 1904.

Glossary of Technical Terms

bāguà 八卦 (trigrams), the 8 combinations of sequences of three *yáo* 爻 (line) each of which may be *yīn* or *yáng*, representing aspects of the natural world: sky, earth, wind, thunder, water, fire, mountain, marsh; the basis of the divinatory system *Zhouyi* and its interpretation as the *Yijing*.

bǎijiā 百家 (Hundred Schools), flourishing of intellectual thought in the pre-Qin period, somewhat inaccurately portrayed as distinct "schools" by Han dynasty scholars and thereafter.

báimǎfēimǎ 白馬非馬 (white horse not horse), thesis defended by Gongsun Long.

bèi 誖 (self-contradictory/perverse), contrary to accepted practice; in logical contexts it can have the more specific meaning of self-contradictory, also written as 悖 outside the *Mojing*.

biétóngyì 別同異 (distinguishing comparison), literally "distinguishing similarity and difference", paired with *hétóngyì* 合同異 (unifying comparison).

bǐ 彼 (that), paired with *cǐ* 此 (this).

bì 必 (necessarily), modal term with a range of uses including entailment.

bǐliàng 比量 (*ānumāna*, inferential knowledge), *yīnmíng* term.

bìrándìdéchū 必然地得出 (necessarily infer), modern term, taken by certain Chinese scholars as the hallmark of logic.

biàn 辯 (disputation), also interpreted as "distinction-drawing", one of the Mohist *míngcíshuōbiàn*.

biànxué 辯學 (study of disputation), used as a translation for "logic" in the later 19th by Joseph Edkins and early in the 20th century by Wang Guowei.

biànzhě 辯者 (dialectician), those skilled in *biàn* 辯 (disputation), who were poorly regarded in the Chinese tradition because of a reputation for sophistry as represented by the *biànzhě èrshíyīshì*.

biànzhě èrshíyīshì 辯者二十一事 (dialecticians' 21 theses), the 21 propositions held by various *biànzhě*, mentioned in the *Tianxia* chapter of *Zhuangzi*.

bùkě 不可 (inadmissible), opposite of *kě* 可 (admissible).

bùmáodùnlǜ 不矛盾律 (Law of Non-contradiction), translation of the western concept, considered as one of the basic laws of logic according to *Putong Luoji*.

bùrán 不然 (is not so), not conforming to reality, contrasting with *rán* 然 (is so).

chōngzúlǐyóulǜ 充足理由律 (Principle of Sufficient Reason), translation of the western concept, considered as one of the basic laws of logic according to some versions of *Putong Luoji*.

cí 辭 (phrase), also interpreted as "statement" or "proposition", one of the Mohist *míngcíshuōbiàn*.

cǐ 此 (this), paired with *bǐ* 彼 (that).

dàgù 大故 (major cause), term apparently introduced in the *Mojing* and contrasted with *xiǎogù* 小故 (minor cause): "When there is a *dàgù*, something is necessarily so; when there is not, something is necessarily not so".

dámíng 達名 (unrestricted name), one of the three types of name, according to the *Mojing*; the others are *lèimíng* and *sīmíng*.

dàn 彈 (slingshot), mentioned by Hui Shi as an obscure word for the purpose of illustrating the method of analogy.

dào 道 (Tao, way), central concept in Chinese philosophy.

dàojiā 道家 (Taoist, Daoist), literally "the school of *dào*", those associated with the views expressed in *Daodejing* and *Zhuangzi*, one of the *bǎijiā* 百家 (Hundred Schools).

dàoxué 道學 (Taoism, Daoism), the study of *dào* and Daoist texts, not to be confused with *dàojiào* 道教 (Daoist religion).

duòfù 墮負 (*nigrahastānaprāta*, falling into failure), *yīnmíng* term for situations leading to failure in argumentation.

fǎ 法 (standard), central Mohist term for a standard of correctness with the degree of objectivity, clarity and universal accessibility provided by a carpenter's tools, e.g. a plum line to determine verticality; used in early Mohist social philosophy and developed further in the *Mojing*, also by the legalists in the narrower sense of "law".

fǎjiā 法家 (legalist), one of the Hundred Schools concerned with the concept of law and other aspects of government that do not rely on the virtue of rulers, whose thought is synthesised in the *Hanfeizi*.

fēi 非 (not/is not), nominal negation, extended to "is not this", and so more abstractly "incorrect", contrasting with *shì* 是 (this/is this).

fójiàoluóji 佛教逻辑 (Buddhist logic), modern Chinese term for logical thought arising from the Buddhist tradition, including that originating in India and developed in China and elsewhere, practically synonymous with *yīnmíng* 因明 (*hetuvidyā*, theory of reason).

fóxué 佛學 (Buddhism), study of Buddhist thought and texts.

gǎnxìngsīwéi 感性思维 (emotional thinking), Chinese Marxist term for thinking determined by the senses or feelings, often contrasted with *lǐxìngsīwéi* 理性思维 (rational thinking).

gù 故 (reason/cause), this is a term that indicates some kind of implication without a clear distinction between reason and cause; it also means "therefore".

guàyáocí 卦爻辭 (line statements), interpretations given to the individual lines of the *bāguà*.

guīmiùfǎ 归谬法 (reductio ad absurdum), modern Chinese term translating the western concept.

guóxué 國學 (Chinese classical studies), used in the late Qing dynasty to refer to the sum of Chinese traditional knowledge and culture in contrast to that being introduced from outside, becoming popular again in recent times with the establishment of a *guóxuéyuàn* 国学院 (academy of guoxue) in most major Chinese universities.

hé 合 (*upanaya*, application), *yīnmíng* term for the 4th member of the *wǔzhīzuòfǎ* (five-membered argument).

hétóngyì 合同異 (unifying comparison), literally "unifying similarity and difference", paired with *biétóngyì* 別同異 (distinguishing comparison).

huǐyùzhīmíng 毀譽之名 (appraisal name), term from the *Yinwenzi* for names involving subjective evaluation.

jiānbái 堅白 (hard-white), term for combinations, like hardness and whiteness, that can "fill" each other, discussed in the *Mobian* and *Gongsunlongzi*.

jié 结 (*nigamana*, conclusion), *yīnmíng* term for the 5th member of the *wǔzhīzuòfǎ* (five-membered argument).

kě 可 (admissible), term of approval for an issue under debate.

kuàngwèizhīmíng 況謂之名 (contextual name), names concerning a subject's evaluative reaction to an object, such as love and disgust, from the *Yinwenzi*.

lèi 類 (kind), central concept of early Chinese philosophy and especially Mohist thought, defined in terms of similarity and difference, and the basis of *tuīlèi* 推類 (kind-based inference).

lèimíng 類名 (classifying name), one of the three types of name, according to the *Mojing*; the others are *dámíng* and *sīmíng*.

lèitóng 類同 (sameness of kind), the basis for *tuīlèi* 推類 (kind-based inference).

lèituī 類推 (kind-based inference), also known as *tuīlèi*.

lǐ 理 (principle), central metaphysical concept of neo-Confucianism, but in the pre-Qin period it has a less technical meaning.

lǐ 禮 (ritual propriety), central concept of Confucian philosophy including social etiquette, ritual performance and role-specific norms such as those of being a father or ruler, son or minister.

lìcí 立辭 (hold a proposition), within the context of a debate, the proposition is defendable: to hold a proposition without being clear about how it arises is stupid 《墨子・大取》: 立辭而不明於其所生（忘）*{妄} 也.

líjiānbái 離堅白 (separating hard from white), view that qualities such as hardness and whiteness that pervade an object can nonetheless be "separated", attributed to Gongsun Long, opposite to the Mohist *yíngjiānbái* 盈堅白.

lìwùshíshì 曆物十事 (Huishi's 10 theses), sequence of ten propositions attributed to Hui Shi in the *Tianxia* chapter of *Zhuangzi*.

lǐzéxué 理則學 (study of rational principles), another translation of "logic" first used in 1918 by Sūn Yìxiān 孫逸仙 (Sun Yat-sen).

liánzhūtǐ 連珠體 (genre of thread beads), literary genre appearing after the Han dynasty, in which argumentation is disguised by means of various conventional devices within a fixed form.

liùshísìguà 六十四卦 (hexagrams), 64 combinations of pairs of *bāguà*, each of which is given an interpretation in the *Zhouyi*.

lǐxìngsīwéi 理性思维 (rational thinking), Chinese Marxist term for thinking determined by the intellect, often contrasted with *gǎnxìngsīwéi* 感性思维 (emotional thinking).

lùnlǐxué 論理學 (study of rational discourse), Japanese term for "logic" from 1869, used in translation to Chinese from 1898.

luójí 逻辑 (logic), phonetic loan from English, introduced by Yan Fu in his *Mule Mingxue* and proposed as the preferred term by Zhang Shizhao in his *Lùn Fānyì Míngyì* 《論翻譯名義》(On the translation of names and meaning) *Kouk Fung Po*, Shanghai, 1910.

máodùn 矛盾 (contradiction), literally "spear" and "shield", with the meaning of contradiction deriving from a story in *Hanfeizi*.

míng 名 (name), also controversially interpreted as "concept", one of the Mohist *míngcíshuōbiàn*, of central interest both in its relation to *shí* 實 and in the topic of *zhèngmíng* 正名.

míngbiàn 名辯 (names and argument), topic of *míngbiànxué*.

míngbiànxué 名辯學 (study of names and argument), combination of *míngxué* 名學 and *biànxué* 辯學 used by modern scholars to refer to discussions of logical thought in ancient China.

míngcíshuōbiàn 名辭說辯 (logico-linguistic categories), literally "name, phrase, explanation, disputation", a sequence of categories discussed in the *Mojing* and *Xunzi*.

míngjiā 名家 (School of Names), those pre-Qin thinkers concerned with discussions about language, such as Gongsun Long, Deng Xi and Hui Shi, one of the Hundred Schools.

mínglǐ 名理 (names and reasons), term for "logic" dating from 1631 and used in the *Minglitan*.

mínglǐxué 名理學 (study of names and reasons), see *mínglǐ*.

mìngwùzhīmíng 命物之名 (name for things), names based on external features of objects, which can only be grasped through senses such as sight or touch, from the *Yinwenzi*.

míngxué 名學 (study of names), term for "logic" dating from 1895 (Yan Fu).

mòbiàn 墨辯 (Mohist disputation), later Mohist theory of *biàn* 辯 (disputation).

mòjiā 墨家 (Mohist), followers of the teachings of Mo Zi, flourishing in the 5th to 3rd centuries B.C.E. but extinct from the Qin dynasty; the later members of this school were the authors of the *Mobian* and are often referred to as "Later Mohists"; one of the Hundred Schools.

mòxué 墨學 (Mohism), study of Mohist texts and ideas.

móu 侔 (parallelizing), one of the *pìmóuyuántuī*, "comparing propositions and letting all proceed" 《墨子・小取》: 比辭而俱行也.

páizhōnglǜ 排中律 (Law of the Excluded Middle), translation of the western concept, considered as one of the basic laws of logic according to *Putong Luoji*.

pì 譬 (analogy), also the method of reasoning by analogy.

pì 辟 (illustrating), one of the *pìmóuyuántuī*, "referring to other things in order to clarify one's own case" 《墨子・小取》: 辟也者舉他物而以明之也.

pìmóuyuántuī 辟侔援推 (four modes of reasoning), discussed at the beginning of *Mozi Xiaoqu*.

pǔtōngluójí 普通逻辑 (common logic), syllabus for logic instruction in most Chinese universities, derived from the Russian education system, and including basic logic laws, concepts, judgements, inference, and argumentation, and occasionally induction but no discussion of probability or mathematical logic.

qīnzhī 親知 (experiential knowledge), one of the three types of knowledge discussed in the *Mojing*; the others are *shuōzhī* and *wénzhī*.

rán 然 (is so), conforming to reality, contrasting with *bùrán* 不然.

rújiā 儒家 (Confucian), one of the *bǎijiā* 百家 (Hundred Schools), literally the "school of ritual specialists" of which Confucius was one, but later identified with those following his teachings such as Mencius, Xun Zi and the many scholars that followed them.

rúxué 儒學 (Confucianism), the study of Confucian texts and ideas.

sānwùlùnshì 三物論式 (form of three things), modern Chinese term for the form of argumentation proposed in the *Mojing* involving three things: *gù* 故 (reason/cause), *lǐ* 理 (principle) and *lèi* 類 (kind).

sānzhīlùnshì 三支論式 (*trayāvayava*, form of three branches), *yīnmíng* term for the form of argumentation proposed by Dignāga as an improvement of the *wǔzhīzuòfǎ* 五支作法 (*pañcāvayava*, five-membered argument), composed of *zōng* 宗 (*pakṣa*, thesis), *yīn* 因 (*hetu*, reason) and *yù* 喻 (*dṛṣṭānta*, example).

sānzhǒngbǐliàng 三种比量 (*trividham anumānam*, three types of reasoning), *yīnmíng* term for three ways of gaining knowledge from inference.

shí 實 (object), also interpreted as "reality" or more neutrally "stuff", what language talks about, understood in relation to *míng* 名 (name).

shì 是 (this/ is this), literally "this" but with an extended use as an affirmation "is this" and so more abstractly "correct", contrasting with *fēi* 非.

shìfēi 是非 (this/not-this), the distinction between *shì* 是 (correct) and *fēi* 非 (incorrect) classification, e.g. of whether something is or is not an ox.

shuō 說 (reasoning), also interpreted as "inference" or "explanation", one of the *míngcíshuōbiàn* 名辭說辯.

shuōzhī 說知 (inferential knowledge), one of the three types of knowledge discussed in the *Mojing*; the others are *qīnzhī* and *wénzhī*.

sīmíng 私名 (private name), one of the three types of name, according to the *Mojing*; the others are *lèimíng* and *dámíng*.

tánbiàn 談辯 (argumentation), used, but only once, by Mo Zi: "one who can argue argues, one who tells stories tells stories"《墨子・耕柱》: 能談辯者談辯，能說書者說書.

tónglèixiāngtuī 同類相推 (inference from sameness of kind), inference from different kinds is inappropriate, e.g. concerning the length of a piece of wood and the night《墨子・經說下》: 木與夜孰長 (B6).

tóngpǐn 同品 (*sapakṣa*, similar instance), *yīnmíng* term for things similar to the subject of the thesis in the sense that they possess the property attributed in the *zōng* (thesis); for a *tóngpǐn* to qualify as a *tóngyù* (positive example) it must also possess the property attributed in the *yīn* (reason).

tóngyù 同喻 (*sādharmyadṛṣṭānta*, positive example), *yīnmíng* term for one of the two parts of *yù* (example); the other part of *yù* (example) is *yìyù* (negative example).

tuī 推 (inferring), one of the *pìmóuyuántuī*, a method by which one uses one's opponents own ideas to refute him, sometimes associated with the method of *reductio ad absurdum*.

tuīlèi 推類 (kind-based inference), the central Mohist conception of inference, also known as *lèituī* 類推 (kind-based inference).

wànwù 萬物 (ten thousand things), referring to all that is part of the natural world.

wéishíbǐliàng 唯识比量 (*vijñāptimātrānumāna*, argument for mere-consciousness), Xuan Zang's argument for the Yogācāra tenet that the object of vision is not separate from visual consciousness.

wéihūqíbǐcǐ 唯乎其彼此 (Law of Identity), translation of the western concept, considered as one of the basic laws of logic according to *Putong Luoji*.

wénzhī 聞知 (testimonial knowledge), one of the three types of knowledge discussed in the *Mojing*; the others are *qīnzhī* and *shuōzhī*.

wényán 文言 (classical Chinese), literary language used from the pre-Qin period up until the reforms of the 20th century; despite significant changes, the older forms remained intelligible to scholars and officials throughout; also known as *gǔwén* 古文 and *gǔhànyǔ* 古漢語.

wú 無 (lacks), contrasting with *yǒu* 有.

wùnán 誤難 (*jāti*, erroneous refutation), *yīnmíng* term for erroneous refutation.

wǔxíng 五行 (five phases), basic aspects of change, also known as the five elements: *mù* 木 (wood), *huǒ* 火 (fire), *tǔ* 土 (earth), *jīn* 金 (metal) and *shuǐ* 水 (water).

wǔzhīzuòfǎ 五支作法 (*pañcāvayava*, five-membered argument), *nyāya* term for a form of inference in five steps: *zōng* 宗 (*pakṣa*, thesis), *yīn* 因 (*hetu*, reason), *yù* 喻 (*dṛṣṭānta*, example), *hé* 合 (*upanaya*, application), *jié* 结 (*nigamana*, conclusion).

xiào 效 (exemplar), or exemplify, lit. to imitate, Mohist term for making a *fǎ* 法 (standard) 《墨子・小取》: 效者為之法也.

xiǎogù 小故 (minor cause), term apparently introduced in the *Mojing* and contrasted with *dàgù* 大故 (major cause): "When there is a *xiǎogù*, something is not necessarily so; when there is not, something is necessarily not so" 《墨子・經說上》: 有之不必然，無之必不然 (A1).

xīn 心 (heart/mind), the organ of reason and emotion according to Chinese philosophy.

xīnxué 新學 (new studies), late Qing dynasty movement involving such scholars as Yan Fu and Liang Qichao, who were influenced by ideas from the West but who wanted to create something new, different from both the Chinese tradition and western thought; inspired by earlier scholars such as Wei Yuan.

xīnyīnmíng 新因明 (*hetuvidyā*, new yinming), phase of *yīnmíng* following Dignāga, contrasted with the earlier *nyāya*.

yáng 陽 (sunny side), one of the two aspects of the conception of the world as in constant change, paired with *yīn* 陰 (shady side), central to Chinese philosophical interpretations of the *Yijing*.

yáo 爻 (line), line in the *bāguà* 八卦 (trigrams).

yì 意 (intention), also interpreted as "idea".

yì 義 (right/appropriate), standard for being right or wrong.

yìpǐn 異品 (*vipakṣa*, dissimilar instance), *yīnmíng* term for things dissimilar to the subject of the thesis in the sense that they do not possess the property attributed in the *zōng* (thesis); for a *yìpǐn* to qualify as a *yìyù* (negative example) it must also not possess the property attributed in the *yīn* (reason).

yǐshuōchūgù 以說出故 (explaining reasons), literally "by means of explanations bring out reasons", a phrase in the *Xiaoqu*.

yìxué 易學 (study of the changes), study of the ancient divinatory text *Zhouyi* and the book containing its subsequent commentaries, *Yijing*.

yìyù 異喻 (*vaidharmyadṛṣṭānta*, negative example), *yīnmíng* term for one of the two parts of *yù* 喻 (*dṛṣṭānta*, example); the other part of *yù* 喻 is *tóngyù* 同喻 (*sādharmyadṛṣṭānta*, positive example).

yīn 因 (*hetu*, reason), *yīnmíng* term for the 2nd member of the *wǔzhīzuòfǎ* and *sānzhīlùnshì* argument forms, also the name of the predicate of that proposition.

yīn 陰 (shady side), paired with *yáng* 陽 (sunny side).

yīnmíng 因明 (*hetuvidyā*, theory of reason), style of reasoning originating in India and introduced to China in the 7th century, also known as "Buddhist logic", divided into an ancient phase including the *Nyāyasūtra* and a new phase from Dignāga and onwards; the sanskrit term "hetuvidyā" is reserved for the later phase.

yīnsānxiàng 因三相 (*trairūpya*, three conditions for reason), *yīnmíng* principles for good reasoning, concerning the relation of the *yīn* (reason) to the *zōng* (thesis), *tóngpǐn* (similar instance) and *yìpǐn* (dissimilar instance) respectively.

yíngjiānbái 盈堅白 (merging hard-white), opposite to Gongsun Long's *líjiānbái* 離堅白.

yǒu 有 (has), contrasting with *wú* 無.

yù 喻 (*dṛṣṭānta*, example), *yīnmíng* term for the 3rd member of the *wǔzhīzuòfǎ* (five-membered argument) and *sānzhīlùnshì* (form of three branches), also "*udāharaṇa*".

yùtǐ 喻體 (*dṛṣṭāntakāya*, example-statement), principle exemplified by *yù* (example).

yǔyánluójí 语言逻辑 (linguistic logic), formal approaches to the syntax, semantics and pragmatics of natural language.

yùyī 喻依 (*dṛṣṭāntāśraya*, example-base), object used for *yù* (example).

yuán 援 (adducing), one of the *pìmóuyuántuī*; "if it is so in your case why may not it be so in mine too?" 《墨子・小取》: 援也者，曰「子然我奚獨不可以然」也.

zhènglǐ 正理 (*nyāya*, correct principle), ancient school of Hinduism and the theory of judgement and reasoning it proposed, especially in the *Zhenglijing*.

zhèngmíng 正名 (correcting names), doctrine concerning the relationship between *míng* 名 (name) and *shí* 實 (object), discussed mostly by Confucians.

zhīlèi 知類 (understanding kinds), condition needed for *lèituī*.

zhōngguó luójí 中国逻辑 (Chinese logic), Chinese traditional logical thought from the pre-Qin period, including that in the *Mojing* and other reflections from the Hundred Schools.

zhōngguó luójíshǐ 中国逻辑史 (history of Chinese logic), also "logic in China", referring both to Chinese traditional logical thought from the pre-Qin period and the broader study of logical ideas in China, including *yīnmíng* 因明 and the reception of western logic.

zhòngxiào 中效 (match exemplar), Mohist term for corresponding to a *xiào* 效 (exemplar) and so conforming to a *fǎ* 法 (standard).

zōng 宗 (*pakṣa*, thesis), *yīnmíng* term for the 1st member of the *wǔzhīzuòfǎ* (five-membered argument) and *sānzhīlùnshì* (form of three branches), also the name of the subject of that proposition.

zōngyǒufǎ 宗有法 (*dharmin*, subject of the thesis), *yīnmíng* term for the subject of the *zōng* (thesis), which Xuan Zang insisted should be excluded from the *tóngpǐn* (similar instance) and *yìpǐn* (dissimilar instance) to avoid circular reasoning.

About the Editors

Liu Fenrong 刘奋荣 is Professor of Philosophy at Tsinghua University, Beijing, China.

Jeremy Seligman 谢立民 is a Senior Lecturer in Philosophy at the University of Auckland, New Zealand.

About the 5 Questions Series

The 5 Questions Series from **Automatic Press** ♦ $\frac{V}{T}$P is a collection of books with short interviews based on 5 questions presented to some of the most influential and prominent scholars in a wide variety of fields, ranging from logic to the philosophy of medicine. We hear their views on their expert field, its aim, scope, future direction and how their work fits in these respects.

Index

A System of Logic, 206
adducing, 16, 217
admissible, 11, 118, 210, 211
Against War, 203
Ai Yuese, 193, 201
Analects, vi, 18, 182, 189, 204
analogy, 12, 16, 213
Ānando, 83
anti-fatalism, 3
ānumāna, 209
Aphorisms on Correct Principles, 37
application, 84, 211, 215
appraisal name, 140, 211
Approaching Eloquence, 158, 203
argument for mere-consciousness, 88, 215
argumentation, 11, 214
Aristotle, 19
Arithmetical Classic of the Zhou Gnomon, 208
astronomy, 100
Autumn Floods, 206

bāguà, 101, 209, 211, 212, 216
bǎijiā, 209, 210, 214
báimǎfēimǎ, iv, 38, 111, 113, 123, 139, 140, 182, 183, 203, 209
Baimalun, 67, 104, 111–113, 123, 124, 203, 204
Ban Gu, 165, 167, 193
Bao Seng, 89, 193
bèi, 48–50, 118, 130, 141, 209
biétóngyì, 101, 209, 211
bì, 115, 209

bǐ, 11, 209, 210
bǐliàng, 209
bìrándìdéchū, 99, 209
biàn, 10, 11, 19, 29, 35, 38, 105, 115, 119, 120, 125, 138, 146, 149, 167, 168, 209, 213
biànxué, 11, 12, 21, 29, 39, 47, 50, 51, 58, 60, 65, 66, 99, 113, 209, 213
biànzhě, 15, 101, 115, 125, 209, 210
biànzhě èrshíyīshì, 15, 101, 125, 126, 209
Bianjing, 11, 203
Bianxue, 197, 203
Bianxue Qimeng, 193, 201, 203, 205
Rens Bod, vi, xi, 197
Book of Changes, 151, 207
Book of Jin, 39, 204
Book of Odes, 44, 206
bùkě, 118, 210
bùmáodùnlǜ, 11, 105, 210
bùrán, 189, 210, 214
Buddhism, 19, 40, 66, 81, 82, 87, 88, 91, 121, 142, 176, 211
Buddhist logic, 18, 36, 38, 89, 121, 134, 193, 195, 197, 199, 210

Canons A, 204
Canons B, 204
Chan-kuots'e, 207
Charakasamhitā, 37, 85
Chen Chengze, 62, 193

Chen Hansheng, 116, 193, 202
Chen Na, 37, 193, 201
Chen Rongjie, 186, 193
Chen Yinque, 61, 193
Chung-Ying Cheng , viii, 193
Cheng Zhaoxia, 83, 193
Cheng Zhongying, 193, 201
Chinese classical studies, 5, 211
Chinese logic, 2–5, 7, 12, 15, 20, 29, 39, 40, 44–47, 52, 53, 56–58, 60, 61, 66, 67, 69, 71–77, 99, 103, 112, 122, 127, 138, 139, 141, 142, 149, 151–154, 167–169, 171, 172, 177, 185, 188, 217
Janusz Chmielewski, 122, 124, 195
chōngzúlǐyóulǜ, 210
Chou-i, viii, 208
Ch'u-tz'u, 203
Chuang Tzu, 199
Chuang-tzu, 208
Chuci, 166, 196, 203
cí, 10, 11, 33, 107, 108, 110, 134, 138, 157, 161, 210
cǐ, 50, 209, 210
Classic of Disputation, 11, 203
Classic of Way and Power/ Virtue, 203
classical Chinese, 215
classifying name, 211
Commentary on Nyāya Sūtra, 37
Commentary on the Final Part of the Nyāyapraveśa, 37, 206
Commentary on the Nyāyapraveśa, 37, 206
Common Logic, 206
common logic, 62, 213
Compendium of Charaka, 37
Compendium on Means of Valid Cognition, 87, 88, 91, 204
conclusion, 84, 211, 215
Confucian, 3, 4, 17, 46, 59, 67, 75, 96, 97, 113, 129, 130, 145, 146, 152, 153, 169, 175, 176, 194, 196, 198, 207, 214, 217
Confucianism, 17, 18, 66, 121, 145, 152, 176, 186, 214
Confucius, vi, 11, 17, 18, 21, 96, 101, 112, 145, 146, 149, 153, 175, 176, 195, 204, 207, 214
contextual name, 140, 211
contradiction, 30, 112, 204, 212
correct principle, 217
Correct Reading of the Mohist Canons, 70
correcting names, 11, 124, 146, 153, 175, 217
Corrections and Interpretation of the Mohist Canons, 205
Critical Edition of the Mozi, 206
critical interpretation of antiquity, 58, 169
Critical Survey of the Mozi, 73, 205
Criticisms 1, 206
Cui Qingtian, viii, xi, 14, 45, 71, 193

dàgù, 29, 30, 108, 210, 215
dámíng, 106, 210, 211, 214
Da Xi Zhu, 193, 202
dàn, 12, 13, 210
dào, 8, 118, 152, 154, 210
dàojiā, 210
dàoxué, 66, 152, 210
Daodejing, vi, 97, 118, 196, 203, 204, 208, 210
Daoism, 66, 116, 152, 176, 186, 199, 203, 208, 210
Daoist, iii, 67, 116, 152, 153, 167, 188–190, 196, 210
Daoist Canon, x, 203
Daozang, x, xii, 203
Daqu, 3, 19, 157, 161, 203, 205
Democritus, 19
Deng Xi, 9, 96, 194, 213
Dengxizi, 97, 203
Dharmakīrti, 20, 82–84, 86–92, 194

dharmin, 83, 87, 217
dialectician, 39, 125, 126, 152, 194, 209
dialecticians' 21 theses, 15, 101, 127, 209
Dialetical Chapters of the Mozi, 118, 124, 126, 157, 205
Dignāga, 18, 20, 35–38, 82–93, 193, 194, 201, 204, 206, 207, 214, 216
Discourse on the Stages of Yogic Practice, 207
Discussion of the Chinese Classics, 204
disputation, 11, 19, 29, 35, 105, 125, 167, 209, 213
dissimilar instance, 83, 85–87, 90, 216, 217
distinguishing comparison, 101, 209, 211
Doctrines of Mo Zi, 72, 208
Dong Zhitie, xi, 33, 61, 194
dṛṣṭānta, 36, 84, 85, 214–217
dṛṣṭāntakāya, 36, 85, 86, 110, 217
dṛṣṭāntāśraya, 36, 85, 109, 110, 217
Du Xiushi, 27
duòfù, 38, 210

Joseph Edkins, 58, 193, 203, 209
emotional thinking, 26, 211, 212
erroneous refutation, 38, 215
Erya, 158, 203
example, 36, 84, 85, 214–217
example-base, 36, 85, 217
example-statement, 36, 85, 86, 217
exemplar, 215, 217
experiential knowledge, 213
explaining reasons, 216
Explanations of the Canons A, 204
Explanations of the Canons B, 204
Exploration of Names and Principles, 9, 99, 194, 201, 205

fǎ, 210, 215, 217
Fa Cheng, 194, 201
fǎjiā, 210

falling into failure, 38, 210
Fang Keli, 71, 194
Fang Ketao, 194, 201
Fangbianxinlun, 37, 203
fēi, 189, 210, 214
fēimìng, 3
Feigong, 203
Feng Yaoming, 194, 201
Feng Youlan, 101, 113, 124, 126, 185, 194
five phases, 123, 215
five-membered argument, 36, 37, 84, 85, 211, 214, 215, 217
fójiàoluóji, 210
fóxué, 66, 211
form of three branches, 36, 214, 217
form of three things, 109, 214
four modes of reasoning, 168, 213
Chris Fraser, vii, 48, 130, 158, 194
Fu Fanji, 194, 201
Fu Jizhong, 95, 96
Fucha Yena, 194, 202
Yiu-Ming Fung, viii, 194
Fung Yu-lan, 194
Francisco Furtado, 18, 51, 99, 194, 196, 205

gǎnxìngsīwéi, 26, 211, 212
Gateway to Logic, 37, 83, 87–89, 92, 207
Gautama Buddha, 19
Ge Baoluo, 194, 202
Ge Lizhen, 194, 201
Ge Ruihan, 116, 135, 194, 201
Jane Geaney, vii, 194
Geng Zhencheng, 95
genre of thread beads, 40, 212
Gongsunlongzi, 97, 113, 118, 121, 123, 124, 152, 194, 197, 204, 205, 207, 211
Gongshu Pan, 67, 68, 194
Gongsun Long, iv, 9, 11, 19, 31, 38, 39, 46, 49, 67, 96,

101, 103, 104, 111–113, 122–124, 126, 139–141, 152, 153, 182, 183, 194, 203, 204, 209, 212, 213, 216
A. C. Graham, vi, ix, xii, 11, 116, 122, 124–126, 132, 134, 135, 157, 176, 184, 194, 204
Grammar of Mr. Ma, 61, 205
Marcel Granet, 122
Great Exegesis of Yinming, 36, 207
Great Exegesis of Yinming: Abridged with Commentary, 36, 207
Great Pick, 161, 203
gù, ix, 107–110, 211, 214
Gu Yanwu, 169, 194
guàyáocí, 101, 211
guīmiùfǎ, 211
Guōdiànchǔjiǎn, 97
guóxué, x, 5, 134, 193, 196, 197, 199, 211
Guo Zhanbo, 12, 195, 207
Guodian bamboo slips, 97
Guogulunheng, 35, 199, 204

Han Fei, 30, 153, 195
Hanfeizi, 13, 30, 112, 154, 189, 195, 204, 206, 210, 212
Chad Hansen, iv, xi, 48, 116, 124–127, 157, 161, 193
Christoph Harbsmeier, xiii, 126, 195
hard-white, 133, 211
has, 189, 217
hé, 84, 211, 215
He Moye, 195, 202
He Shen, 24, 25
hétóngyì, 101, 102, 209, 211
heart/mind, 115, 215
hetu, 19, 36, 38, 84, 87, 109, 110, 214–216
Hetucakra-ḍamaru, 82, 86, 165, 193, 207
hetuvidyā, viii, 8, 14, 15, 18, 32, 35–40, 65, 67, 83–88, 90–93, 189, 193, 194, 201, 206, 207, 211, 216
hexagrams, 101, 212
history of Chinese logic, x, xiii, 1–9, 11, 13–15, 17, 18, 27–29, 32, 33, 35, 36, 39–41, 43, 46, 52, 53, 55–61, 65–71, 74, 95–97, 99, 105, 111–114, 138, 139, 141, 142, 145, 178, 182, 190, 193–199, 217
History of Pre-Qin Argumentation, 207
hold a proposition, 108, 109, 212
Hou Wailu, 96
Hsiao-ch'ü, 123, 207
Hsün-tzu, 207
Hsün Tzu, 198
Hu Maoru, 8, 195, 204
Hu Shi, x, 11, 19, 69, 72, 73, 99, 124, 182, 185, 195, 207
Hu Shih, 195
Huainanzi, 166, 196, 204
Huang Shaoji, 51, 195
Huang Xinchuan, 82
Huangdineijing, 100, 102, 204
Hui Shi, 9, 12, 13, 15, 96, 98, 99, 101, 139, 141, 154, 172, 195, 206, 210, 212, 213
huǐyùzhīmíng, 140, 211
Huishi's 10 theses, 15, 96, 212
Human Nature is Vile, 148
Hundred Schools, 197, 206, 209, 210, 213, 214, 217

I-ching, 151, 207
illustrating, 213
In the World, 206
inadmissible, 11, 13, 118, 210
inference from sameness of kind, 68, 214
inferential knowledge, 209, 214
inferring, 50, 68, 74, 215
intention, 216

Internal Classic of the Yellow Emperor, 204
Interpretation of the Mohist Canons, 205
Introduction to the Study of Names, 205
is not so, 189, 210
is so, 189, 210, 214

Ja Nuzi, 195, 201
jāti, 215
Ji Zhigang, 6
Jia Qing, 25
jiānbái, 133, 204, 211
Jianbailun, 204
Jiang Weiqiao, 9, 195, 204
jié, 84, 211, 215
Jie Xian, 87, 195, 202
Jifu, 204
Jiliang, 87, 88, 204
Jin Yuelin, 27, 195, 205
jīngxué, 66
Jingshuoshang, 3, 204, 205
Jingshang, 3, 158, 204, 205
Jingshuoxia, 3, 204, 205
Jingxia, 3, 158, 204, 205
Jingyan, 37, 195, 206
Jinshu, 39, 51, 196, 204, 205
Ian Johnston, 199
Ju Zonglin, vii, 195

kě, 118, 210, 211
kind, ix, 100, 108, 211, 214
kind-based inference, 14, 16, 31, 58, 68, 74, 98, 100, 211, 212, 215
Kong Zi, 195
kuàngwèizhīmíng, 140, 211
Kuiji, 36, 195, 207
Kung-sun Lung, 194

lacks, 189, 215
Lao Tzu, 195
Lao Zi, 8, 153, 195, 199, 203
Law of Identity, 11, 215

Law of Non-contradiction, 11, 24, 30, 105, 167, 168, 188, 189, 210
Law of the Excluded Middle, 11, 61, 105, 167, 168, 188, 189, 213
Lecture Notes on the Study of Rational Discourse, 204
Hsien-Chung Lee, 196
Jer-Shiarn Lee, 196
Michiel Leezenberg, 196
legalist, 67, 113, 195, 204, 210
Legends of the Warring States, 207
lèi, ix, 100, 108–110, 185, 211, 214
lèimíng, 106, 210, 211, 214
lèitóng, 4, 211
lèituī, 31, 58, 74, 98, 100, 212, 215, 217
lǐ, ix, 108–110, 148, 212, 214
Li Baoheng, 65
lìcí, 108, 212
líjiānbái, 101, 102, 212, 217
Li Jinxi, 62
Li Renbo, 196, 202
lìwùshíshì, 15, 125, 212
Li Xianzhong, 196, 202
lǐxué, 66
Li Yuese, 12, 65, 196, 202
lìzéxué, 21, 212
Li Zhexian, 196, 202
Li Zhizao, 18, 51, 58, 99, 194, 196, 201, 205
liánzhūtǐ, 40, 41, 212
Liang Qichao, x, 19, 51, 59, 60, 69, 72, 134, 196, 205, 208, 216
line, 101, 209, 211, 216
line statements, 101, 211
linguistic logic, 217
Liu An, 165, 166, 168, 196, 203, 204
Liu Fenrong, 69, 196
Liu Peiyu, iv, vii, viii, 8, 10, 14, 196
liùshísìguà, 101, 212
Liu Xie, 9, 10, 165–169
Liu Zhiji, 166

lǐxìngsīwéi, 26, 211, 212
Logic, 205
logic, 21, 212
Logic of the Mojing, 205
logico-linguistic categories, 10, 32, 60, 213
Longshu, 196, 202
Lu Kasi, 196, 202
Lu Sheng, 11, 39, 51, 67, 75, 196, 203, 205
Lu Xun, 21, 177
Luan Tiaofu, 134, 196
Thierry Lucas, xi, 196
lùnlǐxué, 9, 21, 212
Lunlixue, 195, 204
Lunlixue Jiangyi, 204
Lunyu, 204
Luo Dan, 148, 196, 202
luójí, 21, 212
Luoji, 27, 195, 205
Luojizhiyao, 58, 59, 73, 199, 205
Lü Buwei, 49, 196, 205
Lü Cheng, 81, 92, 196, 207
Lü Shuxiang, 62, 196
Lüshichunqiu, 13, 116, 118, 119, 196, 205

major cause, 210, 215
máodùn, 30, 112, 204, 212
maodun, 25
Mashiwentong, 61, 62, 205
match exemplar, 75, 217
mechanisation of mathematics, 5
Mencius, 145, 153, 196, 205, 214
Meng Zi, 49, 196
Mengzi, 132, 182, 196, 205
merging hard-white, 101, 216
meta-study, 46
mìng, 11, 161
míng, 10, 11, 15, 33, 38, 61, 104, 106, 107, 115, 124, 134, 138–141, 146, 153, 161, 162, 175, 212, 214, 217
míngbiàn, 28, 30, 76, 113, 212
míngbiànxué, vi, viii, 12, 14, 15, 28, 29, 31, 32, 39, 40, 60, 65, 66, 74, 77, 99, 113, 212
míngcíshuōbiàn, 10, 32, 33, 35, 60, 138, 167, 209, 210, 212–214
míngjiā, 52, 213
mínglǐ, 9, 99, 213
mínglǐxué, 21, 213
mìngwùzhīmíng, 140, 213
míngxué, 11, 12, 21, 29, 36, 39, 47, 60, 65, 66, 99, 113, 145–147, 149, 198, 213
Minglitan, 9, 18, 50, 51, 58, 99, 194, 196, 198, 201, 205, 213
Mingshilun, 11, 46, 204, 205
Mingxue Qianshuo, 32, 198, 203, 205
minor cause, 210, 215
mòbiàn, 19, 20, 29, 76, 213
mòjiā, 213
Mo Tzu, 197
mòxué, 213
Mo Zi, 3, 11, 19, 20, 47–49, 51, 60, 67, 68, 72, 75, 96, 153, 182, 183, 185, 194, 197, 205, 213, 214
Mobian, vii, x–xii, xv, 3, 11, 121, 123, 129, 157–162, 197, 203, 205, 207, 211, 213
Mobianzhuxu, 39, 51, 67, 196, 204, 205
Mohism, 39, 116, 186, 213
Mohist, 3, 4, 11, 18, 19, 29, 31, 35, 36, 39, 47–52, 58, 67–69, 71, 73–75, 96, 101, 104–109, 112, 113, 116–119, 121–125, 130–135, 145–147, 149, 151–153, 157, 161, 167–169, 176, 182, 188, 189, 196–198, 205, 209–213, 215, 217
Mohist Canons, 3, 116, 119, 167, 168, 182, 189, 205
Mohist disputation, 19, 29, 213
Mojing, x, 3, 11, 15, 29, 30, 32, 36, 46, 48, 51, 52, 60, 67, 97,

98, 101, 103, 104, 106–109, 112, 114, 116, 132–135, 141, 157, 183, 185, 194, 196, 197, 201, 203–205, 209–211, 213–215, 217
Mojing de Luojixue, 135, 137, 197, 205
Mojing Jiaoshi, 134, 196, 205
Mojing Jiegu, 198, 205
Mojing Zhengdu, 70, 198
móu, 112, 116, 213
Mozi, 3, 10, 51, 61, 69, 107, 119, 129, 132, 157, 161, 199, 202–205
Mozi Xiaoqu, 168, 213
Mozi Xue'an, 73, 205
Mozixiangu, 51, 195, 197, 206
Mule Mingxue, 32, 198, 206, 212

Nāgārjuna, 37, 196, 203
name, 10, 61, 115, 124, 134, 139, 146, 153, 161, 175, 212, 214, 217
name for things, 140, 213
names and argument, 28, 212
names and reasons, 9, 99, 213
Nanyi, 206
Narratives of the Changes, 101, 207
necessarily, 115, 209
necessarily infer, 99, 209
Joseph Needham, 12, 65, 122, 126, 165, 196
negative example, 86, 215, 216
nèishèngwàiwáng, 96
neo-Confucianism, 66, 212
neo-Daoism, 66, 142
new studies, 66, 216
new yinming, 216
nigamana, 84, 211, 215
nigrahastānaprāta, 210
not/is not, 189, 210
nyāya, 39, 84, 215–217
Nyāyamukha, 37, 83, 207
Nyāyapraveśa, 206
Nyāyasūtra, 18, 35, 37, 84, 216

object, 16, 124, 141, 146, 153, 175, 214, 217
On Equalising Things, 132, 206
On Hard and White, 204
On Names and Objects, 205
On Pointing at Things, 207
On Reasoning, 37, 206
On the Heart of Skilful Means, 37, 203
On the Wheel of Reason, 86, 207
On Understanding Change, 207
Ōnishi Hajime, 8, 82, 193, 195, 204
Outline of Logic, 59, 73, 205

páizhōnglǜ, 11, 213
pakṣa, 36, 38, 84, 110, 214, 215, 217
Pan Ku, 193
pañcāvayava, 36, 84, 214, 215
parallelizing, 112, 213
Paramārtha, 199
Gregor Paul, vii, 194
perception, 93
philosophy, 66
phrase, 10, 134, 161, 210
pì, 12, 13, 213
pìmóuyuántuī, 74, 112, 168, 213, 215, 217
positive example, 86, 214–216
Pramāṇasamuccaya, 87, 88, 204
pratyakṣa, 93
Preface to the Mohist Dialectical Chapters, 11, 205
Primer in the Study of Disputation, 203
Primer on Logic, 92, 206
principle, ix, 108, 212, 214
Principle of Sufficient Reason, 23–25, 105, 210
private name, 214
pǔtōngluójí, 62, 63, 213
Putong Luoji, 7, 11, 105, 198, 206, 210, 213, 215

qīnzhī, 107, 108, 213–215
Qinshihuang, 24, 197
Qiushui, 206, 208

Qiwulun, 132, 135, 206, 208

rán, 189, 210, 214
rational thinking, 26, 211, 212
reason, 19, 36, 84–87, 214–216
reason/cause, ix, 108, 211, 214
reasoning, 10, 11, 214
Records of the Grand Historian, 206
Rectification of Names, 207
reductio ad absurdum, 48, 50, 188, 211
Ren Bode, 197, 201
right/appropriate, 216
ritual propriety, 148, 212
Dan Robins, vii, 196
rújiā, 214
rúxué, 66, 152, 214
Rushilun, 37, 199, 202, 206
Ruzhenglilun, 14, 18, 36, 189, 198, 206, 207
Ruzhenglilun Houshu, 37, 206
Ruzhenglilun Luechao, 37, 206
Ruzhenglilun Wenguishu, 37, 198, 206

sādharmyadṛṣṭānta, 110, 215, 216
sage within, king without, 96, 97
sameness of kind, 4, 211
sānwùlùnshì, 109, 110, 214
sānzhīlùnshì, 36, 109, 214, 216, 217
sānzhǒngbǐliàng, 214
Sanzang, 87
sapakṣa, 83, 86, 87, 89, 214
School of Names, 9, 11, 46, 67, 69, 96, 97, 101, 119, 121, 145, 146, 152, 188, 194, 213
self-awareness, 93
self-contradictory/ perverse, 141, 209
Jeremy Seligman, 198
separating hard from white, 101, 212
shady side, 101, 216
Shen Jianying, iv, 197

Shen Youding, iv, 14, 28, 43, 69, 103, 104, 135, 137, 197, 205
shì, 189, 210, 214
shí, 10, 15, 38, 124, 141, 146, 153, 161, 162, 175, 212, 214, 217
shìfēi, 214
Shih-chi, 206
Shih-ching, 44, 206
Shiji, 165, 168, 197, 206
Shijing, 44, 206
Shiyi, 101, 206, 207
Shu Xi, 165, 166
shùxué jīxièhuà, 5
shuō, 10, 11, 13, 107, 138, 214
shuōzhī, 107, 108, 214, 215
Shuoyuan, 118
sīmíng, 210, 211, 214
Śīlabhadra, 87, 195
Sima Qian, 165–168, 197, 206
similar instance, 83, 85–87, 89, 90, 214, 216, 217
slingshot, 210
Small Pick, 123, 207
Song Saihua, 197
Songs of Chu, 203
Spring and Autumn Annals of Mr. Lü, 205
Ssu-ma Chien, 197
standard, 210, 215, 217
study of Chinese medicine, 100
Study of Disputation, 203
study of disputation, 11, 21, 58, 66, 209
study of mind, 66
study of names, 11, 21, 36, 60, 66, 99, 145, 146, 186, 213
study of names and argument, 29, 39, 60, 65, 99, 212
study of names and reasons, 21, 213
Study of Rational Discourse, 204
study of rational discourse, 9, 21, 212
study of rational principles, 21,

212
study of the changes, 74, 100, 216
study of the classics, 66
subject of the thesis, 83, 86, 87, 214, 216, 217
Sun Yirang, ix, x, 51, 106, 195, 197, 206
Sun Zhongyuan, vii, 5, 14, 60, 67, 68, 76, 118, 130, 197
sunny side, 101, 216
Sunzi Bingfa, 189
Sunzi's Art of War, 189
svasaṃvedana, 93

tánbiàn, 11, 214
Tan Jiefu, 197
Tang Mingjun, 197
Tang Shiqi, 6
Tang Yongtong, 84
Tao, 210
Tao-te-ching, 203
Tao-tsang, x, 203
Taoism, 152, 210
Taoist, 210
Tarkaśāstra, 37, 206
ten thousand things, 12, 215
Ten Wings, 206
testimonial knowledge, 107, 215
that, 11, 50, 209, 210
The Association of the History of Logic, 104
The Development of the Logical Method in Ancient China, 73, 99, 207
theory of reason, 18, 35, 211, 216
Thesaurus Linguae Sericae, 195, 202
thesis, 36, 84–86, 214–217
this, 50, 209, 210
this/is this, 189, 210, 214
this/not-this, 214
Three Baskets, 87
three conditions for reason, 85, 86, 216
three origins of logic, 15, 32, 65, 73, 75, 76, 103, 109

three types of reasoning, 87, 214
Tianxia, 15, 101, 125, 206, 208, 210, 212
tónglèixiāngtuī, 68, 214
tóngpǐn, 83, 85, 86, 89, 90, 214, 216, 217
tóngyù, 86, 214–216
Tongbianlun, 204, 207
trairūpya, 38, 82, 85, 86, 216
trayāvayava, 36, 38, 82, 109, 110, 214
trigrams, 101, 209, 216
Tripiṭaka, 87
trividham anumānam, 214
tuī, 47, 50, 68, 74, 215
tuīlèi, 3, 14, 31, 58, 68, 74, 211, 212, 215
Têng Hsi, 194

understanding kinds, 49, 68, 217
unifying comparison, 101, 209, 211
unrestricted name, 210
upanaya, 84, 211, 215
Upāyakauśalyahṛdaya śāstra, 37, 203

vaidharmyadṛṣṭānta, 110, 216
Vātsyāyana, 37, 194
vijñāptimātrānumāna, 88, 215
vipakṣa, 83, 86, 87, 90, 216

wànwù, 12, 215
Wang Dianji, 14, 28, 43, 103, 197
Wang Guowei, 11, 58, 197, 203, 209
Wang Kexi, vii, xi, 11, 45, 197
Wang Li, 62, 198
Wang Xianjun, 8, 198
Wang Zanyuan, 70, 198
way, 16, 118, 210
wěi, 133
wéishíbǐliàng, 88, 215
Wei Yuan, 216
wéihūqíbìcǐ, 11, 215
Wen Gongyi, 14, 71, 198
Wen Gui, 37, 198, 206

Wen Gui's Commentary on the Nyāyapraveśa, 37, 206
Wen Jiabo, 22
wénzhī, 107, 108, 214, 215
Wenxin Diaolong, 9, 166
wényán, 215
White Horse Discourse, 104, 123, 203
white horse not horse, iv, 38, 111, 123, 139, 152, 194, 203, 209
Wing-Tsit Chan, 193
Works of Deng Xi, 203
Works of Gongsun Long, 204
Works of Han Fei, 204
Works of Mencius, 205
Works of Mo Zi, 205
Works of the Masters of Huainan, 204
Works of Xun Zi, 207
Works of Yinwen, 207
Works of Zhuang Zi, 208
wú, 189, 215, 217
Wu Feibai, 106, 198, 205
Wu Jiaguo, 7, 198
Wu Kanmin, 22
wùnán, 38, 215
Wu Wenjun, 5, 6, 198
wǔxíng, 123, 204, 215
wǔzhīzuòfǎ, 36, 37, 84, 211, 214–217

Xianqin Bianxueshi, 207
Xianqin Mingxueshi, x, 182, 195, 207
xiào, 75, 215, 217
xiǎogù, 29, 30, 108, 210, 215
Xiaoqu, ix, 3, 47, 49, 68, 75, 116, 123–125, 132, 136, 157, 205, 207, 216
Xie He, 165, 167, 168
Xie Limin, 198, 202
xīn, 115, 215
xīnxué, 66
xīnxué, 66, 216
xīnyīnmíng, 216

xìng, 133
Xing 'e, 133, 148
Xiong Shili, 36, 207
Xu Liangying, 65
Xu Zongze, 9, 198
xuánxué, 66, 142
Xuan Zang, 14, 18, 36, 37, 48, 82, 83, 87–90, 92, 189, 195, 198, 202, 206, 207, 215, 217
xùngǔxué, 58, 169
Xun Zi, 10, 11, 19, 29, 44, 46, 67, 96, 112, 122, 133, 145–149, 153, 177, 195, 198, 207, 214
Xunzi, 32, 60, 97, 116, 119, 121, 129, 132, 133, 148, 157, 182, 189, 207, 213

Yan Fu, 11, 32, 36, 52, 60, 99, 198, 203, 205, 206, 212, 213, 216
Yan Shigu, 59, 198
yáng, 101, 123, 204, 209, 216
Yang Wujin, vii, 50, 125, 183, 198
yáo, 101, 209, 216
yì, 161, 216
yìpǐn, 83, 85, 86, 90, 216, 217
yǐshuōchūgù, 107, 216
yìxué, 74, 77, 100, 216
yìyù, 86, 215, 216
Yijing, viii, 14, 74, 100, 101, 151, 153, 207–209, 216
yīn, 19, 20, 36, 84–86, 101, 123, 204, 209, 214–216
yīnmíng, 4, 8, 9, 14, 18–21, 29, 31, 32, 35, 36, 85, 86, 172, 188, 209–211, 214–217
yīnsānxiàng, 85, 216
Yinci, 30
yíngjiānbái, 101, 212, 216
Yinlunlun, 207
Yinmingdashu, 36, 195, 207
Yinmingdashu Shanzhu, 36, 207
Yinwen, 139–141, 198, 207
Yinwenzi, 97, 139, 141, 198, 207,

211, 213
Yinwenzi Dadaoshang, 140
Yizhuan, 101, 151, 206, 207
yogācāra, 93
Yogācārabhūmi-śāstra, 87, 207
yǒu, 189, 215, 217
yù, 36, 84, 85, 214–217
yùtǐ, 36, 85, 217
yǔyánluóji, 27, 197, 199, 217
yùyī, 36, 85, 217
yuán, 217
yuányánjiū, 46
Yujia Shidilun, 207

Zhai Jincheng, iii, xi, xiii, 45, 198
Zhang Dainian, 104, 113
Zhang Dongsun, 56, 198
Zhang Jialong, iv, 62, 81, 199
Zhang Lianshun, 83
Zhang Shizhao, 58, 59, 72, 73, 199, 205, 212
Zhang Taiyan, 35, 36, 199, 204
Zhang Yan, 199, 202
Zhanguoce, 13, 207
Zhanguoce Qicesi, 58
Zhao Yuanren, 62, 199
Zhao Zhongli, 65
Zheluo Jiabenji, 37
Zhen Di, 37, 199, 202, 206
zhènglǐ, 217
zhèngmíng, 11, 111–113, 124, 146, 147, 149, 153, 175, 195, 198, 207, 212, 217
Zheng Weihong, 199
Zhenglijing, 37, 217
Zhenglimenlun, 14, 18, 37, 83, 189, 198, 207

Zhenglishu, 37
Zhengming, 11, 29, 44, 46, 67, 146, 157, 207
zhījué, 93
zhīlèi, 49, 68, 217
Zhiwulun, 204, 207
zhōngguó luóji, 4, 217
zhōngguó luójishǐ, 217
Zhōngguóluójíshǐ Yánjiùhuì, 104
zhòngxiào, 75, 217
zhongguoluojishi, 139
Zhongyong, 154
Zhou Book of Changes, viii, 208
Zhou Gucheng, 80
Zhou Liquan, 27, 103, 199
Zhou Shan, iv, xi, 16, 154, 199
Zhou Wenying, 14, 82, 199
Zhou Yunzhi, iv, 8, 14, 80, 113, 199
Zhoubisuanjing, 116, 208
Zhouyi, viii, 29, 31, 58, 60, 74, 100–102, 151, 207–209, 212, 216
Zhu Zhikai, 79, 199
Zhuang Zi, 39, 49, 98, 99, 122, 125, 126, 139, 153, 154, 177, 195, 199, 206, 208
Zhuangzi, 15, 96, 101, 116, 118, 121, 125, 126, 129, 131, 132, 154, 199, 206, 208, 210, 212
Zhuge Yintong, 81
Zimozi Xueshuo, 72, 208
zìwǒyìshí, 93
zōng, 36, 84–86, 214–217
zōngyǒufǎ, 83, 217
Zuozhuan, 116

www.ingramcontent.com/pod-product-compliance
Lightning Source LLC
Chambersburg PA
CBHW022005160426
43197CB00007B/279